The Reconstruction of Workplace Conflict Resolution

Many attempts have been made in recent decades by liberal market economies to reconstruct public workplace conflict resolution agencies in response to major changes in patterns of workplace conflict. These have often been hampered or stymied by political schisms, stalemate or inertia. The radical reconstruction of conflict resolution in Ireland marks out a major exception to the international pattern and represents a case of successful adaptation and innovation in conflict resolution services and supports. Drawing on detailed primary research, and aimed at scholars, policy makers, professionals and students, this book examines the drivers of innovation in the Irish case and shows how the new state agency for workplace conflict resolution, the Workplace Relations Commission, operates and maintains the confidence of employers, unions, people at work and government. The Irish case is considered in comparative context, and current strategic challenges facing the Workplace Relations Commission are assessed.

William K. Roche is Full Professor of Industrial Relations and Human Resources at the College of Business, University College Dublin. He is a graduate of UCD and completed his doctorate at the University of Oxford, where he was Heyworth Memorial Prize Research Fellow of Nuffield College. He has held visiting professorships at the University of South Australia, Adelaide and at the University of Melbourne and the Cyprus International Institute of Management. He was a Jean Monnet Fellow at the European University Institute, Florence. He is a Fellow of the Geary Institute for Public Policy at UCD.

Paul Teague is Emeritus Professor of Management at The Queen's University Belfast. He holds a PhD from the London School of Economics and has been a Fulbright Scholar at the University of Massachusetts. He is a Fellow of the Irish Academy of Management. He has written widely on the themes of the employment relations consequences of deeper European integration, social partnership and employment performance, workplace conflict management and human resources in the recession. He has published over 50 papers in top-tier journals on these themes.

Denise Currie is a Reader in Human Resource Management at Queen's Business School. She is also a graduate of Queen's Business School, where she completed her PhD on conflict management in business networks (2010). Her current activities lie broadly in employee relations with particular interest in the various dynamics and organizational processes that are integral to creating positive working environments. Specifically, she has interests in workforce conflict, cooperation and collaboration, wellbeing, and diversity and inclusion.

Routledge Research in Employment Relations
Series editors: Rick Delbridge and Edmund Heery
Cardiff Business School, UK

Aspects of the employment relationship are central to numerous courses at both undergraduate and postgraduate level.

Drawing from insights from industrial relations, human resource management and industrial sociology, this series provides an alternative source of research-based materials and texts, reviewing key developments in employment research.

Books published in this series are works of high academic merit, drawn from a wide range of academic studies in the social sciences.

52. **Employment Relations as Networks**
    Methods and Theory
    Edited by Bernd Brandl, Bengt Larsson, Alex Lehr, Oscar Molina

53. **Employment Relations and Global Governance**
    The Dialogue between the Global Unions and the IFIs
    Yvonne Rueckert

54. **Trade Unions and the British Industrial Relations Crisis**
    An Intellectual Biography of Hugh Clegg
    Peter Ackers

55. **Workers, Power and Society**
    Power Resource Theory in Contemporary Capitalism
    Edited by Jens Arnholtz and Bjarke Refslund

56. **The Reconstruction of Workplace Conflict Resolution**
    The Road to the Workplace Relations Commission in Ireland
    William K. Roche, Paul Teague and Denise Currie

The Reconstruction of Workplace Conflict Resolution

The Road to the Workplace Relations Commission in Ireland

William K. Roche, Paul Teague and Denise Currie

Routledge
Taylor & Francis Group
NEW YORK AND LONDON

First published 2025
by Routledge
605 Third Avenue, New York, NY 10158

and by Routledge
4 Park Square, Milton Park, Abingdon, Oxon, OX14 4RN

Routledge is an imprint of the Taylor & Francis Group, an informa business

ISBN: 978-1-032-85017-7 (hbk)
ISBN: 978-1-032-85838-8 (pbk)
ISBN: 978-1-003-52005-4 (ebk)

DOI: 10.4324/9781003520054

Typeset in Galliard
by codeMantra

Contents

Figures

Preface

Over recent decades, public workplace conflict resolution agencies have come under significant pressure to reconstruct their identities, priorities and operations to adapt to changing patterns of conflict in workplaces. These pressures have been felt with particular intensity across the liberal market economies of the English-speaking world. Agencies' capacities to adapt and reconfigure their services have varied significantly. Some, such as in New Zealand and Australia, have grappled with sharp changes in the tempo and direction of political reform programmes. Others, such as in the United States, have been stymied by inertia and stalemate arising from deep political schisms around workplace conflict and how, if at all, it should be addressed. Ireland stands out as a national case where radical change and adaptation have been led by conflict management professionals unencumbered by political clashes or conflicting ideologies.

The Workplace Relations Commission is the major public institution for resolving workplace conflict in Ireland. The Commission came into being in 2015 when four pre-exiting agencies (five, if the statutorily independent Rights Commissioners hosted by the Labour Relations Commission are included) were merged in an improbable, radical and highly effective initiative in public service reform. The creation of the new agency was a response to long-understood problems of fragmentation, complexity, duplication and dysfunctionality in the State's provision for resolving conflict in workplaces. The reform process was led by professional conflict management leaders, seizing the opportunity afforded by the global financial and fiscal crisis to initiate and oversee major reforms. But the road to the Workplace Relations Commission was long and began before the State was founded. This book locates the emergence of the Commission in the 'voluntary' industrial relations system largely inherited at the foundation of the State. Fragmented and limited dispute resolution practices consistent with this tradition were created in the Irish Free State. These were replaced after the War by the Labour Court – for long the cardinal institution of voluntary dispute resolution. Over time, debates arose about the effectiveness of the Court, especially in the face of escalating industrial conflict and a growing industrial relations crisis during the 1970s and into the 1980s. The response was to create the Labour Relations Commission in 1991. Evidence of intensifying dysfunctionality as the Commission shared the pitch with a growing series of independent agencies addressing different facets of workplace conflict finally resulted in the creation of the Workplace Relations Commission in 2015. In the background of these developments were a series of long-term trends in the nature of workplace conflict and pressures for change and reform. In Ireland's voluntary industrial relations system the role of the state was confined to providing employers, unions and people at work with supports for resolving their differences through conciliation or adjudication. They remained free to avail of or decline these supports as they saw fit. Within the Irish voluntarist tradition, neither industrial relations nor conflict resolution was politicized or marked by sharp differences of posture or philosophy on the part of the main political parties.

As this book shows, voluntarism has also changed significantly. The original voluntarist dispute resolution system made little substantive public provision for the resolution of individual employment grievances. Pre-Labour Court conflict resolution practices, like those of the Court itself, focused on the voluntary resolution of collective disputes between employers and unions. Individual disputes in the main were taken up and resolved by unions on behalf of their members through collective bargaining with employers. Alternatively, they were sometimes resolved through the civil courts. The latter route to settlements was expensive and risky and therefore out of the reach of most working people. The inauguration of Rights Commissioners in 1970 marked a shift towards the public provision of conflict resolution for those claiming to have experienced individual employment grievances. The subsequent explosive growth in new and extended employment rights brought in its train a dramatic growth in the incidence of individual grievances, initially addressed by Rights Commissioners and subsequently by the Workplace Relations Commission's adjudication service. The rise of individual dispute resolution, involving claims that employers had infringed employment rights, inevitably heralded the 'juridification' of conflict resolution. Adjudicators in public dispute resolution agencies were now required to frame decisions within the law and those decisions were legally enforceable. At the same time, a long-term decline occurred in the demand for public collective dispute resolution services. While collective disputes remained on the whole amenable to voluntary dispute resolution by public agencies, resort to the civil courts, especially by employers, also became more common.

This book focuses on the two major 'first ports of call' for workplace conflict resolution in Ireland: the Workplace Relations Commission and the Labour Relations Commission. The background to the creation of the Labour Court is also examined in detail – the Court being the first public conflict resolution agency of wide jurisdiction created by the State. Debates surrounding the effectiveness of the Court are also examined as an important background feature of reforms that led to the establishment of the Workplace Relations Commission. The focus on the Labour Relations Commission and Workplace Relations Commission is in no way intended to relegate the central role played by the Labour Court in Ireland's workplace conflict resolution system. The Court remains a central and highly effective institution for resolving both collective disputes and individual grievances that remain unresolved following the efforts of the Workplace Relations Commission. While the Labour Court was formally repurposed in 2015 as an appellate agency for unresolved conflicts and like the Workplace Relations Commission has been significantly affected by the juridification of conflict resolution, the Court's services are perhaps more familiar than those of the agencies on which this book focuses. The operation of the Court has also remained relatively stable over time.

Efforts by public conflict resolution agencies internationally, as in Ireland, to reconstruct and even reinvent themselves in response to the changing nature of conflict in workplaces and associated external and internal pressures have not gone unnoticed. This book is one outcome of a major international research project undertaken to study these efforts, co-ordinated with colleagues at the Industrial and Labor Relations School of Cornell University, New York: Ariel Avgar, Alex Colvin and Harry Katz. The project studied changes in public provision for conflict resolution in six English-speaking or 'Anglo-American' countries with institutional and legal affinities: the United States, the United Kingdom, Ireland, Australia, New Zealand and Canada.

Both in that study and in writing this book we have accumulated significant debts that we wish to acknowledge with gratitude and appreciation. First, we wish to thank our research collaborators from the international project for valuable and insightful comments on drafts of reports on developments in Ireland. Ariel Avgar, Alex Colvin, Harry Katz, Katrina Nobles, Deborah Hann, Paul Latreille, David Nash, Richard Saundry, Erling Rasmussen, Mark Bray, Johanna Macneil, Dionne Pohler and Bradley Weinberg all contributed valuable feedback on our work for this book. Practitioner members of the International Industrial Relations Agencies network of public conflict resolution agencies also provided helpful feedback in a series of webinars, in particular senior staff of the Workplace Relations Commission. We owe a particular debt of gratitude to Liam Kelly, staff and board members of the Workplace Relations Commission and the Labour Relations Commission who consented to be interviewed for the study, in some cases more than once. Both agencies have generously supported our research over the years on developments in conflict resolution in Ireland, and we want to express our appreciation for their openness and professionalism towards our research. Other conflict resolution leaders, professionals, advisors and commentators also consented to be interviewed for this book and provided valuable comments and insights. The authors are responsible for the analysis and interpretation presented in this book.

Dr Kieran Mulvey has encouraged and supported our work over many years and has contributed to the development of a substantial body of research on developments in conflict resolution in Ireland.

We wish to thank the series editor of Routledge Research in Employment Relations, Ed Heery, for his encouragement. We are also indebted to three anonymous reviewers for their helpful and constructive comments. Our thanks also to Brianna Ascher and Jessica Rech at Routledge/Taylor & Francis for guiding our manuscript towards publication with great professionalism and support.

Our research on the wider international project and on the developments in Ireland reported in this book was supported by funding from the Industrial and Labor Relations School of Cornell University, from the College of Business at University College Dublin and from Queen's Business School at Queen's University Belfast.

We owe a particular debt of gratitude to Bernie Cramp at UCD for her excellent and skilful editorial support for our work.

Our research on this book draws on multiple sources and these are detailed in the first chapter. Suffice it to note here that for the convenience of readers and for consistency with other source references, the archival sources drawn on in Chapter 2 are cited in the text by using the names of persons or bodies that created the records, with full archival source details provided in the references section of this book.

William K. Roche
Paul Teague
Denise Currie
Dublin and Belfast
April 2024

1 Reconstructing workplace conflict resolution in liberal market economies

Introduction

Industrial relations institutions that govern the labour market are varied and wide-ranging in nature. They include collective bargaining systems, employment and labour law regimes and the vast array of agencies dedicated to either devising and enforcing employment standards or helping to solve workplace problems and conflicts. These institutions exist primarily to ensure that people are treated fairly at work and that orderly relationships exist between unions, employees and their employers. Some industrial relations systems have been more successful than others in realizing these core objectives. Clearly, multiple factors can influence the performance of any industrial relations institution, but a key indicator will be the extent to which they are able to keep pace with unfolding developments in work and employment (Locke et al. 1995). If institutions are not fully aligned with labour market dynamics, then it's almost certain that their functioning will be impaired in one way or another – a governance gap emerges between labour market institutions and the behaviour of firms and employees.

Governance gaps in labour markets are likely to create a range of distortions in an employment system. Consider wage setting: if pay levels do not move in line with productivity improvements, then all sorts of problems can arise: pay levels and rates running ahead of productivity are likely to stoke up inflationary pressures; alternatively, if they fall behind productivity, then inequality is likely to arise as the share of output going to capital increases, with the labour share declining, usually by a commensurate amount (Blanchflower 2019). Or take the example of training and skill formation. If training systems are disorganized, not only are they unlikely to produce sufficient numbers of the skilled workers being demanded by employers, but they may also trigger all sorts of negative externalities in the labour market: employers, for example, may choose to invest minimally in training and instead poach required skilled workers from other firms: while such decisions may be rational for individual firms, at the aggregate level, the result is

DOI: 10.4324/9781003520054-1

chronic underinvestment in training within an economy. Governance gaps can also creep into employment law regimes (Thelen 2004). For so long so much of employment legislation was developed on the assumption that the typical employee was male, worked full time and was directly employed by a stand-alone firm. All these assumptions have taken a battering in recent decades due to the boundaries of firms becoming more permeable and a-typical forms of employment growing massively. Much has been done so that employment legislation catches up with the new realities of work and employment. But, it would be heroic for anyone to conclude that full regulatory alignment has been restored between employment legislation and contemporary labour market dynamics (Pulignano 2023).

Other examples could be set out, but the basic point is that the ongoing challenge for any type of industrial relations institution is to remain aligned with the ebb and flow of ground-level developments in that part of the labour market which it is responsible to govern. On this point, there is pretty much wide agreement. Despite this consensus, surprisingly little is known about what these institutions do to remain aligned and what happens if a gap emerges between the activities of an industrial relations institution and the actual dynamics of the labour market area which it is supposed to be governing. Sparse knowledge also exists on other critical questions such as how institutional misalignment is detected and how strategies to correct the problem are designed and implemented – and whether or not they are successful. In other words, the processes of change and renewal that industrial relations institutions follow in an effort to remain relevant in fast-changing labour markets largely continue to remain a black box.

The purpose of this book is to address this deficiency in the literature by examining how and why the public regime in Ireland charged with helping to solve workplace conflict and maintain a stable, peaceful industrial relations environment more generally was overhauled to create the Workplace Relations Commission (WRC). It also assesses the challenges the new agency faced as it sought to establish organizational legitimacy amongst relevant stakeholders. Thus, this book is an attempt to throw light upon reform processes associated with the making and remaking of a public regime for workplace conflict resolution, a longstanding important industrial relations institution particularly in Anglo-American liberal market economies. To provide a comprehensive account of these reform processes, this book first explains why liberal market economies need public agencies to help resolve workplace disputes and conflicts more than coordinated economies. So that the reform process that led to the creation of the WRC is fully understood the book also sets out important contextual information by explaining earlier momentous decisions first to establish the Labour Court in 1946 and then to create the Labour Relations Commission (LRC) in the early 1990s.

But, most of all the book seeks to place the establishment of the WRC in the context of changing patterns of workplace conflict and other changes external to conflict management agencies that created pressures for change in the delivery of conflict resolution services. In the background to the reform process that led to the established public regime for workplace conflict resolution being abandoned and the WRC being created was a major shift in the character of workplace conflict involving a long-run decline in collective conflict, particularly in the incidence and volume of strike activity, and a rise in the incidence of grievances and alleged infringements of employment rights by individual employees. This book charts the effects of these and related changes on the reform process, on service provision and resourcing and on the character of public conflict resolution service provision.

A recurring theme that runs throughout the book is how governments and public agencies have responded to the slowly unfolding yet important changes that have been occurring in Ireland and elsewhere to the nature of workplace conflict. In the past, conflict at work immediately conjured up the image of large-scale strikes causing a fair degree of disruption to organizations, the economy and the wider public. But for some time now collective forms of industrial dispute have been on the decline almost everywhere. Notwithstanding a significant escalation in industrial conflict in some European countries and beyond in the recent past, across countries, strikes and associated forms of industrial action are at an all-time low. This does not mean that workplace conflict has withered away, merely that it is taking a different form. Workplace conflict has become less collective and more individual in nature. Various developments have fuelled this shift from collective to individual-based workplace conflict. The huge growth of individual employment rights over the past 20 years or so has opened up a more effective legal route for employees seeking to redress employment grievances. Changes in work organization such as team working have led to the proliferation of relationship-based conflict, which is largely individual in character.

The shift from collective to individual forms of workplace conflict has created multiple challenges for trade unions and employers. But it has also created challenges for public dispute resolutions bodies. These bodies were mostly first created in the early parts of the twentieth century – with Anglo-American countries being the pioneers. In the beginning, almost everywhere governments created public dispute resolution agencies to assist trade unions and employers, who had become entangled in difficult-to-settle collective industrial disputes, find a pathway to a peaceful settlement: their *modus operandi* was to maintain stable and orderly collective industrial relations.

But the widespread decline of collective conflict and growth of individual forms of workplace conflict is a challenge to this *modus operandi*. For example, the traditional methods used by public agencies to help resolve collective bargaining disputes – which were in the main about pay and working conditions – were conciliation, 'facilitation' or 'interest-based bargaining'. But, different methods are needed to address individual forms of workplace conflict that are mostly relationship-based. Investigations and mediation rather than conciliation and interest-based bargaining are required to deal with problems such as claims of sexual harassment or unfair treatment of one form or another. Thus, the prospect lurked of public dispute resolution agencies – in Ireland and elsewhere – offering conflict management services that were not fully synchronized with the changing dynamics of workplace conflict in organizations. Compounding this problem is the emergence, albeit unevenly across many countries, of various forms of individual and collective 'alternative dispute resolution' (ADR) in firms that represent a conscious effort to 'internalize' most aspects of conflict resolution within organizations. In some instances, organizations have sought to create some form of 'private conflict resolution system'. If these emerging internalized systems take hold and become widespread, a huge disconnect would open up between the conflict resolution services provided by public agencies and how organizations actually go about solving workplace problems. Sooner or later, the question would be asked: what is the purpose of having a public agency to support workplace conflict resolution in organizations? Even if this precipice was not reached, the growth of more elaborate conflict management arrangements in organizations is bound to alter in some manner the interface between public conflict resolution agencies and their various clients and stakeholders. So multiple external pressures as much as anything created the impetus for the overhaul of public workplace conflict services in Ireland.

We will be returning to these pressures soon enough, but first, it is necessary to provide an answer to the most basic of questions: why is a public agency necessary to help solve problems and conflicts at the workplace in liberal market economies?

Why public agencies are necessary for the resolution of workplace conflict

The employment relations systems of advanced economies vary a great deal. The institutions used to incorporate people into working life – employment regulations, wage-setting processes, skill and training regimes and so on – exhibit strong national peculiarities. Yet it would be misleading to push this divergence argument too far. A longstanding argument in the literature suggests that although distinctive, national employment relations systems can be grouped together into broadly similar subsets. A classic distinction often made is between the voluntarist industrial relations systems of liberal market economies and the corporatist industrial relations systems of coordinated market economies (Teague and Currie 2016). For the most part, the six countries making up the Anglo-American world are considered to be the family of voluntarist industrial relations countries whilst most north European countries are viewed as being partially or fully paid-up members of the corporatist club.

It is not that each national employment relations system making up the two different categories possesses the exact same institutional configurations. Rather, they tend to exhibit similar characteristics and function in broadly similar ways. But significantly, employment relations systems in coordinated economies are generally viewed as being more effective than voluntarist employment relations systems at solving employment and work-related problems (Batt et al. 2010). A key distinguishing feature of trade unions and employer organizations in many coordinated economies is their capacity to formulate collective strategies, negotiate collective agreements and implement collective policies outside and above the firm. Through exercising these capabilities, trade unions and employer organizations create a coordinated interface between micro and macro dimensions of the labour market. Firms are provided a certain latitude to develop their own policies and procedures to meet the idiosyncratic challenges of their particular commercial circumstances. At the same time, they are also tied to economy-wide or sector-wide collective agreements that balance and codify the conflicting interests of employers and trade unions at the aggregate level. Policies and procedures are put in place to ensure effective compliance with what is for all intents and purposes a quasi-collective contract. Such highly coordinated labour market arrangements do not arise spontaneously or hold together by one-sided-trust arrangements between the parties. They are sustained by employer organizations and trade unions making promises that each believes to be credible. Thus, the glue that holds together coordinated labour markets is deeply embedded credible commitments that employer organizations and trade unions make to each other: each party makes an assurance about the behaviour to the other, but at the same time provides an assurance of their own behaviour and abilities. Credible commitments forge and sustain two-sided trust arrangements.

The upshot of this peculiar institutional design of corporatist employment relations systems is that their primary actors, employers and unions, have greater internal capacity to solve problems across a range of employment-related matters including pay-setting, skill formation and conflict management. In relation to conflict management, consider the case of Sweden, long considered a leading coordinated economy. Traditionally, the Swedish industrial relations system has been characterized by exceptionally high trade union density rates, well-organized employer associations and a well-developed institutional framework that enables either collective bargaining or other forms of collective engagement between trade unions and employers at the national, sector and workplace levels. Although the functioning of this institutional framework has frayed in recent decades, it nevertheless remains more or less intact. As a result of a series of historical political and industrial agreements, a premium is placed on the ability of the collective bargaining system to solve workplace conflict *internally*. If disputes arise and cannot be resolved at the workplace, then progressively senior trade union and employer representatives are drafted in until the problem is settled. A similar procedure operates for problems that arises at the regional or national level. Over the years, this system has proved to be remarkably successful in ensuring that workplace conflict, whether it is large or small, is resolved quickly and to the broad satisfaction of the involved parties. Effectively the management of workplace conflict is internalized within the collective bargaining system (see Teague 2009).

Two main consequences arise from workplace problems being addressed in such a manner. One is that little or no provision exists for individuals to pursue a workplace grievance outside the formal collective bargaining structure. The only route open to them is to enter the mainstream judicial system, which can be a protracted and costly affair. The other is that Sweden, in common with other coordinated economies, has no need for an elaborate system of public bodies to assist the resolution of workplace problems. The only public agencies set up to handle workplace conflict in Sweden are a small conciliation/mediation office, which employs only a handful of staff and an Employment Tribunal that sits infrequently. For all intents and purposes, the system for the resolution of workplace conflict operates autonomously from state intervention (Teague 2009). A series of complementary procedures and mechanisms inside and outside firms are used to ensure that a resolution to workplace conflict is reached within the employment relations systems and does not leak out into the public arena.

Liberal market economies do not have a comparable internal capacity for employers and trade unions to solve problems by themselves. In most liberal market economies, the so-called Anglo-American economies, the key organizing principle of the employment relations system is voluntarism. A voluntary system of industrial relations is premised on freedom of contract and freedom of association, which across the Anglo-American world gave rise to free collective bargaining, on the one hand, and the relative legal abstention from employment relations, on the other hand (Teague 2013). The next chapter of the book examines the origins and evolution of the Irish voluntarist system of industrial relations in detail. But the important point for the discussion here is that voluntarist employment relations systems tend to be more decentralized, with employment and work-related decisions by firms usually only weakly influenced by external institutional arrangements. Trade unions tend to be fragmented and prone to pursuing their own sectional interests whilst employer organizations seldom have the capacity to constrain the behaviour of firms with regard to pay, training or most other policies related to the management of the employment relationship, including dispute resolution. The institutional design of most voluntarist employment relations systems militates against them having the capacities to formulate collective strategies, negotiate collective agreements and implement collective policies outside the firm, which is such a distinctive feature of coordinated economies. With only flimsy internal mechanisms to resolve workplace disputes, the big problem with voluntarist employment relations systems is that of how to assure labour market order and stability (Colvin and Darbishire 2013). As a result, there is a real danger of an unresolved workplace conflict spilling over and triggering further disputes or generating economy-wide contagions of mistrust and suspicion between employers and employees. Across the Anglo-American world, governments reached the conclusion that they could not sit idly by and watch collective bargaining negotiations descend into open conflict with potentially huge economy-wide negative effects. The response everywhere was to establish some form of institutional framework of state-provided dispute resolution facilities to assist in the settlement of workplace disputes, when necessary. Public agencies and arrangements to support the resolution of workplace conflict were thus set up to compensate for the institutional weaknesses and failures of voluntarist employment relations systems.

In a sense by creating public agencies to help resolve employment dispute resolution, governments were recognizing workplace conflict as a negative labour market 'externality' that required a public policy response. They were rejecting the rational self-interested world of mainstream economics that suggested conflict at work or elsewhere should neither be deep-seated nor protracted: disagreeing parties should have the capacity to calculate when it is in their self-interest to resolve a conflict. Governments were more hard-nosed as their working assumption was that in the real world such utilitarian behaviour does not always prevail, with negative consequences for individual organizations and the wider economy. Sometimes, disputes and disagreements can get so embittered that one or all of the parties involved parties persist with the conflict way beyond the time when it was in their interests to reach a settlement. Disputes of this kind are not only self-harming but can also be difficult to settle as the red mist of conflict blurs the parties' pathway to an acceptable resolution. When workplace conflict is difficult to resolve, the organizational and human costs can be significant. Days can be lost due to some form of industrial action, sickness and absenteeism rates can be high, and management-employee relations can become strained. Disharmony at the workplace can impede organizations from creating adaptable structures to succeed in today's challenging business environment.

Moreover, the effects of workplace conflict may not be confined to a particular organization or group of employers. Organizations seldom operate fully in their own bubble and thus any conflict they experience may produce wider spillover effects. If too many firms in a particular economy experience workplace conflict, then it is likely that various forms of contagion will arise. A more permissive environment is created for both collective and individual workplace disputes. In terms of collective conflict, labour market norms emerge that promulgate mistrust and even conflict between employers and trade unions, creating a cool climate for the fostering of cooperative employment relations inside organizations. In terms of individual disputes, employees start to mimic each other's behaviour when they become involved in workplace disputes: this sort of behaviour explains the growing acceptability of using lawyers to resolve individual disputes at the workplace. Contagions of this kind suggest that labour market failures have arisen in relation to workplace conflict: employment disputes are likely to be more prevalent, the cost of addressing these problems is relatively high and the impact on organizational and economy-wide performance is appreciable. Because this dimension to workplace conflict is external to individual organizations but internal to the industrial relations system, it is difficult for an individual or group of firms to address effectively these externalities. As a result, public intervention is needed.

The role of public agencies for workplace conflict resolution

Thus, across the Anglo-American world, governments, often towards the end of the nineteenth century as union organization expanded, sparking employer organization and resistance, arrived at the conclusion that public agencies were needed to be an integral part of the architecture of voluntarist employment relations systems. The nature, purpose and organizational characteristics of these public agencies vary a great deal across countries, but all tend to carry out at least one of the following three key functions. One is to establish the norms – rules would be too strong a word – that should govern workplace relations, particularly in terms of demarcating acceptable and unacceptable behaviour. A number of activities are usually carried out to this end:

- Collective bargaining is supported and commonly union recognition is advocated.
- Public servants or publicly appointed neutral parties are made available to employers and unions to support dispute resolution.
- Information systems are created so that organizations and employees are aware of their legal rights and obligations.
- Advice is provided to organizations about the significance of particular employment laws and what constitutes good people management policies.

- Advocacy is used to promote employment practices considered to be best-in-class
- Training is provided to ensure that organizations have the expertise and know-how to address workplace conflict effectively.
- Some type of quasi-judicial process is provided within the employment relations system.

These processes can perform an important role: they can give public agencies the authority to bring together disputing parties involved in an employment conflict, with a view to reaching a settlement. This 'convening power' is particularly useful when relationships between disputing parties have reached an impasse. It also requires agencies to possess a range of services that enables them to address workplace conflict quickly and decisive. As a result, almost all public dispute resolution agencies in the Anglo-American world have the capacity to deliver some form of conciliation/facilitation, mediation and adjudication or arbitration. A further potential role for public agencies is not only to deliver efficient and fair conflict resolution services but also to prevent workplace disputes by launching initiatives that promote cooperative employment relations at the workplace: greater collaboration between employers and employees has the direct effect of crowding out adversarialism from workplace relations.

From the very beginning, debate has raged about the appropriate mission and activities of public agencies for workplace conflict resolution. In some countries, this debate is on-going. For example, an old chestnut is whether public agencies should concern themselves solely with resolving disputes or whether they should also have responsibility for more proactively preventing conflict by trying to influence the type of employment relations followed by employers and employees. One view is that public agencies should 'stand above' employer-employee interactions and only intervene when relationships between the two become embittered for one reason or another. In other words, public agencies should seek first and foremost to be 'neutral' so that they are in a better position to help employers and employees resolve their disagreements. Without the 'neutrality' principle being upheld, so the argument goes, a public agency runs the risk of being tarnished as pro-business or pro-trade union. The counter-argument is that making 'neutrality' a coveted characteristic of public agencies for workplace dispute resolution runs the danger of adversarial employment relations going unchallenged. If the collective bargaining system is riven with a 'them and us' mentality, then employers and employees are encouraged to adopt unreasonable stances and then drag the dispute resolution agencies into the subsequent bargaining games they play: public agencies get captured by the employer-employee interactions they are seeking to stand above. From this perspective, the role of a public agency is framed differently. It is not simply about these agencies intervening when appropriate to address a workplace dispute but also to be part of an on-going wider process that seeks to build trust and cooperation between employers and employees at the workplace: as much emphasis is placed on conflict prevention as conflict resolution. This debate has not been decided decisively in favour of either position so most public agencies continue to grapple with this tricky matter. Thus, although public agencies to support the resolution of workplace conflict exist across the Anglo-American world, debates continue in each country about how such bodies should be constituted and what services they should deliver.

International developments in public conflict resolution agencies

The result of these debates has been considerable cross-country diversity in the exact organizational make-up of public conflict resolution agencies. Despite organizational diversity, there is currently wide agreement across these agencies that they are facing challenging times. All the agencies agree that emerging developments, mostly outside their control, are threatening to make them less purposeful if not less relevant. Some of these developments are country-specific. In Australia and New Zealand, for example, political pressures representing different party approaches to the resolution of workplace conflict have created an exceptionally turbulent policy environment in which public agencies are obliged to operate: conservative governments have encouraged the resolution of workplace problems by firms themselves, assigning a fairly minimalist role to the public agencies set up to assist the resolution of employment disputes. In contrast, Labour Governments have sought to strengthen the role of these public agencies. In other countries such as Canada, the pressure on the public conflict resolution agencies has arisen from changing jurisprudence in the approach towards worker rights and collective action. And in yet other countries, like in the United Kingdom, the public agencies, most notably Acas, have been under pressure for some time to demonstrate the public value (in terms of its use of taxpayer funds) that arise from their activities. In the United States, the dramatic decline in union density has created an imperative to reevaluate the structures and assumptions of the existing dimensions of its conflict resolution system.

Despite the existence of country-specific challenges, a number of similar pressures are evident across countries that threaten to reconfigure the public dispute resolution landscape. Many of the developments pointed out above in relation to Ireland are also occurring in other Anglo-American countries. All have experienced some form of decline in collective manifestations of conflict and an increase in the expression of individual workplace tensions and grievances. Similarly, all countries have experienced a fall in union density, with countries like the United States and Australia seeing dramatic declines. Australia saw a decline from 41 per cent union density in 1990 to 12.5 per cent in 2022. In Great Britain, collective bargaining coverage declined from 70 per cent in 1979 to 26 per cent in 2019. Other countries, such as Canada, saw more modest declines, but even here, there was a large enough reduction in unionization to affect public agencies' work. Across countries the decline in union representation and collective bargaining coverage was most pronounced in the private sector, resulting in a changing mix of collective conflicts in the workplace including more public sector disputes. The decline in collective conflict is not just seen through the reduction in strike frequency but also in the dominant role played by traditional collective bargaining and labour-management relationships for a growing proportion of the workforce in many countries. In almost every Anglo-American country, union decline led to reductions in the demand for collective conflict resolution supports and services. In the United States, for example, the dramatic decline in union density has led to a bifurcated system for resolving disputes with vastly different modes of access to dispute resolution agencies and in their 'jurisdiction' with non-union workers relying, mostly, on private and individual systems set up by firms.

Side-by-side, with the decline in collective representation in Anglo-American countries, there has been an expansion of individual employment rights. Without addressing the question of a causal connection between these patterns, expansion of rights and decline of unionization, it is clear that both trends have placed a significant pressure on public dispute resolution agencies and have necessitated a realignment of practices and procedures. The legislatively driven expansion of employee rights has had clear implications for the functioning of the public agencies charged with the resolution of workplace conflict. Australia and the United States offer examples of how dramatic increases in individual employment rights have important consequences for the type of conflicts that dominate the conflict resolution system. In Australia, the most prevalent conflicts that make it into the system are now based on individual employment rights and involve issues such as unfair dismissal, bullying and sexual harassment. Across countries, it is evident that the growth in individual employment rights and protections affects the dominance of legal framing around workplace conflict and, in many ways, decouples the adjudication and resolution of workplace conflict from union membership.

Consistent with the trends set out earlier in relation to Ireland, all Anglo-American countries have witnessed an expansion of employment arrangements that depart from the traditional employer–employee relationship. Everywhere there has been a growth platform-mediated employment arrangements, such as ride-sharing or food delivery, which has created a new group of workers that commonly benefit from neither collective nor individual employment protections. These changes also have implications for both the type of conflicts that might arise between workers and firms and also the ability of different public agencies to address such conflict given existing mandates and organizational structures. In Great Britain, for example, an expansion of such arrangements has heavily influenced the strategic choices made by the main public dispute resolution agency, Acas.

Thus, across the Anglo-American world, multiple pressures are emerging, some of which are country-specific and others more universal in character, that are challenging the established ways pubic workplace conflict resolution agencies do things. It is not an overstatement to suggest that the core traditional mission – the over-arching policy purpose – of public conflict resolution agencies is being called into question. For most of the twentieth century, the key purpose of these agencies was to maintain stable and orderly collective industrial relations. For sure, most public agencies still need the internal capacity and expertise to address collective industrial disputes, especially as the incidence of strikes and other forms of collective action have been on the rise recently across the Anglo-American world. But, it is unlikely that resolving collective disputes will continue to be the mainstay mission of these agencies in light of the changes that are occurring to work and employment. The traditional strongly collectivist organizational ethos of these agencies seems increasingly misaligned with the growing individualized nature of most contemporary workforce conflict. Accentuating the problem is that most of the agencies are finding it difficult to influence conflict resolution in non-union firms or connect fully with precarious workers. Moreover, the seemingly relentless growth of private forms of conflict resolution makes it increasingly untenable for agencies to cocoon themselves from such challenges and cling to their long-established collectivist mission.

Thus, the external environment is giving arise to foundational challenges to the traditional conflict resolution landscape. The obvious question that arises is how will public conflict resolution agencies respond? Should they adopt a radical strategy aimed at transforming their core mission, which in practice would mean nurturing a new organizational identity and renewing their internal capabilities to deliver a broader, more sophisticated range of services? Or should they choose the more incremental strategic option, that would involve gradually recombining internal capabilities and slowly building up new services? The aim would be to reconstitute their conventional core mission by stealth.

Efforts by public conflict resolution agencies to reconstruct and even reinvent themselves in response to the changing nature of conflict in workplaces have not gone unnoticed. A recent study of public dispute resolution agencies in six Anglo-American countries – Ireland, the United States, the United Kingdom, Canada, Australia and New Zealand – assesses how they responded to the multiple pressures swirling around them (Avgar et al. 2023). The study highlighted that the different institutional structures, political regimes and dispute resolution priorities that prevail in different Anglo-American are heavily influencing the degree to which a national public dispute resolution agency will pivot to include a broader range of conflicts and disputes that do not conform to the traditional unionized and collective model.

The comparative study also emphasized that the WRC stood apart from public agencies in other countries, with the possible exception of Canada, in several important ways. Perhaps, the most marked distinction is that unlike other countries, state-provided workplace conflict resolution services in Ireland have never been heavily politicized or subject to political schism and polarization. In countries like Australia and New Zealand, the role of conflict resolution institutions has been deeply politically contested. As a result, reform programmes in these countries have not been primarily or directly motivated by concerns to align public conflict resolution bodies with unfolding changes in the nature of workplace conflict. Instead, they have been largely driven by political ideology, which puts the dispute resolution bodies on something of a roller-coaster journey as their mission and purpose radically oscillated depending on which political party was elected to office. In Ireland, the workings of the conflict resolution bodies have never been captured by political ideology. As evident in our analysis of the establishment of the Labour Court and subsequent developments, these bodies have carried out their work in the context of broad-based political support. They have consistently enjoyed the full imprimatur of government, which not only strengthened their organizational legitimacy, but also allowed their work to be carried out in a largely politically uncontested manner. Equally important, it allowed for reforms and changes to be introduced in a manner that first and foremost sought to address problems that had been identified with the operation of the public regime for workplace conflict management by public servants and conflict resolution professionals. This book analyses the genesis, nature and significance of these reforms.

Using the public policy literature to understand workplace conflict resolution change

Creating the WRC in 2015 as the go-to place to resolve almost all forms of workplace conflict in Ireland, whether big or small, represents a highly significant public policy moment. It brought to an end a public policy regime that delivered workplace conflict resolution services through a number of specialized bodies that operated more or less independently from each other. The WRC was deliberately designed to sweep away institutional fragmentation by creating a single, all-encompassing agency to provide dispute resolution services. In this sense, its creation can be viewed as an act of transformative public policy. Viewing the setting up of the WRC in such a manner allows the analysis to draw upon a rich public policy literature to understand and explain how change and reform were initiated and enacted to recast the delivery of public workplace conflict resolution services in Ireland.

One important strand of the public policy literature that can be usefully employed relates to policy entrepreneurship (Cairney 2017). In fact, the study of the creation of the WRC provides a textbook example of how policy entrepreneurship can unlock policy stasis. From the 1990s onwards, state conflict resolution services became manifestly dysfunctional due to growing fragmentation represented by multiple agencies with widening and overlapping jurisdictions.

The LRC, while recognized at the time as the main agency for resolving workplace conflict, shared the pitch with a number of other agencies: the Employment Appeals Tribunal (EAT), the Equality Tribunal, the National Employment Rights Authority (NERA), the National Centre for Partnership and Performance and the National Implementation Body. The case for the reform of workplace conflict resolution services had become manifest from the early 2000s. Multiple reviews and reports highlighted the deficiencies of fragmentation but gained little traction at senior government level. The big problem was that no incentive for change existed: each agency consistently met the goals that were set for it and as a result more or less disregarded arguments that everyone would be better off if greater coordination were introduced into the delivery of conflict management services. Meantime, as workplace conflict, particularly collective employment relations problems, was more or less stable, the case for change, least of all, radical change, within senior government circles, was not apparent. The underlying need for change did not transmit into a policy imperative for change.

The policy entrepreneurship literature speaks about unanticipated events, 'windows of opportunity', that can potentially dislodge policy blockages and create the space for policy innovation (Mintrom 2019). An opportunity to reform conflict resolution bodies arrived with the global financial crisis in 2008, the resulting Great Recession and programme of fiscal austerity in Ireland. Very rapidly the macroeconomic environment changed dramatically, creating a climate for policy reform that seemed unimaginable up to that point. Two senior conflict resolution 'insiders' or professionals were game changers as they transformed the underlying need for reform debate into a coherent and plausible policy plan for the reconfiguration of all state conflict resolution agencies. They did so by developing a radical vision and blueprint that involved the merger of four agencies (five, if the formally independent Rights Commissioners service, operating within the WRC is included) and the repurposing of the Labour Court.

In developing the radical plan, the two professionals performed all the 'classic' actions of policy entrepreneurs (see Cohen, 2016): (1) they properly 'framed' the problem facing public workplace conflict management as one of institutional fragmentation. Equally, important, they were persuasive in arguing that not only was radical change an imperative, but it was also feasible; (2) they developed policy solutions in a careful manner so that their reform proposals directly addressed the root cause of the problem and in a way that generated supporters and minimized disaffection; (3) they were acutely aware that their case for reform would not be won by simply developing smart policy proposals. As a result, they were very active in building a policy coalition involving politicians and senior civil servants to advance their ideas; (4) they were ruthless in portraying the Great Recession as an unprecedented opportunity to overhaul the existing policy infrastructure decisively and quickly.

However, the two professionals did not exhibit some of the main traits often associated with policy entrepreneurs – being driven to see innovation and change for its own sake or to advance their own careers. In many ways, the professionals acted more like the policy leaders portrayed in Selznick's (1957) classic study *Leadership in Administration*. For Selznick, the key purpose of a policy leader was to develop, maintain and, if required, disrupt the functioning of an organization or institution should it not be realizing its core mission. Organizational integrity, he maintained, could not be achieved if the policy leader themselves did not act with integrity to govern, adapt and reform the organization for which they were responsible. From this perspective, the two professionals can be viewed as being motivated to renew the organizational integrity of workplace conflict management agencies.

A second part of the public policy literature that is used in the assessment concerns how public agencies acquire legitimacy. A recurring theme in this literature is that a public agency does not acquire legitimacy either automatically or spontaneously. Instead, it emphasizes that a series of interrelated internal and external challenges require addressing to secure organizational legitimacy (Scott 2001). Internally, organizations have to address three overlapping challenges: (1) resources and capabilities have to be mobilized and coordinated to meet the tasks and goals set for the organization; (2) the capacity has to be developed not only to identify and codify important unfolding trends, but also to respond to these quickly; (3) an organizational mentality and culture needs to be fostered that accepts, even celebrates the need for continuous renewal. These challenges were particularly pressing for the new WRC, not least because it was established as a single agency to deliver an all-encompassing range of conflict management services, including conciliation, mediation, adjudication and enforcement. The skills and expertise needed to conduct these activities are quite diverse. Thus, the new WRC faced the daunting challenges of not only coordinating these heterogeneous capabilities, but also of developing an overarching organizational culture that integrated each constituent part of the organization.

The external challenges an organization faces when trying to build legitimacy are largely twofold. One is the need to establish boundaries that delineate the work and functions of the organization in a manner that is recognized and accepted by all relevant external parties and that responds to major external pressures and trends. The other involves the internal challenge of acquiring a distinctive organizational identity and status amongst the constituencies to which the organization is delivering services: the organization has not only to be known for what it does but have the reputation for delivering its services efficiently and effectively (see Dowling and Pfeffer 1975). These tasks were particularly difficult for the WRC in its formative years as it was the subject of considerable adverse commentary by users and stakeholders – not helped, it may be added, by the new senior management team declaring it would deliver a 'world class' conflict resolution service. These were trying enough times for the leadership of the new agency for they were acutely aware that without gaining organizational legitimacy the WRC would face on-going internal and external struggles to gain acceptance. However, the new agency successfully weathered these initial turbulences and has now secured the confidence and respect of users and stakeholders. The manner in which the WRC navigated its way through these challenges holds lessons about what a public service agency can do to gain organizational legitimacy.

Thirdly, the study uses the public policy literature to show in concrete fashion how complex public policy change involves not only its design, but also its implementation. It highlights that no automatic transmission mechanism exists to connect the need for policy reform with the actual development of policy proposals to effect change. Policy malfunctioning can persist for years without any concerted corrective action being launched. In other words, connecting the need for policy reform with actual policy change rarely occurs spontaneously. It needs deliberate, conscious efforts (Brouwer and Huitema 2018). On paper, a range of methods could be used to make the connection, but this book emphasizes policy leadership and entrepreneurship. However, it immediately needs highlighting that the kind of leadership displayed by senior conflict resolution professionals that led to the creation of the WRC, and indeed, earlier leadership by the public servants largely responsible for creating the LRC, marks Ireland off from programmes of reform in public provision of workplace conflict resolution internationally. Many of the long-run trends in patterns of workplace conflict evident in Ireland have been apparent also in other advanced economies. However, reform of conflict resolution agencies in other English-speaking countries with legal and institutional affinities with industrial relations in Ireland has been deeply politicized, resulting in either reforms reaching an impasse or change being purely ideologically driven and subject to sharp changes in direction and momentum.

In telling the story about the creation of the WRC, this book also reveals a process of change that stands apart from some of the mainstream approaches to how public policy reform takes place. Consider first the rational approach to public policy making. On this approach, public policy change occurs through a clinical and sequential process of rational design (Mintrom, and Norman 2009). First of all, those driving the public policy change or innovation identify, scrutinize and put into consistent order those objectives and other values that lie at the centre of the new policy. Then an assessment is made of all possible means of achieving the identified objectives and values, including examining all possible consequences from employing each of the possible means. After these tasks have been completed, a combination of policies and arrangements should emerge that will enable the realization of all the designated objectives and values (Saint-Martin and Rothmayr Allison 2011). However, the creation of the WRC was not the result of such calculative strategic action. Instead, the pathway to its creation involved developing proposals for change that were less concerned with adopting 'best-in-class' solutions and more focused on ensuring that they fitted with the Irish context and would gain approval from stakeholders and government alike.

The story about how the WRC was set up also defies the 'mudding-through' approach to doing public policy – the main alternative to more rationalist models of public policy making. According to this classical paradigm, public policy makers and civil servants make decisions based on the basis of a fairly limited range of information and analysis. Thus, for example, Charles Lindblom, the godfather of the muddling-through approach, suggests that policy makers have not got the time or resources to identify and analyse comprehensively every policy option and thus almost always follow a more constrained process that involves making limited comparison and conducting only partial analysis (Lindblom 1959). As result, due to bounded rationality, lack of time and resources, policy makers muddle through, which leads to policy development being heavily incrementalist in character. Thus, for the proponents of the muddling-through approach, public policy decision-making is hard-wired against radical change: only rarely will dramatically different new policies be introduced. Instead, the emphasis is on developing policies that build on existing arrangements, with the emphasis on making tweaks here and there in an evolutionary manner (see Thelen 2009).

Throughout the 1990s and the noughties, the Irish public policy regime to support the resolution of workplace conflict seemed to embody all the traits of the muddling-through model. Radical change was shunned. Policy changes were introduced in fits and starts usually in response to new developments in relation to the changing character of workplace disputes and changes in employment law. But these changes were always introduced in a manner that was respectful of existing public agencies with a workplace conflict resolution role; great care was taken not to disrupt established policy bailiwicks and competences. The emphasis was very much on making pragmatic adaptations that sought to ensure that public policy was keeping pace with unfolding workplace conflict developments without disturbing too much inherited ways of doing things. Thus, the public policy regime seemed to be configured in a way that made it impenetrable to transformative policy change. And yet within a short period of time, the policy regime for workplace conflict resolution was turned upside down, with five separate agencies being replaced by one. In defiance of the strictures (and preferences) of the muddling-through approach, the creation of the WRC, like the earlier creation of its parent body the Labour Court, suggests that a public policy regime can be simultaneously wedded to an incremental way of doing things and remain open to radical policy change. Thus, assessing how the state has gone about trying to maintain a low workplace conflict environment in Ireland reveals some fascinating insights into how the strengths and weaknesses of alternative approaches to how public policy is formed and implemented but also how it can change overtime.

Public dispute resolution in Ireland

Thus multiple issues have to be considered when assessing the effectiveness of Ireland's public policy regime to support the resolution of workplace conflict. This book explores these issues for the first time in a systematic and in-depth manner. The assessment starts with a context-setting analysis of the country's 'voluntary system of industrial relations' and the place of conflict resolution within voluntarism. It identifies the role of the state in conflict resolution and the origins of an enduring cross-party political consensus on the reform of workplace conflict resolution, which is such a peculiar feature of the Irish case. The strong challenges to voluntarist industrial relations and dispute resolution during the first decades of the twentieth century are highlighted to emphasize that Ireland could easily have travelled an alternative pathway to voluntarism in the way it organized employer-employee relations. The patchwork of dispute resolution and wage fixing bodies in existence before the establishment of the Labour Court are examined. The role of Sean Lemass, as the architect of the Labour Court, is explored, as are the stark differences between Lemass's original vision for the Court and the institution established in 1946 – revealing by then the strength of voluntarism in shaping collective conflict resolution. The establishment of the Court also reveals the absence of political division and politicization – features of the reform process that would carry over into the creation of the LRC and WRC.

A careful examination is conducted of the establishment, governance and operation of the LRC. Established in 1991, the LRC was soon to become the pivotal public agency institution for workplace conflict resolution. Changing patterns of industrial conflict, marked by long-run decline in collective conflict and the growth in individual grievances focused on employment rights, are seen as having a strong impact on Commission services, particularly conciliation, Rights Commissioners and advisory. The assessment also views the new, unfolding forms of workplace conflict as the main underlying reason for the growing organizational fragmentation of public conflict resolution services that occurred during the 1990s. As a result of fragmentation, multiple bodies were responsible for the delivery of these services, including the EAT, the Equality Tribunal, the NERA, the National Implementation Body and the National Centre for Partnership and Performance. Further still, the changing nature of workplace conflict acted as a catalyst for the emergence of new ADR practices and other 'private conflict resolution' processes within workplaces.

The creation of the WRC in 2015 out of a radical merger of four existing agencies is examined as is its governance, operation and management. A careful assessment is made of the impact of changing patterns or service demand and delivery on the work of WRC. The sustained and continuous efforts made by the WRC to foster a coherent and integrated organizational culture in the context of having to develop a range of quite diverse conflict resolution and labour market enforcement services are described. The trials and tribulations experienced by the WRC as a result of the Zelewski case and Supreme Court judgement are considered.

An important issue that this book seeks to explain is how and why change occurs in the public dispute resolution regime for workplace conflict. To this end, a detailed analysis is provided of external and internal pressures for the reform of the workplace conflict resolution agencies, beginning with the Labour Court and extending to the LRC and the wider highly fragmented multi-agency system of conflict resolution. The industrial relations crisis of the 1970s contributed to the creation of the LRC by splitting the conciliation service from the Labour Court to become the pivotal service of the LRC. The effects of changing patterns of conflict, particularly the sharp rise of individual rights mediation and adjudication, are analysed, as are the effects of growing workforce diversity. The impact of the global financial crisis and fiscal crisis of the State and the opportunity for reform of the radical 'Mulvey-Deering' reform proposals are examined to explain the creation of the WRC.

Because COVID-19 had such a profound effect on Irish life, the assessment presented in the book would be incomplete if an analysis was not made of the impact of the pandemic on service delivery in the WRC. Thus, the rapid adjustments made to existing modes of service delivery and the import of new models of delivery on services are described to gain a view of how well the WRC coped with this health emergency. The abiding effects of the pandemic in leading to areas of innovation in services are also reviewed. This assessment of how the WRC coped with the challenges of COVID-19 is part of a wider assessment of how the organizational character of public conflict resolution agencies has changed with the creation of the WRC. It is argued that the WRC is less an institutional enabler of collective dispute resolution than a provider of a range of workplace conflict resolution services, with a primary concern to mediate or adjudicate on individual rights-based complaints and grievances. The new challenges and competencies involved in this shift are considered.

Overall, the assessment presented in the book should bring into open view the changes in public dispute resolution bodies that have occurred with the creation of the Labour Court, LRC and the WRC. It should also provide a clearer picture of the major pressures leading to reform and their effects on the character of workplace conflict resolution. Most notably, three 'turning points' are identified in the reform of conflict resolution: the transition from wartime to normal economic conditions that led to the Labour Court, the 1970s escalation in industrial conflict and industrial relations crisis that led to the creation of the LRC and the global financial crisis and fiscal crisis that influenced the creation of the WRC. The pattern of reform involving public servants and conflict management professionals rather than politicians is highlighted. Developments in Ireland are compared to politicized reform programmes in other English-speaking countries. Finally, the analysis identifies the strategic challenges that are currently being faced by the WRC as it shapes to address effectively workplace conflict in the period ahead.

Research methods

A range of research methods was used to collect the data for this study. First of all, a large volume of primary source materials informed the analysis. These included annual reports, strategy and policy documents and work programmes of the LRC and WRC and annual reports of other conflict resolution and employment rights agencies: the EAT, Equality Tribunal, Labour Court and the NERA. Archival research in the National Archives of Ireland and UCD Archives was also undertaken, with a view to examining the foundations of conflict resolution in Ireland within the wider voluntarist system of industrial relations, inherited from the United Kingdom. Other primary source materials included a range of policy papers, reviews, speeches, public addresses and conference presentations by ministers and by figures centrally involved in reform initiatives. Also included are reform proposals, submissions and feedback documents pertaining to the creation of the LRC and WRC, generated by the Department of Labour and successor departments responsible for the conflict resolution and employment rights agencies.

The authoritative weekly industrial relations organ, *Industrial Relations News*, was drawn on extensively to provide contemporary coverage of reform initiatives and debates, as well as reports on the website of the state broadcasting authority, RTE and reports by other media outlets. Judgements of the Irish High and Supreme Courts and associated documentation were also referenced. Personal documents not in the public domain were also provided by figures centrally involved in reform processes. These primary sources were backed up with a wide range of articles by academics and practitioners.

Secondly, statistical data on trends and patterns in referrals to conflict resolution and employment rights agencies and on the resourcing of services within agencies were compiled from annual reports of agencies, supplemented by data made available by the WRC. Data on trends in industrial conflict were obtained from the data series and archives of the Central Statistics Office. CSO data on numbers of employees in the workforce or at work were used to adjust these data for changes in the size of the workforce. Other sources of statistical data reported are referenced to the secondary sources in which they are reported.

Thirdly, interviews were conducted with leaders and senior professional staff of the LRC and WRC, with board members of both agencies and with figures centrally involved in reform initiatives. In all nine leaders and senior professional staff and six board members of the LRC and WRC were interviewed. One interview with a significant figure involved in the reform process leading to the creation of the WRC was undertaken in a detailed question-and-answer format over the Internet. Face-to-face interviews were generally of one or more hour's duration. Most interviews were recorded and post-interview summaries were compiled highlighting the main issues arising from interviews.

A second round of interviews, involving 14 senior member staff of the WRC, was conducted in September 2022 to examine the response of the WRC to the COVID-19 pandemic, and specifically how services were delivered under the constraints imposed by lockdown and other public health restrictions. The opportunity was also taken to update our initial interviews in relation to strategy and policy initiatives in the WRC. Interviews were also conducted with two conflict management professionals to explore the effects of the pandemic on the private provision of individual conflict resolution services (mainly mediation) and collective conflict resolution. Both were prominent and highly experienced professionals with and extensive network connections with peers and service users.

2 Voluntarism and conflict resolution in Ireland

Introduction

The road to the Workplace Relations Commission began before the state was founded. The institutional and political roots of workplace conflict resolution in Ireland lie deep within the 'voluntarist' industrial relations system that Ireland inherited from the United Kingdom, reinforced by a political system established after Independence that essentially avoided the politicization of industrial relations. This chapter examines the emergence of Ireland's conflict resolution institutions and practices. These were challenged during the turbulent first two decades of the twentieth century but survived more or less intact. The incremental development of a patchwork of conflict resolution and wage-fixing institutions of limited coverage followed during the 1920s and 1930s. During the wartime Emergency wages were controlled and the latitude for industrial conflict was narrowed significantly. The ending of wartime wage controls and an anticipated surge in wage claims and strike activity led to a turning point in the institutional framework for resolving workplace conflict. The Minister for Industry and Commerce, Sean Lemass, enacted reforms leading to the establishment of the Labour Court in 1946. The character of the Court was at variance with Lemass's original vision of a quasi-judicial institution that would align wage fixing with government economic policy. Lemass was the first and was also to be the last political architect of workplace conflict resolution in Ireland. His Labour Court would dominate the field for close on half a century.

The institutional roots of voluntarist conflict resolution

The independent Irish State inherited from the United Kingdom a 'voluntarist' industrial relations tradition and associated provisions for conflict resolution. Voluntarism involves employers and unions ordering their mutual dealings as they see fit, with the state's role largely confined to supporting

DOI: 10.4324/9781003520054-2

dispute resolution where conflict cannot be prevented or resolved through collective bargaining between employers and unions. State support for conflict resolution stops short of compulsion. Collective bargaining largely proceeds without state interference, other than possibly attempts to use moral suasion to avoid disputes or to bring the pressure of public opinion to bear on the parties to reach reasonable settlements. Consistent with the voluntarist tradition, it is a canon of union involvement in collective bargaining that entanglement with the courts should be avoided and that legislative measures that threaten such entanglement should be resisted.

The genesis of the voluntarist tradition in the United Kingdom and associated postures by employers, unions and the state has been traced in Alan Fox's magisterial study, *History and Heritage: The Social Origins of British Industrial Relations* (1985). Fox claims that by the late nineteenth-century sections of Britain's business, political and administrative elites had largely accepted trade unions and collective bargaining on pragmatic grounds. Sharp divisions of opinion nevertheless persisted between and within these parties on such issues as union recognition, collective bargaining, wage determination and the freedoms unions should be accorded within the law to represent members and undertake industrial action. The radical left within the trade union movement alleged that the promotion of compromise by the state was a conspiracy against the interests of the working class (Davidson 1978). Employers and their industrial associations repeatedly launched offensives and counter-offensives against unions, in particular unions organizing unskilled workers (Middlemas 1979: ch. 2). Yet, 'respectable' unions came to be viewed by sections of elite employer, political and administrative opinion as positive agents of the social integration and social control of the working class. Collective bargaining between employers and trade unions willing to accept rather than overthrow the status quo was viewed as a socially and politically progressive institution (Fox 1985: chs. 4–5).

With the advance of the voluntarist position, a series of laws sought to provide space for unions to operate within the law, most notably the Trade Union Act 1871, and the Conspiracy and Protection of Property Act 1975. The pivotal Trade Disputes Act 1906 sought to protect unions against the application of common law doctrines and principles by a hostile judiciary, especially in circumstances where industrial action was contemplated or occurred. The creation of the Labour Department of the Board of Trade in the late 1880s – the Board being the government's pivotal division for interfacing with the business world – led to continuous efforts to institutionalize and support collective bargaining and dispute resolution (Fox 1985: 246–255). The Department's labour policy worked by 'cajoling, persuading [and] leaning on the parties to ... conflict' (Fox 1985: 251, quoting Colin Crouch). The Department sought also to substitute conciliation by professionals, including former union officials, for direct ministerial intervention in industrial disputes (Middlemas 1979: 58–63). The Labour Department was instrumental in leading legal reforms promoting voluntary dispute resolution, in particular the Conciliation Act 1896, and its leaders also supported the liberalization of the law on industrial disputes, at the same time harbouring reservations about trade union power and the extent to which the law ought to be reformed (Davidson 1978).

Developments in industrial relations in Ireland largely mirrored developments in the United Kingdom – notwithstanding the manifold complications introduced by nationalism, unionism and sectarian divisions (Berresford Ellis 1985; Kostick 1996). Many British trade unions organized Irish workers. Boyle estimated that by the end of the nineteenth century, more than 75 per cent of Irish trade union members were organized by British unions (Boyle 1988: 125–126).[1] Emmett O'Connor's definitive *A Labour History of Ireland* (2011) reveals the strong parallels and overlaps between the development of trade unions and industrial relations in Ireland and Britain in the nineteenth and early twentieth centuries. Moreover, strike activity in Ireland from the 1890s broadly reflected UK strike waves and their accompanying economic and labour market influences (Cronin 1979: ch. 3; O'Connor 2010: chs. 3–5). Following practice in Britain, the UK Labour Department of the Board of Trade promoted conciliation in serious disputes in Ireland, such as a 1907 general strike in Belfast and the Great Dublin Lockout of 1913 (Berresford Ellis 1985: 180–181; O'Connor 1988: 86–87). During the Dublin lockout, the Labour Department's chief conciliator, Sir George Asquith, presided over a court of inquiry into the dispute. When the inquiry failed to resolve the dispute, an Industrial Peace Committee was convened by a number of prominent citizens, with no better outcome (Morrissey 2007: 79–81).

Other than such cataclysmic disputes, labour histories of the era record little direct involvement by the Labour Department in conflict resolution in Ireland, even in significant conflicts, such as the Wexford Lockout of 1911–1912, which convulsed the town and caused widespread hardship. Here, as in other disputes, national and local luminaries and members of parliament were prevailed on to intervene, while the corporation also sought to broker settlement (Roche 2012: 42–44).

Militancy, repression and challenges to conflict resolution[2]

The fledgling voluntarist practice of state-assisted facilitation of dispute resolution was challenged by two cycles of acute industrial conflict in the early twentieth-century Ireland. The first occurred from the early 1900s to the outbreak of the First World War and the second spanned the period from 1917 until the early years of the Irish Free State.

Figure 2.1 Strike Activity in Ireland 1910–1921.

Source: Data obtained from David Fitzpatrick, 'Strikes in Ireland 1914-1921', Saothar, 6, Table 3.

Figure 2.1 presents the trend in strike activity during these periods. During the first cycle, mass unionization by unskilled and semi-skilled workers and demands for union recognition and collective bargaining triggered a series of lockouts in major towns and cities, beginning in Belfast (1907), Cork (1909), Wexford (1911–1912) and culminating in the Dublin lockout (1913). The mass unionization of general workers during this period triggered such widespread, intense and prolonged disputes that what amounted to class conflict ensued in cities and towns around Ireland. In all these conflicts and many smaller disputes, employers sought to resist and break the 'new unions', particularly the syndicalist Irish Transport (and General) Workers' Union (ITGWU).

The second cycle of industrial conflict spanned the later years of the First World War, War of Independence and the Civil War, petering out in the early years of the Irish Free State. As evident in Figure 2.1 during the second cycle strike activity involved a significantly higher number of both strikes, workers involved and working days lost (excepting the year of the Great Dublin Lockout, 1913) During this cycle wartime economic conditions coupled with the collapse of civil order during the War of Independence and Civil War led to a wave of industrial conflict involving more socially radical instances of militancy. The shift to compulsory labour-intensive tillage farming coupled with buoyancy in food production and other industries led to a dramatic increase in unionization during the latter years of the First World War. The collapse in civil order, as the Royal Irish Constabulary came under attack and retreated to barracks, and the tactics and iconography of the Bolshevik revolution lent the new militancy a socially radical edge. While the great majority of strikes, even at the apex of industrial conflict between 1918 and 1920, concerned mundane issues surrounding wages, a spate of factory occupations occurred and 'soviets' were established across a range of industries, particularly in Munster (O'Connor 1988). Land seizures and cattle drives were also common, especially in the West (O'Connor 1980; 1988; Kostick 1996: ch. 5).

The underground Dáil Government's Department of Labour continued the practice instituted by the UK Board of Trade (and from 1916 a newly established Ministry of Labour), by intervening in industrial disputes to promote settlements. The Department was established in April 1919, when the Dáil appointed Countess Markievicz Minister for Labour. The Department's work properly commenced in August, when premises and staff were secured. The activities of the Department were hampered by interference by the British military with postal correspondence and by Markievicz's attempts to evade arrest, by her imprisonment and the imprisonment of substitute ministers (Arrington 2016: ch. 13). The executive of an English union was reported to have been opposed to intervention of the Department that might have resulted in a separate settlement for Irish members. Operating with little more than a handful of core staff, the Department was responsible for dispute resolution, assisting Irish members of some British unions to establish Irish organizations, managing the 'Belfast Boycott' on goods from Northern Ireland,[3] establishing an employment agency for police officers who were expelled or resigned from the Royal Irish Constabulary and unemployed Volunteers, and establishing an unemployment insurance scheme (Dáil Eireann Secretariat Department of Labour 1920–1922a). Dáil interventions in disputes were significantly more frequent than earlier conciliation efforts by the Board of Trade. Figure 2.2 shows that interventions by the Department peaked around the period when industrial conflict was the highest and most intense.

Conciliation and arbitration efforts by the Department involved ministers, substitute ministers, senior officials and TDs. The greater part of the Department's work in dispute resolution however was undertaken by agents engaged throughout the country and paid for their activities. As the Department's work evolved, it sought to improvise a set of principles and structures for dispute resolution. In 1919, it was agreed to

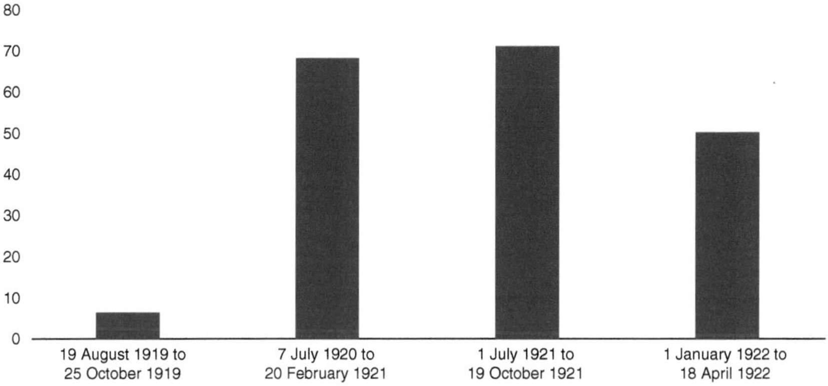

Figure 2.2 Disputes in Which the Department of Labour Intervened 1919–1922.

establish a national conciliation board for the settlement of trade disputes (Dáil Eireann Secretariat Department of Labour 1920–1922b). In 1920, the Department set out a series of principles for arbitration. This might occur only in circumstances where both parties recognized the authority of the Dáil and where direct engagement between the parties was unable to resolve disputes (Dáil Eireann Secretariat Department of Labour 1920–1922c). The Department sought funds to pay board members as it was deemed not currently advisable to appoint permanent officials to such roles or to ask parties in dispute to pay. Where conciliation failed, it was deemed that chairs of conciliation conferences should not arbitrate unless requested to do so by the parties (Dáil Eireann Secretariat Department of Labour 1920–1922d). Labour and union leaders were consulted on the further formalization of conciliation and arbitration board practices. The parties to a dispute were to be invited to elect representatives to a conciliation board, chaired by a neutral party or a person appointed by the Dáil. Unless a work stoppage has already occurred, none should occur pending the deliberation of the board. Failure of the board to resolve the dispute should, on consent by the parties, lead to arbitration by an agreed party, or a person appointed by the Dáil (Dáil Eireann Secretariat Department of Labour 1920–1922e).

The Department reported to the Dáil in March 1921 that 'in view of the frequency of strikes and lockouts throughout the country, it would be manifestly impossible for the Department to intervene directly' and suggested the creation of a system of conciliation boards in all local authority areas (Dáil Eireann Secretariat Department of Labour 1920–1922e). 'Violent land disputes' were to be referred to Dáil arbitration courts (Dáil Eireann Secretariat Department of Labour 1920–1922c). Little remaining activity by the British Ministry of Labour was reported. However, pre-emptive action was taken in the case of local government disputes. In August 1920, The Department reported that

> having ascertained that the enemy government contemplated establishing machinery for the purpose of dealing with the salaries and wages of public officials ... all public authorities were circularized suggesting a scheme for the amicable settlement of disputes between such bodies and their officials and employees.

The conciliation boards recommended were to consist of two or more representatives of each side and an agreed chair, or a chair appointed by the Minister for Labour (Dáil Eireann Secretariat Department of Labour 1920–1922f). A year later, 70 councils had adopted the proposal and established conciliation-arbitration boards (Dáil Eireann Secretariat Department of Labour 1920–1922g). Over and above these initiatives, the Department was also instrumental in establishing Commissions following disputes in 1922 in canals and retail tailoring and in creating joint industrial councils at sectoral and district levels in co-operative and propriety creameries (Dáil Eireann Secretariat Department of Labour 1920–1922h).

By 1921, conflict had escalated to such a degree that the Dáil mandated the Ministers for Labour, Trade and Commerce and Agriculture to confer with a view to 'taking any steps necessary to prevent the starting of a class war' (Dáil Eireann Secretariat Department of Labour 1920–1922i). Markievicz, similarly alarmed, warned the cabinet of the 'imminence of social revolution' (Mitchell 1974: 141–142). As conflict became more socially militant and radical, the Dáil and subsequently the Provisional Government turned to repression to re-establish order and protect private property. The Government supported farm employer actions in cutting wages as farm prices fell after 1920 and recession deepened in the years that followed (Costello 2003: ch. 5; O'Connor 1988). Other wage cutting disputes were also supported by a combination of repressive measures and attempts to promote conciliation and establish commissions of inquiry (O'Connor 1988: 112–113). The IRA were deployed to restore order in land seizures and occupations, while the National Army broke up Soviets that remained extant at the end of the Civil War (O'Connor 1988: 127–131; Kostick 1996: ch. 5). Combining conciliation, arbitration and repression the Government of the new state sought to manage often intense and sometimes radical industrial conflict until civil order was restored following the War of Independence and Civil War:

> Conscious of its status as midwife of the new regime, the cabinet was anxious to maintain the values of liberal democracy. In so far as this was achieved, it was realized through the paradox of withholding the

> conventions of liberalism until after the crisis phase. The security forces that acted against trade unionists in 1922 and 1923 did not act within the law, were ill disciplined and often openly partisan.
>
> (O'Connor 1988: 163)

By the mid-1920s, the Independent Irish state had secured civil order, aided by the reluctance of labour and trade union leaders to foment radical social activism and support head-on challenges to private property during the militant phase of industrial action from 1920 to 1922. As civil order was restored, wage levels declined in line with prevailing recessionary conditions and repression was no longer a prominent feature of industrial dispute resolution.

The general posture and activities of the Dáil and Free State government mirrored those of the Board of Trade by involving employer and union representatives in dispute resolution and prioritizing conciliation over arbitration. Suppression was resorted to where the nature of conflict meant that these activities were redundant or failed. The Dáil also followed a dual-track strategy by deploying underground Republican Arbitration Courts to settle industrial and land disputes (Dáil Eireann Debates, 17 August 1921; Kostick 1996: 104; Kotsonouris 1994). The underground courts largely operated on the basis of established juridical procedure. As Kotsonouris (1994: 133) remarked, their 'procedure, law and precedent were those of the courts they replaced'.

A Fragmented patchwork of institutions: conflict resolution in the Irish Free State

The Provisional Government, now determined to keep the state out of long-term engagement with industrial disputes, soon abolished the Dáil Department of Labour and transferred its activities to the Department of Industry and Commerce. Republican conciliation and arbitration bodies were discontinued, the courts were reconstituted and ad hoc commissions of inquiry replaced the former 'semi-official back-up [conciliation] service of the Department of Labour' to prevent or resolve disputes (O'Connor 1988: 155–156). National and departmental 'Whitley Councils' charged with negotiating pay and conditions had been created in the pre-treaty Irish civil service. These were abolished by the Irish government in 1924, as they were viewed as inconsistent with state sovereignty over public expenditure (Maguire 2005: chs. 4 and 9).

Arrangements for dispute resolution in the Irish Free State remained both fragmented and of limited coverage. The Conciliation Act 1896, the Industrial Courts Act 1919 and the Reports of the Whitley Committee on Relations Between Employers and Employed 1919 provided the legislative basis for conciliation and adjudication in industrial disputes (Mortished 1947/1948). With 'prominent public men commonly acting as mediators or arbitrators' in industrial disputes, few permanent voluntary dispute resolution arrangements existed (Quinn 1952: 44). Incrementally, joint industrial councils, charged with negotiating pay and resolving disputes, were created in flour milling (1933), Dublin printing and allied trades (1934), the Dublin newspaper industry (1936), bacon curing (1936), woollen, worsted, linen and cotton (1938), sugar manufacturing (1938), hosiery (1941), rosary beads (1941) and tanning (1944).

While Whitley reports had made provision for worker participation in management in firms covered by joint industrial councils, in Ireland these bodies operated at sector level and were confined to collective bargaining over pay and conditions and dispute resolution (Mortished 1947/1948: 674). Joint conciliation boards had been established in Dublin transport, Dublin pawnbroking trades, licensed vintners trade, the boot and shoe industry and railways and the building industry in Dublin and Cork (Quinn 1952: 45). These bodies were mainly chaired by public servants from the Department of Industry and Commerce, appointed by the minister – in some cases chairs alternated between employer and worker members – and comprised employer and union nominees. Collective agreements and dispute resolution proposals were non-binding. Provisions under the Industrial Courts Act 1919 permitting the state to establish *ad hoc* arbitration boards to resolve individual disputes were not availed of. This was attributed to the fact that the parties to disputes could not be compelled to accept arbitration, while unions and employers favoured dispute resolution via voluntary collective bargaining (Committee on Vocational Organization 1943: para. 342). Invoking powers available under the Industrial Courts Act 1919, ministers could also establish industrial courts, with the primary objective of establishing the facts at issue in disputes of public importance. Industrial courts, which comprised independent chairs and could also involve equal numbers of employers and workers outside the firms or industries in dispute, were established in a number of instances: Dublin Tramways (1929), the Grand Canal Company (1935), Linen and Cotton Industry (1937), the Sugar Company (1937) and Dublin Bakeries (1940). While industrial courts could issue recommendations on how disputes might be resolved, they had no powers to compel the parties to accept these recommendations. Nevertheless, in all instances, the recommendations of the courts had been accepted by the parties in dispute (Committee on Vocational Organization 1943: para. 342; Mortished 1947/1948: 674; Quinn 1952: 45).

The Conditions of Employment Act 1936 provided for the registration of collective agreements, whereupon they became legally enforceable.

No provision was made however for registered agreements to contain dispute resolution procedures. In the event, only one agreement was registered (in hosiery). This was attributed to the government's reluctance to register agreements making provision for standard wage rates throughout industries, irrespective of location (McCarthy 1977: 183). The Agricultural Wages Act 1936 established an agricultural wages board comprising a chair, neutrals and employer and worker members, all nominated by the minister; district wage committees of similar composition were also established. The wage boards and committees were charged with fixing legal minimum wage rates for agricultural workers, but again no conflict resolution procedures were provided for.

A number of trade boards had been established prior to the foundation of the State and others were added during the 1930s. These were charged with fixing binding minimum wages in low-pay industries (the so-called 'sweated trades') with low levels of unionization. They were again representative of employers and workers but made no provisions for dispute resolution. Trade boards were created in tailoring; paper box; sugar confectionery and food preserving (1909); hand embroidery; shirt-making (1913); tobacco; aerated waters; boot and shoe repairing; brush and broom making; rope, twine and net; women's clothing and millinery; button making (1919); general waste materials; reclamation; packing (1934); handkerchief and household piece goods (1935). The Shops (Conditions of Employment Act) 1938 established a shops wages board on the model of trade boards to fix legal minimum wage rates for shop workers. Ireland joined the International Labour Organization in 1923 and the right to join trade unions was enshrined in Article 40 of the 1937 Constitution.

Most collective bargaining, dispute resolution and wage-fixing bodies had been established during the 1930s against a background of the rapid expansion of industrialization and industrial employment. Many dispute resolution arrangements were Dublin based. Most bodies were established by Fianna Fail governments and some were established at the behest of bodies set up under legislation, such as the Cereals Act 1933 and the Pigs and Bacon Act 1935.

With industrialization and economic revival during the 1930s, trade union membership and density rose sharply, as did wage levels. As evident in Figure 2.3, the incidence and prevalence of industrial conflict also increased.

Dispute resolution bodies could provide careers or career enhancement for employers and union representatives. That there was a demand for positions in dispute resolution bodies became evident when representative wage tribunals were established during the wartime Emergency. McCarthy (1977: 246) quotes a union leader's irritation at what they saw as the 'unseemly

Figure 2.3 Strike Activity 1923–1945.

scramble among unions … for seats on … tribunals' notwithstanding union opposition to wage controls and wider legislative measures that sought to promote union rationalization.

Over and above the industry-specific wage-fixing and dispute resolution bodies that existed, a small group of conciliators worked in the Department of Industry and Commerce, providing voluntary dispute resolution support to employers and unions. These public servants intervened in a significant number of disputes during the 1920s and 1930s. While interventions peaked during the early 1920s, the later years of the 1930s saw a steady rise in the annual incidence of voluntary dispute resolution by departmental officials (Quinn 1952: 48–49). As is clear from Figure 2.3, the conciliation staff of Industry and Commerce appear to have been successful in averting work stoppages in a significant number of industrial disputes.[4]

Figure 2.4 shows the relative significance of conflict resolution methods in use from 1923 to 1939. It is evident that direct negotiations between the parties, without third-party involvement, were the most widely used means of settling disputes. Conversely, arbitration was little used. Voluntary conciliation was widely used – presumably provided in the main by conciliation staff of the Department of Industry and Commerce. The remainder of disputes ended without successful negotiation, possibly through the capitulation of one party or the other (Figure 2.5).

Figure 2.4 Involvement of Trade and Industries Branch of the Department of Industry and Commerce in Disputes.

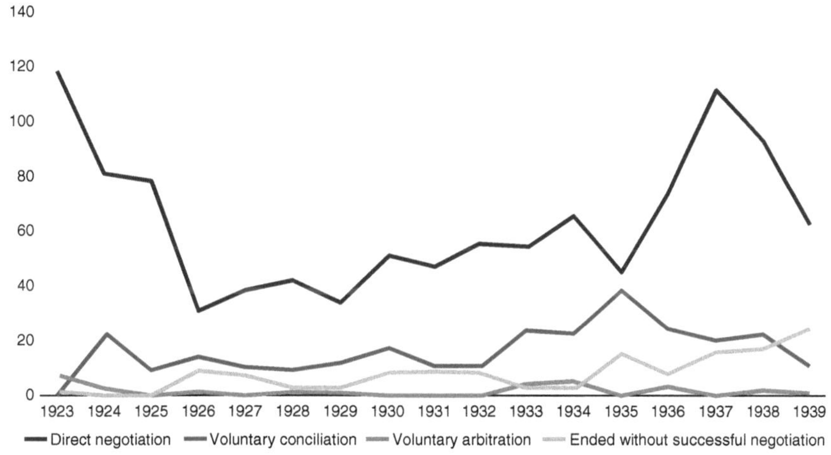

Figure 2.5 Modes of Dispute Resolution 1923–1939.

Wartime wage controls and the foundations for post-war reforms of dispute resolution

The prevailing patchwork of conflict resolution and wage-fixing bodies was suspended during the wartime Emergency by new arrangements to control wages. Responding to fears that wage rises were fuelling inflation and following threats of statutory controls on wages, the Government introduced the Emergency Powers (No. 83) Order in 1941 under the 1939 Emergency Powers Act. The Order effectively froze wages at their 1941 levels

(Article 6), suspended all statutory pay fixing bodies (Article 8) and set aside immunities for unions engaged in strikes under the Trade Disputes Act 1006 (Article 9).[5]

Significant trade union opposition to wage controls, involving mass public demonstrations, led to consultations between the relevant Minister, Sean Lemass, and the Irish Trade Union Congress (ITUC). The original Order was amended in 1942 through the Emergency Powers (No. 166) Order and further amended through subsequent orders. What emerged was a system of advisory wage tribunals, comprising a chair, employer member and employee member – the latter two members appointed by the Minister from panels established for the purpose of administering pay increases. The system operated by first establishing or confirming standard pay rates in industries and then recommending pay rises ('bonuses') related to changes in the cost of living index. While pay rises recommended and achieved significantly lagged the high prevailing rate of inflation, some 800 ministerial orders for pay awards were issued by 1943 (McCarthy 1977: 250).

Some commentators viewed the wartime wage tribunals as forerunners of the Labour Court (McCarthy 1977: ch. 7). Tribunals held investigations into applications for pay rises, heard submissions and issued recommendations (to the Minister). While tribunals were not the first pay fixing arrangements to involve employer and worker representatives in investigating wage claims or disputes, as evident from the patchwork of such arrangements that had evolved by the outbreak of war, they were certainly the first national system of this kind and aspects of their composition and procedure were to resemble those of the Labour Court.

The Labour Court and the creation of an integrated national dispute resolution system

The ending of wage controls in 1946 and an anticipated scramble for pay rises, likely accompanied by a surge in industrial conflict, led to the creation that year of the Labour Court. While the Court was to become for many years the pivotal institution of the voluntarist system of collective bargaining and dispute resolution, original ideas about the character of the Labour Court envisaged a very different kind of institution. Lemass was the architect of the Labour Court, but he initially sought to create an institution that would supervise wages in accordance with the economic imperatives of the post-war economy. In a 1942 'Memorandum on Labour Policy', Lemass considered institutional changes that might be required following the ending of the war. He expected 'many labour disputes with the passing of wage control, coupled with the influence of wages in the UK' (Lemass 1942). Lemass's original blueprint for the Labour Court emerged in a Memorandum for Government in 1944 (Department of Industry and Commerce 1944a). Lemass revealed that he had raised 'in a very general way' with the ITUC the idea that consideration should be given to the 'possibility of avoiding a return to the old methods of strikes and lockouts as the sole effective means of securing wage adjustments'. Lemass declared that he found the Congress 'very receptive' to this proposal (Lemass 1944a).

His plan was to establish a Commission that would inquire into the relationship of wage policy to national economic development. This would supplant the current 'more or less haphazard methods of determining wages and conditions'. He envisioned that the Commission might ultimately lead to the establishment of a permanent body to observe and report periodically on the economic and social significance of wage movements. His Departmental Memorandum (Department of Industry and Commerce 1944a) noted that informed by the experience of wartime wage control machinery (which was not regarded as suitable to peacetime), it was the view of the Minister that there seemed to be a 'necessity to examine the desirability and practicality of establishing normal machinery for the determination and alteration of wage rates in at least certain industries and in certain circumstances' (Department of Industry and Commerce 1944a). Lemass proposed that the Commission would be composed mainly of employer and labour organizations. The Commission would also examine the desirability of making wage rates legally enforceable and of giving judicial effect to collective agreements (Department of Industry and Commerce 1944a).

Commenting on the Memorandum, Departmental officials noted that the wartime wage tribunals had accustomed both employers and workers to the notion of arbitration in matters of remuneration (Department of Industry and Commerce 1944b). Observations on the reform proposals by the Department of Finance claimed that they would 'involve something little less than a revolution in the methods … followed up to the present' (Department of Finance 1944a). A follow-on Memorandum to government by the Minister of Finance was clearly designed to counter the formal presentation of Lemass's proposals. The Finance Memorandum observed that the Minister for Finance

> cannot but feel that the terms of reference [of the Commission] would be construed by organizations of employers and employees as suggesting a desire for vigorous state regulation of wages and the establishment of something in the nature of compulsory arbitration.
>
> (Department of Finance 1944b)

The Department opposed pursuing an issue canvassed in Lemass's memorandum of relating wages to the cost of living and observed that voluntary collective bargaining on the whole had operated quite successfully.

The Department of Industry and Commerce's Memorandum was presented to the Government in October 1944 and was agreed subject to minor amendments. It contained a more specific proposal that the planned Commission would consider the

> desirability and practicality of establishing machinery for the determination and alternation of wages rates and for the avoidance and settlement of trade disputes, whether in respect of wage rates or other matters; the making of wage rates legally enforceable on a national or local basis, the giving of judicial effect to collective agreements and the creation of tribunals for the interpretation and application of such agreements.
> (Department of Industry and Commerce 1944a)

The Memorandum noted that if government agreement was obtained in principle, draft terms of reference for the Commission would be submitted for observations and amendments to the employer federations and the ITUC.

Lemass next engaged in consultations with the ITUC, declaring that he would hesitate to propose the establishment of the Commission if the Irish Trade Union Congress felt for any reason unable to participate in its work (Lemass 1944b). The ITUC responded that it did not like the idea of a commission as it would be unduly slow in producing results and because its objectives would be more effectively realized through discussions on a less formal basis between union and employer representatives under the auspices of the Department of Industry and Commerce (Lemass 1945a). The ITUC indicated that while it would accept machinery to facilitate dispute resolution when direct negotiations had failed, compulsory arbitration would not be acceptable. The ITUC delegation sought draft proposals for the machinery of dispute resolution for informal discussion by unions.

Lemass continued to press for engagement around the 'general issue of wage policy' and held to the view that any machinery established to avoid disputes needed to be guided by 'general principles' and that his proposed Commission might define these (Lemass 1945a). A document was prepared outlining a draft agenda for a discussion with the ITUC and the Federated Union of Employers (FUE). This reflected issues covered in the various memoranda but also contained a comment that legislative proposals for dispute resolution would be more effective if approved by employers and workers than if forced on either party (Department of Industry and Commerce 1945a). As well as Congress, Lemass held meetings with FUE.[6] Planned joint meetings with employers and unions were then impeded by the split that occurred in the ITUC in 1945.[7] Lemass corresponded with FUE and both union confederations, the ITUC and the Congress of Irish Unions (CIU), stating that the imminent ending of wartime wage controls made progress in establishing new dispute resolution arrangements a matter of special urgency.

He now also proceeded to develop his proposals in detail, holding meetings and receiving responses on issues of detail from ITUC and CIU. The Congresses stated their opposition to limitations on the right to strike, the need for 'minimum compulsion', the 'avoidance of lawyers' and stressed the importance of a new body functioning 'in a flexible and common sense way rather than in a formal legal manner'. They also insisted that the body's decisions should be 'applicable only where parties had voluntarily submitted to it' (Department of Industry and Commerce 1946). Draft heads of the bill establishing the Labour Court were sketched by Lemass – famously in a child's copybook (Horgan 1987: 123). The split between unions continued to hamper bipartite or tripartite meetings – Lemass repeating his concern to colleagues that the Government should not be seen to 'impose a position on the parties' or to be 'committed to a definite policy' (Department of Industry and Commerce 1945b).

The final Industrial Relations Bill 1946 emerged from Lemass's rounds of consultations with union and employer bodies. The Bill represented a significant departure from Lemass's original idea to create a body that would align wages with economic development and deliver binding decisions in wage and other disputes. Lemass's original plan had been to replace the existing patchwork of conflict resolution and wage-fixing bodies and the 'haphazard' wage rises that resulted from these institutions and collective bargaining. As outlined, this would be accomplished first by establishing a commission, with representation from employers and unions, that would develop a set of principles for a wage policy. These, in turn, would guide a permanent dispute resolution body that would enjoy judicial powers and deliver binding decisions. This plan appears to have been tempered and altered in the main on the basis of consultations with union leaders, who opposed the idea of a commission, insisted that a permanent dispute resolution body could not operate on the basis of compulsion, enjoy judicial authority or even involve lawyers.

In the end, a body that had originally been intended to form the core of a radical corporatist reconstruction on wage bargaining and dispute resolution became instead the pivotal institution of voluntarist industrial relations. Lemass's corporatism envisaged union and employer associations becoming subordinate to the state and prevailed upon to accept policies seen to accord with the public interest (Bew and Patterson 1982: ch. 1; Girvin 1989: ch. 5; Dunphy 1995: ch. 5; Lee 2012: ch. 4; McCarthy 1977: 535–536; Roche 2009). Instead, the Labour Court would operate on the basis of principles and practices initially institutionalized by the Labour Department of the Board of Trade. This legacy was retained by the Dáil's Department of Labour and by the Free State and became enshrined in the patchwork of dispute resolution and wage-fixing institutions both inherited from the British administration and created during the 1930s. Conciliators working in the Industries' Branch of the Department of Industry and Commerce applied the same principles and practices in seeking to assist employers and unions to resolve disputes.

When Lemass introduced the Industrial Relations Bill in the Dáil, he made it clear that union and employer representatives with whom he had consulted were not committed to his proposals in principle or in detail. Yet he was at pains to insist that he sought to act as an instrument of their interests:

> I wish to say first, however, that I do not regard this Bill as a Government measure in the ordinary sense. It is a measure designed to facilitate trade unions of workers and employers in adjusting their difficulties concerning wages and conditions of employment and I can say that, within very wide limits, it will be framed as they want it framed, subject to the willingness of the Dáil as a whole to accept what is proposed. I regard myself merely as the instrument for bringing the Bill before the Dáil, steering through its various stages and bringing it into operation when enacted.
> (Dáil Eireann Debates, 25 June 1946)

So, as Lemass saw it, the Bill would only work if all the parties affected regarded it as a useful measure. He welcomed proposals to improve the Bill from across the House. It was not, he said, proposed to make its provisions compulsory, except to the extent that parties voluntarily and knowingly submit themselves to it in their own interests. To this end, he stated that he did not believe in compulsory arbitration imposed by law, which, in the last resort, would involve the regulation of wages by the state (Dáil Eireann Debates, 25 June 1946). Employers and unions could opt to rely solely on negotiations, or on 'old-time weapons of lockouts and strikes', or they could have resorted to the Court. Their freedom to take industrial action would not be impaired in any way. Labour Court decisions would be non-binding recommendations, unless the parties to investigations agreed to be bound by these. While the Court would enjoy the powers of the High Court to summon witnesses and hear evidence under oath, no provision was made for the involvement of lawyers in any aspect of the Court's work.

What remained of Lemass's original core principle that wages should be adjusted and disputes resolved in the public interest had become one of a set of criteria guiding Labour Court recommendations (Industrial Relations Act 1946, Article 68(1)):[8]

> The Court, having investigated a trade dispute, shall make a recommendation setting forth its opinion on the merits of the dispute and the terms on which, in the public interest and with a view to promoting industrial peace, it should be settled, due regard being had to the fairness of the

> said terms to parties concerned, and the prospects of the said terms being acceptable to them (Industrial Relations Act 1946)

Lemass emphasized in his contribution to the debate that the 'Government decided that the primary obligation was to secure [sic] that industrial disputes should be avoided or resolved in a practical, common-sense way' (Dáil Debates, 25 June 1946). Investigations, hearings and recommendations would be delivered by divisions of the Court comprising a Chair and a worker and employer member, appointed by the Minister from panels of union and employer nominees. Conciliation officers (public servants) would mediate in disputes in the first instance and formal investigation would ensue only if conciliation failed. Trade Boards would become Joint Labour Committees and Joint Industrial Councils could register with the Court and would maintain their current activities without interference by the Court, unless they chose to avail of the Court's services. Collective agreements could be registered and become legally binding.

A major feature of the Dáil debates on the Bill was the absence of party divisions on Lemass's proposals. Fine Gael Opposition Leader, Richard Mulcahy, stated his party's position clearly at the outset of his contribution to debate on the Second Stage of the Bill:

> I should like to say, first, that we can meet the Minister saying that we approve generally the principle behind this measure. I see no reason at all for objecting to its Second Reading, nor do I foresee that, in Committee, anything is likely to arise that would prevent the Minister getting machinery of the kind he is looking for to bring workers and employers more directly and more closely together and settling matters related to remuneration and conditions.
>
> (Dáil Eireann Debates, 25 June 1946)

Throughout the Bill's passage into law debate largely surrounded technical issues and matters of detail, concerning, for example, the scope of the new dispute resolution arrangements – in particular which occupational groups would be included or excluded. The most trenchant critic of the Bill, as well as of Lemass's general approach, was Fine Gael TD and former Minister for Industry and Commerce, Patrick McGilligan. McGilligan was critical in particular that the Court would operate in the absence of a policy on wages. To this Lemass responded:

> I have not attempted in introducing this Bill to formulate a wages policy. … The Government necessarily took powers to control wages during the war. It is proposing to relieve itself of these powers. It certainly does not contemplate retaining any measure of direct control of

> wages which would enable it to implement a wages policy. I expressed the view in introducing the Bill that a national wages policy must emerge as a result of agreement and cannot possibly be established by means of compulsion. The Government will not be powerless. As I pointed out, through its tariff policy, through its price control measures, and by various devices, including exhortation and criticism, it will be able to influence the views of others and the general trend of wage policy. But in the long run that must come as a result of a wider understanding of the national interests and, particularly, of the interests of the workers in relation to economic development.
>
> (Dáil Eireann Debates, 25 June 1946)

This was somewhat disingenuous. Lemass's original vision involved a Commission, representative of unions and employers, formulating a wage policy that would guide the Court's deliberations – a proposal dropped following union objections.

Lemass's Bill became the Industrial Relations Act 1946, with few significant amendments. The Dáil adopted Lemass's proposals following little opposition to the Bill's approach or institutional arrangements. The first Chairman of the Labour Court, Ronald Mortished, was appointed by Lemass. Mortished had a background as an activist in public service trade unions and the labour movement and had also worked for a time for the International Labour Organization.

At the same time as Lemass was consulting with unions and employers and in the process reworking his earlier proposals into the idea of a Labour Court grounded in voluntarist principles, he was also working on a parallel set of proposals for post-war economic policy. These appeared again to call into question the role finally envisaged for the Labour Court. A wide ranging 1945 'Memorandum on Full Employment' returned to industrial relations and wage fixing. Influenced by UK Keynesian policy proposals in pursuit of full employment, Lemass again put forward the view that the regulation of wages would be necessary in an economy pursuing full employment, noting that 'free wage bargaining in full employment might lead to constant upward pressure on money wage rates' and that 'in all circumstances the State should have the powers to ensure that in wage negotiations the general public interest is protected' (Lemass 1945b: 25–27).

> The conclusion is inescapable that a full employment policy is incompatible with the old practice of setting wage rates by direct negotiations between employers and trade unions, or by strikes and lock-outs, and that in return for the removal of the fear of unemployment, the workers must be willing to accept the supervision of wage rates by a public authority charged with the responsibility of protecting the real value of

all wages against depreciation through the inflation of prices following higher wage claims.

(Lemass 1945b: 27)

Lemass's ideas now extended to providing for more efficient forms of industrial management and finding ways of overcoming trade unions' resistance to more productive methods of working. He believed that a right of trade unions to 'participate in industrial management would appear to be necessary' and envisaged that this might be achieved through the establishment of works councils within firms and industrial councils within industries (Lemass 1945b: 26–27). His vision was for a 'truly democratic partnership in our industries after the war' (Lemass 1945b: 26). Lemass further stated that his proposals might necessitate a 'compulsory reorganization' of management and the reorganization of the trade union movement.

Following the establishment of the Labour Court, Lemass proceeded to work on an Industrial Efficiency and Prices Bill to give effect to some of his wider ideas. While the idea of the 'supervision of wage rates by a public authority' was dropped, as were works councils, the Bill proposed the establishment of development councils for industry involving representatives of employers, unions and other persons. Councils would promote improved methods of production and the use of labour, training and product and factory design (Industrial Efficiency and Prices Bill 1947).

> The establishment of these development councils would, we think, express in visible form the reality of the partnership between management and workers, express their common interest in the welfare and development of the industry in which they are engaged and provide means—which, in most cases, were lacking heretofore—by which they might discuss these matters which I have mentioned from two viewpoints and achieve useful results by so doing.
>
> (Dáil Debates, 22 October 1947)

The Bill lapsed at its second stage when a general election was called in 1948. Lemass's proposals for further reforms of industrial relations revealed his continued willingness to intervene in economic activity and to promote employer and union engagement in new institutions to support economic development. In 1947, following a sharp escalation in prices, the Government had threatened to introduce statutory controls on pay rises if talks with unions failed to deliver an acceptable voluntary pay agreement (Dáil Eireann Debates, 15 October 1947). In the event, the Chairman of the Labour Court intervened at the behest of the FUE to broker a national wage agreement between it and the two trade union Congresses. In effect, the process involved developing a voluntary national wage policy.

An attempt by Mortished to broker a follow-on national wage agreement in 1951 failed. He then declared that in the public interest the Labour Court did not regard the case for a general increase in wages has having merit, and so could not pronounce in favour of such an increase. This incident, coupled with criticism from sections of unions that the Court was excessively concerned with the public interest and with national economic policy, contributed to Mortished's resignation in 1952 (McCarthy 1977: 541).

While Mortished's fate revealed the limits of the Court's scope to articulate a wages policy, Lemass's corporatist proclivities continued during his time as a Minister and subsequently as Taoiseach. As well as playing a role in brokering national pay agreements, Lemass established a series of neocorporatist tripartite bodies linked with economic planning, including a National Productivity Committee, charged with improving productivity and industrial efficiency, a Committee on Industrial Organization, charged with adapting industries to free trade, and the National Industrial and Economic Council, which involved unions and employers in economic planning and discussions on the development of incomes policy (Roche 1997: 174–175).

The exclusion of public service workers had been a major issue of debate in the passage of the 1946 Bill into law. The Government sought to exclude public servants on the grounds of the principle of 'state sovereignty', arguing that no independent body could issue recommendations affecting public expenditure, which had to remain the preserve of government. The work of the Labour Court was eventually paralleled by a new dispute resolution system in the public service. Prior to independence, civil servants in the UK's Irish administration had access to a Conciliation and Arbitration Board. The board comprised three members, one each representing employers and civil servants and was chaired by a High Court judge. Arbitration was abolished in 1920. As outlined, Whitley Councils, established in the UK public service, were rejected by the Free State government (McGinley 1997: 237). Public service unions continued to press for an effective channel to fix pay and resolve disputes. With most public servants excluded from the Labour Court, a scheme for conciliation and arbitration for civil servants was finally introduced in 1950, followed by schemes for teachers (1954–1955), Gardaí (1962) and local authorities (1963).

The political foundation of voluntarism and conflict resolution

The early political foundations of voluntarism were traced by Fox (1985) to a long-run series of constitutional, social and legislative changes whereby political and business elites in the United Kingdom came to accept unions as positive agents of social integration. Political developments in independent

Ireland were further to reinforce voluntarism and voluntary dispute resolution.

The Republican and Free State Governments, preoccupied with establishing and securing the new state in a 'conservative revolution' or 'counter-revolution', retained the common law, statutes, economic, business and financial institutions inherited from the United Kingdom (Regan 1999). Other than during the War of Independence and Civil War, when governments had coercively suppressed worker militancy and social radicalism and the Emergency when wages were subject to state control, the State largely retained and replicated the industrial relations and dispute resolution legacies inherited from the United Kingdom.

The political foundations of voluntarism and voluntary dispute resolution were to be reinforced by the political system that emerged in the independent Irish State. As has been widely observed, the Irish labour movement refrained from supporting social militancy during the War of Independence in deference to support for the struggle for independence (Berresford Ellis 1985; Kostick 1996; O'Connor 1988). Rank-and-file militancy and social radicalism were also disowned by the ITGWU – the union spearheading the unionization drive and committed to syndicalism (O'Connor 1988: 112).

The Irish party system, formed in the embers of the Civil War, famously defined the identities of the main political parties on the basis of their positions on the 'national question' rather than on the basis of class. In the 'two-and-a-half party system' that long prevailed, the minority Labour Party was confined to opposition or participated in coalition governments, limiting its power and ability to influence government policies.[9] In the early decades of independence, Cumann na nGaedheal and Fine Gael supported economic liberalism and free trade, while Fianna Fail, supported by Labour, promoted protectionist industrialization and embarked on a programme of social and employment legislation during the 1930s.

During the 1930s, Sean Lemass was instrumental in mobilizing trade union and working-class support for Fianna Fail, as the new party set out to create an electoral base across the social class spectrum.[10] Lemass has been described during this period as a 'proto-Keynesian' in his support for public spending and public works as ways of combating unemployment (Dunphy 1995: 148–149). While the major parties remained deeply divided on the national question, a strong measure of political consensus developed on economic and industrial affairs. As Mary Daly (1992: 124) observed on developments during the 1930s:

> … acquiescence to the terms of the Conditions of Employment Act [1934] at a time when Irish political life was deeply riven over nationalist matters reflects a broad consensus for an economic middle ground among employers, workers and politicians.

When Lemass presented his 1946 Industrial Relations Bill, he benefitted from the same political consensus and from cross-party support for the overall thrust of his reform proposals. Lemass's original corporatist vision for the Labour Court had fallen foul of the voluntarist legacy. When he attempted to institute radical change in institutions for wage fixing and the resolution of industrial conflict during the transition to post-war economic conditions, he faced deep resistance embedded in industrial relations legacies favouring adversarial collective bargaining, freedom to undertake industrial action and an insistence that the state should act as an honest broker facilitating voluntary dispute resolution. Ultimately, both the manner in which the Labour Court was configured and the personnel of the Court reflected longstanding postures and practices stretching back to before the foundation of the State. Resistance to any institution perceived as alien to the voluntarist legacy had been borne in on Lemass in his consultations with unions. The practices and the composition of the Labour Court essentially reproduced the modus operandi of pre-Court dispute resolution institutions.

Yet the foundation of the Labour Court still marked a turning point in Irish industrial relations. The Court brought into being the first nationally integrated system of conflict resolution of wide coverage, supplanting the patchwork of institutions that had grown up before and after independence. The process involved in establishing the Labour Court also created a legacy of extensive consultation by government with union and employer bodies in reforming dispute resolution. The same legacy prioritized the achievement of consensus and the avoidance of imposed reforms. Consensus between the main political parties and the search for accord between the direct parties to industrial relations became the established pathway to reform. The broad consensus that existed around industrial relations meant that no clashing ideologies or programmes were promulgated for the reform of collective bargaining or dispute resolution.

Sean Lemass was the first and also the last political architect of conflict resolution in Irish industrial relations. While subsequent politicians shepherded major conflict resolution reforms through the Dáil, none articulated visions of reform comparable to Lemass. Bertie Ahern bore some similarities to Lemass in his corporatist view of pay bargaining and industrial relations, becoming central to the advent and development of social partnership from 1987 (Roche 2009). Earlier, Ahern won support for the Industrial Relations Act 1990 that established the Labour Relations Commission. His Fine Gael ministerial counterpart, Richard Bruton, would also be instrumental in enacting the major reforms that established the Workplace Relations Commission. As later chapters will show, both sets of reforms were developed by public servants and conflict management professionals. Politicians and political parties largely welcomed reform proposals and otherwise kept politics out of the functioning and reform of conflict resolution institutions.

Conclusions

Provisions for workplace conflict resolution in Ireland were shaped by the voluntarist industrial relations system inherited from the United Kingdom. Within this system, employers were encouraged by the state to recognize and accommodate worker interests. Where negotiations failed, conflict resolution was seen as best achieved by boards of third parties, representative of employers and workers, acting on the basis of professional knowledge and competence. These boards could best eschew overly formal or legal procedures and wherever possible issue non-binding or agreed sets of proposals to resolve disputes. These principles and arrangements were to be complemented by legally binding proposals in trades where little union organization existed and exploitation was a persistent risk. This view of conflict resolution was promulgated and instituted by the Labour Department of the Board of Trade. It became enshrined in the foundations of Irish industrial relations and dispute resolution. The significance of British trade unions in Ireland and the emergence of many Irish trade unions as breakaways from British unions contributed to the institutionalization of voluntarism. The voluntarist tradition was challenged in the early decades of the twentieth century by employer resistance to militant syndicalist new unions and then by social radicalism shaped by the First World War, the War of Independence and the Civil War.

Voluntarism was sustained as the new Irish State retained the conflict resolution and wage-fixing institutions established under British rule. To these were added incrementally new bodies following the same features and practices. By the advent of the Second World War, a patchwork of conflict resolution bodies of limited coverage had developed. These were suspended by the Wages Standstill Order and latterly by the operation of wage tribunals. The tribunal system, which involved employer and union representatives, instituted a nationally integrated system of conflict resolution – forming the basis of a new system to emerge with the ending of wartime controls. In preparation for the ending of wartime controls, Sean Lemass developed a radical vision of a corporatist wage fixing and dispute resolution institution that would harness unions and employer bodies to a national wage policy linked to the imperatives of economic development. This vision was diluted in consultations with the trade union bodies that were strongly resistant to compulsion or to making wages subservient to national economic policy. The resulting Labour Court became the cornerstone of Irish voluntarist dispute resolution for nearly five decades.

The politics or non-politics buttressing voluntary conflict resolution also emerged early as the major political parties were formed on national rather than on class lines and came to adopt broadly similar postures towards industrial relations and wage determination. Lemass's eventual proposals for establishing the Labour Court embedded voluntarist principles and enjoyed cross-party political support. Subsequent reform proposals that would lead to the establishment of the Labour Relations Commission and the Workplace Relations Commission enjoyed the same cross-party support. More broadly, the absence of political division around how workplace conflict could best be resolved allowed public servants and conflict management professionals to dominate subsequent reform processes.

Notes

1 Many small local Irish unions had been absorbed by British craft and general unions. Later, numerous Irish trade unions were formed by breaking away from British unions. By 1922, 19 per cent of Irish trade union members were members of the Irish branches of British trade unions, as Irish general unions had grown relatively strongly and new Irish unions had split off from British unions (Roche 1987).

2 This and subsequent sections draw on records held in the National Archives of Ireland and in UCD Archives. For convenience, references in the text to archival records will be cited under the names of people or organizations responsible for creating records. Full archival details are provided under the names of these persons or organizations in the references section of the book.

3 The Boycott was instituted by the Dáil in August 1920 when thousands of Catholic workers were expelled from Belfast firms and incidents of serious sectarian violence occurred.

4 The usage of state-provided voluntary dispute resolution assistance was very significantly lower than the pattern of usage of voluntary conciliation that was to emerge following the establishment of the Labour Court.

5 Contractually agreed pay rises and increments were excluded from the scope of the Act.

6 The reactions of FUE to Lemass's proposals were not recorded in departmental records. FUE's involvement in the 1946 Act is covered only in a cursory manner in the FUE's history (Chubb 1992: 8).

7 The split resulted from simmering tensions between British-based and Irish-based unions – the latter favouring the disbandment of British unions in Ireland (see McCarthy 1977: ch. 5).

8 The public interest criterion was subsequently rescinded.

9 Labour supported the first Fianna Fail Governments and influenced Fianna Fail's Conditions of Employment Act 1934 (Dunphy 1995). The party in the Inter-Party Government of 1948–1951 was instrumental in the introduction of the first Conciliation and Arbitration scheme in the civil service. The Party in government was also involved in developing proposals that would lead to the establishment of the Labour Relations Commission.

10 See Allen (1991) for an analysis of growing support for Fianna Fail among sections of Irish trade union leaders, especially in the Irish Transport and General Workers' Union, and the role this played in proposals to reform the trade union system to the disadvantage of British based trade unions through the Trade Union Act, 1941.

3 The Labour Relations Commission

Introduction

The Labour Relations Commission (LRC) was established in 1991 as part of a programme of reform of industrial relations law that extended to changing the conditions governing industrial action by trade unions. Both the creation of the Commission and the wider reform programme reflected a growth over previous decades in the volume of industrial conflict and associated pressure on the Labour Court – the pivotal institution for conflict resolution for almost four decades. This chapter examines the creation and operations of the LRC and the manner in which the Commission's services evolved over the period during which it assumed the mantle of the State's primary conflict resolution agency from the Labour Court, while occupying a conflict resolution landscape that was becoming increasingly fragmented and opaque through the parallel operation and widening jurisdictions of other conflict resolution agencies: the Employment Appeals Tribunal and the Equality Tribunal, as well as agencies established under social partnership agreements, the National Employment Rights Authority, the National Centre for Partnership and Performance (NCPP) and the National Implementation Body (NIB). As will be shown in the chapter that follows the growing fragmentation of the conflict resolution system represented by multiple agencies was a major factor leading to the reform programme that created the Workplace Relations Commission (WRC) in 2015.

The creation of the LRC in 1991 represented the first major reconfiguration of dispute resolution agencies since the establishment of the Labour Court in 1946. As detailed in Chapter 2, the Labour Court (see Figure 3.1) had been created as a means of handling the transition from wartime control of pay to the resumption of free collective bargaining. Although its architect and political sponsor, Minister for Industry and Commerce and subsequently Taoiseach (Prime Minister), Sean Lemass, had envisaged the Court operating as a public authority supervising wage determination within a corporatist blueprint for economic management

DOI: 10.4324/9781003520054-3

The Labour Court

The Labour Court was established in 1946 to resolve industrial disputes and promote harmonious industrial relations following the ending of wartime wage controls and the resumption of free collective bargaining. Chairpersons and deputy chairpersons, appointed by ministers, and employer and union members, nominated by employer and trade union federations, sat in three-person divisions to investigate and adjudicate on industrial disputes. The Court issued recommendations that were normally non-binding on parties to a dispute. Conciliation officers, subsequently restyled industrial relations officers, provided a conciliation service. The Court was divested of the conciliation service in 1991 with the creation of the Labour Relations Commission (LRC). A rights commissioner service (see below), created in 1970, was also transferred from the Court to the Labour Relations Commission. The remit of the Labour Court changed again following the creation of the Workplace Relations Commission (WRC) in 2005. The Court became an appellate agency for WRC adjudication decisions arising from individual employment grievances, while retaining its investigation function in collective disputes referred for investigation by the WRC, or in which the Court intervenes on its own accord.

Conciliation and Arbitration Schemes

A range of public service grades were excluded from accessing the Labour Court. Instead, a parallel system of conciliation and arbitration was established from the 1950s to resolve disputes involving public service employers and unions representing civil servants, teachers, the police (Gardai) and local government employees. This restriction was subsequently relaxed to permit some public service groups, in particular, local government employees and certain service health workers, to access the dispute resolution services of the Labour Court and subsequently the Labour Relations Commission. The trend of granting access to mainstream conflict resolution services to more public to more public service groups has continued under the Workplace Relations Commission.

Rights Commissioner Service

In 1970 an independent dispute resolution service, 'rights commissioners', was created. Rights commissioners where charged with resolving disputes involving individual employees and small groups of employees, other than disputes connected with rates of pay, hours of work or annual holidays of a body of workers. Under a growing body of employment legislation from the 1990s rights commissioners were assigned jurisdiction to investigate complaints over the violation of employment rights. Depending on the statute under which cases were pursued, rights commissioner decisions could be appealed to the Employment Appeals Tribunal (see below), or the Labour Court – with different appellate channels favoured during different periods. In practice rights commissioners adopted a mediation-arbitration/adjudication posture in resolving employment grievances – seeking to mediate settlements where possible and otherwise issuing adjudication decisions. The Rights Commissioners service was transferred to the Labour Relations Commission (see below) in 1991 and supplanted by a new adjudication service following the creation of the WRC in 2015.

The Employment Appeals Tribunal

The Unfair Dismissals Act 1977 created the Employment Appeals tribunal (EAT), which expanded the remit of the Redundancy Appeals Tribunal established in 1967. Hearings at the EAT were conducted by legally qualified chairs, who presided in conjunction with ordinary members nominated by organizations representative of employers and trade unions. The EAT was assigned jurisdiction over unfair dismissals, redundancies and minimum notice in the event of job losses. The EAT's jurisdiction subsequently expanded under a raft of employment rights legislation enacted during the 1990s. With the exception of cases that remained to be heard, the EAT was supplanted by the newly created adjudication service following the creation of the WRC in 2015.

The Labour Relations Commission

The Labour Relations Commission was established in 1991. The Commission assumed responsibility for the conciliation service hitherto provided by the Labour Court. It was also charged with promoting good industrial relations and facilitating a more active approach to dispute prevention and resolution.

These functions were discharged primarily through its newly created advisory service. The LRC assumed responsibility for the rights commissioner service, and also for equality officers previously operating within the Labour Court and charged with investigating complaints under the employment equality legislation. (This function was transferred in 2004 to the Equality Tribunal). The LRC initiated a collective facilitation/preventive mediation service, a mediation service for parties involved in interpersonal conflict and an early dispute resolution service. The LRC was merged into the newly created WRC in 2015.

The National Centre for Partnership and Performance

In 1997 a new agency, the National Centre for Partnership (re-launched in 2002 as the National Centre for Partnership and Performance) (NCPP) was created. The NCPP sought to foster partnership in firms and public service organizations, guided by a series of framework agreements concluded by employers, unions and government. In seeking to foster good industrial relations, the NCPP's activities overlapped the work of the LRC. The NCPP was abolished in 2010 as part of a programme of agency rationalization and cost cutting introduced to address the fiscal crisis that followed the advent of the Great Recession.

The National Implementation Body

In 2000 employers, governments and unions established the National Implementation Body (NIB) The NIB sought to manage the delivery of the stability and industrial peace provisions of national pay agreement contained in a series of tripartite 'social partnership agreements'. The NIB acted as a kind of virtual agency, providing a distinctive form of networked dispute resolution: mobilizing leaders and influencers within union and employer associations and senior civil servants to resolve disputes that threatened national pay agreements or to cause economic dislocation, frequently by (re)directing unresolved disputes down procedural routes to the LRC and Labour Court. The NIB cased to operate in 2009 following the collapse of social partnership and national pay bargaining.

The Equality Tribunal

The Equality Tribunal (ET) was created in 2004. The investigation and conciliation functions hitherto undertaken by equality and industrial relations officers of the Labour Court under the employment equality acts were transferred to the ET. ET decisions could be appealed to the Labour Court. The ET offered users a mediation service.

The National Employment Rights Authority

In 2007, following a series of scandals and controversies surrounding violations of employment rights, the National Employment Rights Authority (NERA) was established. Provisions for the creation of NERA were contained in the *Towards 2016* social partnership agreement concluded by employers, unions and the government in 2006. Assuming responsibility for the labour inspectors service previously managed within a succession of government departments responsible for employment and labour affairs, NERA was charged with enforcing employment statutes. The Authority possessed powers to inspect businesses and to prosecute employers found to be non-compliant with employment legislation. The activities of NERA were transferred to the Workplace Relations Commission in 2015.

The Workplace Relations Commission

The Workplace Relations Commission was created in 2015 out of a merger of the Labour Relations Commission, the Employment Appeals Tribunal, the Equality Tribunal and the National Employment Rights Authority. The agency is charged with promoting the improvement and maintenance of good workplace relations. The WRC is the primary agency for adjudicating on complaints and grievances by employees under employment rights and industrial relations acts. Early dispute resolution and mediation services are provided. The WRC provides a collective conciliation service for the parties to industrial disputes, as well as advisory, facilitation and allied services. The WRC operates an inspection and enforcement service to ensure compliance with employment law.

Figure 3.1 Agencies for Resolving Workplace Conflict, Applying the Law and Promoting Good Industrial Relations.

Sources: Table compiled from multiple sources.

and development, the Court became the cornerstone and pivotal institution of the voluntary industrial relations system. The Court's three-person divisions, comprising employer and union nominees and chairs (sometimes independently appointed, sometimes promoted from among union and employer deputy chairs and currently appointed through open competition), investigated and adjudicated on industrial disputes. Court hearings were generally preceded by conciliation conferences conducted by industrial relations officers (civil servants) working for the Court. 'Recommendations' issued by the Labour Court were and remain generally non-binding.

The Industrial Relations Act 1990, which created the LRC, contained a wider series of reform measures that encompassed the regulation of trade union ballots for industrial action, the provision of notice of industrial action and restrictions on the capacity of employers to obtain injunctions in industrial disputes (Wallace 2010: 25). Political debate surrounding the 1990 Act focused in the main on this wider package of reform proposals. The Act also contained proposals for the reform of dispute resolution, creating the new agency. Little political conflict or debate surrounded proposals for creating the LRC, which were largely uncontroversial (Mulvey 2010: 46; Wallace 2010: 25). The external pressures for change that led to the creation of the LRC are examined below.

The Commission assumed responsibility for the collective conciliation service hitherto provided by the Labour Court. The LRC also assumed responsibility for the 'Rights Commissioners' service, established in 1970 to resolve employment grievances and disputes involving individuals and small groups, and the Commission also initially took over the equality service previously provided by the Labour Court and subsequently transferred to a new Equality Tribunal (see Figure 3.1). The Commission was also charged with promoting good industrial relations and encouraging and facilitating a more active approach to dispute prevention and resolution. The creation of the LRC was seen as a means of restoring the original purpose of the Labour Court as a 'court of last resort' (Murphy 1997: 297).

The LRC was governed by a tripartite board comprising representatives of unions and employer associations and government appointees. Kieran Mulvey, an experienced public service union leader, was appointed as chief executive. Under the legislation that established the LRC, collective disputes were to be referred to the Commission for conciliation. The Labour Court would not normally investigate a dispute unless it received a report from the LRC that no further effort on its part would contribute to the resolution of the dispute. The LRC established a new advisory service, charged with fostering good industrial relations. The advisory service assisted firms and unions to improve communications, manage change and reorganization more effectively and move away from dysfunctional industrial relations.

The advisory service also worked with 'frequent users' of the LRC's conciliation services to address the reasons for their chronic dependence on third-party involvement in resolving disputes (Morrin 2012). The advisory service provided training in conflict resolution and industrial relations and prepared a series of codes of practice that provided guidance on good industrial relations principles and practices. Codes covered such areas as procedures for grievance, discipline and dispute resolution; the conduct of disputes in essential services and the handling of disputes in firms where employers refused to concede union recognition.

The LRC soon established itself as a successful and authoritative institution, becoming the 'most important industrial relations institution in the state' (Wallace 2010: 26). For nearly a quarter of a century, the Commission was the pivotal state institution for resolving collective disputes (through the conciliation service) and individual employment grievances (through the Rights Commissioners service), while also promoting good industrial relations (through the advisory service).

The core and most highly resourced activities of the LRC were concerned with individual and collective conflict resolution, with fewer resources devoted to the advisory service.

Figures 3.2 and 3.3 reveal one of the key developments over the life of the LRC: the slow and near progressive decline in the demand for collective conciliation and the dramatic growth in the incidence of conflict resolution involving individual employment grievances, handled in the main by Rights Commissioners. The genesis of both trends will be examined below under external pressures for change.

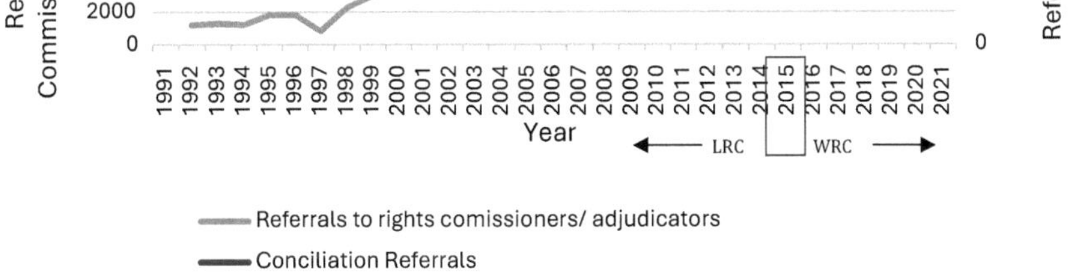

Figure 3.2 Referrals to Conciliation, Rights Commissioners and Adjudication.

Source: LRC/WRC Annual Reports.

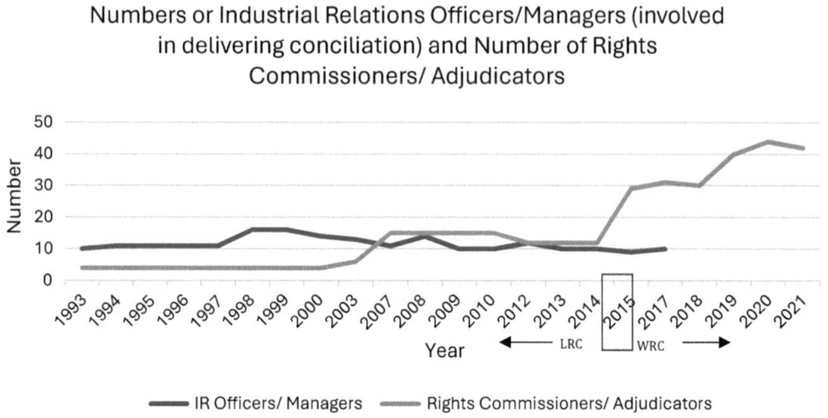

Figure 3.3 Number of Staff Involved in Providing Conciliation and the Number of Rights Commissioners/Adjudicators.

Source: LRC/WRC Annual Reports and data provided by the WRC.

Collective dispute resolution services

Reflecting its roots in the conciliation service of the Labour Court and embodied in the pivotal roles of union and employer association representatives in the governance of the institution, the LRC early on identified conciliation as the agency's most important function (Mulvey 1991, cited in Wallace et al. 2004: 98). Viewed in terms of changing patterns of demand for the services of the LRC and increasingly in terms of the allocation of staff resources (see Figure 3.2), this, however, had ceased to be the case by the end of the LRC's first decade. Although demand slackened for collective conciliation as the incidence and volume of industrial conflict continued to fall, the Commission's conciliation service continued to enjoy a high public profile due to its role and success in resolving large-scale industrial disputes, including disputes in essential services. The service also registered a significant and sustained reduction in the proportion of disputes resolved at conciliation as compared with the track record of the Labour Court (Murphy 1997: 356; Wallace 2010: 35–36). As late as 2004, an incoming Labour Court Chairman still complained of a 'revolving door problem' (*Industrial Relations News*, 29 January 2004), where disputes investigated by the Labour Court were subject to further conciliation following adjudication. For the most part, this problem was tackled through a protocol agreement between the LRC and the Court and a more vigorous approach by the LRC to resolving disputes at conciliation (Duffy 2010: 65; Labour Relations Commission 1991: 7; Murphy 1997: 7; Wallace 2010: 39).[1] Surveys undertaken by the LRC revealed high levels of user satisfaction with the services provided (Wallace 2010: 33).

In addition to its ongoing work in resolving collective disputes through conventional conciliation, the Commission was instrumental in pioneering the provision of a new collective ADR service. Drawing on experience acquired during the 1990s in providing intensive support to management and unions in firms engaged in restructuring and complex change programmes, the LRC developed a 'facilitation' service (McGee 2012: 61–64). Facilitation – though the concept could be deployed in a flexible manner – involved a form of 'assisted bargaining', which turned traditional third-party involvement in dispute resolution on its head. As practised by industrial relations officers working in the conciliation and advisory services, facilitation, described by the Commission as 'preventive mediation/ facilitation' (Labour Relations Commission 2008: 24), involved engaging with employers and unions at the outset or in the early stages of negotiations with the objective of facilitating change, preventing deadlock and heading off industrial disputes (Teague et al. 2015: 229–230). The service was offered when in the view of the LRC it could provide an effective alternative to conventional conciliation subsequent to the parties having become deadlocked (Labour Relations Commission 2008: 24; Roche 2016a; Teague et al. 2015: Ch. 11). Facilitation, as practised by the Commission, was similar in major respects to the role played by third parties in 'interest-based bargaining'. The service was highly flexible and could combine proactive mediation with conciliation where deadlock threatened to hold up, or to derail, assisted negotiations and needed to be tackled in a more conventional manner (Roche 2016a; Teague et al. 2015: ch. 11). Facilitation focused around a variety of workplace issues, including the implementation of changes to work practices and the development of improved workplace procedures. The objective of the facilitation service, as portrayed by the LRC, was to assist parties to reach mutually acceptable solutions. The process also encompassed the LRC's role in chairing joint working parties to implement recommendations arising from LRC-facilitated reviews of industrial relations arrangements inside organizations (LRC Annual Report; 2010). Taking account of differences in how the incidence of facilitation was reported in annual reports, Figures 3.4a and Figure 3.4b show facilitation activities of various kinds were modest but more or less consistent throughout the 2000s before increasing thereafter in the early 2010s.

Between 1987 and 2009 employers, unions and governments negotiated seven successive social partnership agreements that covered pay rises and an expanding array of economic and social policies. The LRC played little role in brokering or monitoring the programmes or pay agreements.[2] However, all agreements contained workplace dispute resolution procedures that provided for the referral of unresolved disputes to the LRC and the Labour Court.

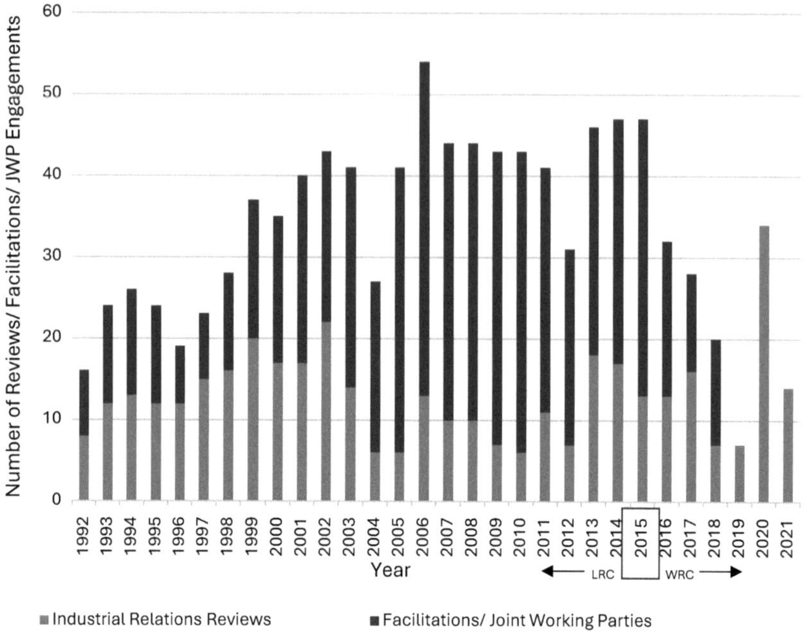

Figure 3.4a Incidence of Facilitation and Related Activities.

Note: The numbers recorded in this graph relate to a number of activities, including the chairing of joint working parties, and preventative mediation/ facilitation where assistance was given for situations where parties anticipate future difficulties. This data needs to be treated with caution as these activities are grouped differently across annual reports and there may be some overlap between activities from one year to the next. Records of 'facilitations and joint working parties' are not available from 2019 onwards but total 'facilitation discussions' / meetings are recorded instead – see Figure 3.4b.

Source: LRC/WRC Annual Reports.

Following the collapse of social partnership in the wake of the Great Recession, the Commission adopted a new role in public service pay bargaining that transposed the practice of facilitation to a new level. Industrial conflict loomed when government austerity measures included unilateral cuts in public service pay. With less than unanimous endorsement by the LRC board, but enjoying political cover at the highest level of government, LRC CEO Kieran Mulvey called publicly for an agreement between the government and the public service unions. The result was that the LRC became pivotal to brokering the 'Croke Park' agreement between the state and public service unions.[3] The 2010 agreement contained pledges of no further cuts in pay or involuntary job losses for the duration of the deal in return for a commitment by public service unions and their members to cooperate with changes to work practices and new staff mobility arrangements

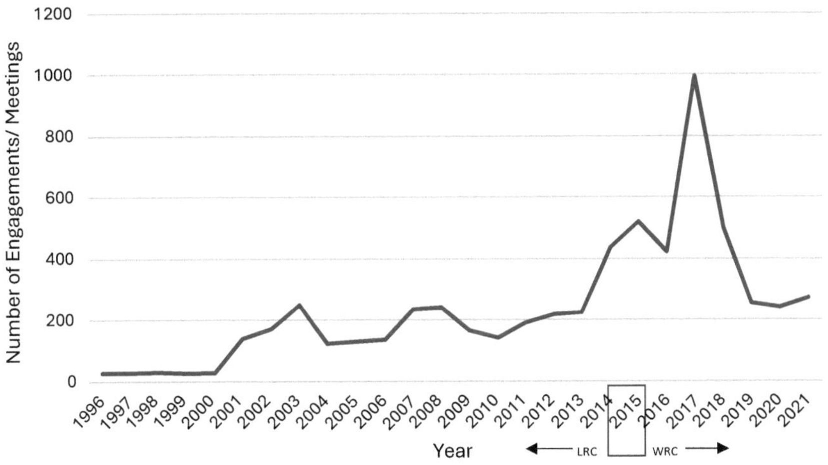

Figure 3.4b Incidence of Facilitation and Related Activities.

Note: The numbers recorded in this graph refer to the total engagements/ meetings held in relation to facilitation and related meetings for Joint Industrial councils, Joint Labour Committees, Conciliation and Arbitration Schemes. From 2016, these numbers reflect 'facilitation discussions' offered by both the conciliation and advisory services.

within and across workplaces. The Commission's role in facilitating collective bargaining in the public service continued in the successor agreement to Croke Park, the 2013 'Haddington Road' agreement (also known as the Croke Park Two agreement). Haddington Road resulted in further agreed pay cuts for higher-earning public servants and increased working hours for many categories. The Haddington Road negotiations involved the chief executive and all the conciliation staff of the LRC facilitating highly detailed negotiations between public service employers and unions representing a wide span of grades and categories. Facilitation activity was combined with some 150 conciliation conferences and was followed up by officers of the Commission chairing a series of oversight committees charged with the smooth implementation of the agreements reached with different public service unions (Labour Relations Commission 2013: 23–24). This initiative was the single most complex conflict resolution initiative in the State's industrial relations history. The role of the LRC (and subsequently WRC's) in facilitating collective bargaining across the public service continued over two subsequent pay agreements, concluded in circumstances of dramatic economic and fiscal recovery. The WRC continued this role in negotiations leading to the public service agreement for the period 2021–2022, ***Building Momentum***, whilst adapting to a negotiation process during COVID-19 in which there were 'far fewer present for a necessarily limited amount of socially distanced face-to-face talks' (***Industrial Relations News***,

26 November 2020). Under all public service pay agreements since 2010, the LRC/WRC was the designated agency for pre-adjudication conflict resolution for categories entitled to access the Commission's services – a role shared with the public service conciliation and arbitration schemes in the case of grades covered by the latter. In the case of *Building Momentum*, unresolved disputes are first brought to the attention of, or considered by, 'sectoral oversight bodies' and then referred to the WRC (Department of Public Expenditure and Reform 2020: 16).

After the collapse of social partnership, a 'protocol agreement' between the Irish Business and Employers' Confederation (IBEC) and the Irish Congress of Trade Unions (ICTU), set out shared priorities for the conduct of collective bargaining in the private sector. The protocol again cemented the role of the LRC as the first port of call in resolving disputes that now frequently centred around concession bargaining initiated by employers (Mulvey 2010: 49–50).

The LRC's statutory duty contained in the 1990 Act to prepare codes of practice to guide grievance and dispute resolution led to the advisory service becoming directly involved in disputes arising from the so-called 'right to bargain' laws and procedures. After unions encountered growing resistance to recognition from the 1980s, a series of changes were made to industrial relations law to enable them to represent members in enterprises where employers refused to concede recognition. Under the code of practice on voluntary dispute resolution provided for in the 2001 Industrial Relations (Amendment) Act and 2004 Industrial Relations (Miscellaneous Provisions) Act, an officer of the advisory service of the LRC could work with the parties to resolve a dispute where an employer refused to engage in collective bargaining. Unresolved disputes, or instances where employers refused to engage with the LRC, could lead to an investigation and recommendation (followed by a legally binding determination) by the Labour Court. The number of cases handled under the voluntary dispute resolution procedure was modest relative to the overall volume of conciliation activity (see Figure 3.5).

The use of the procedure by unions fell away following a judgement by the Irish Supreme Court in 2007. In a case brought by the low fares airline, Ryanair, the Court found that employers might validly claim to engage in collective bargaining with an entity other than a trade union and thus remain outside the jurisdiction of the right-to-bargain procedure and its associated voluntary dispute resolution procedure. In the view of trade unions, the Supreme Court judgement negated the functioning of the right-to-bargain procedure. The reform of the original right-to-bargain laws in 2015 has not changed this picture.

With respect to conciliation activity more generally, the Commission regularly referred in annual reports and other commentaries to its growing complexity. This was attributed to more intense international competition,

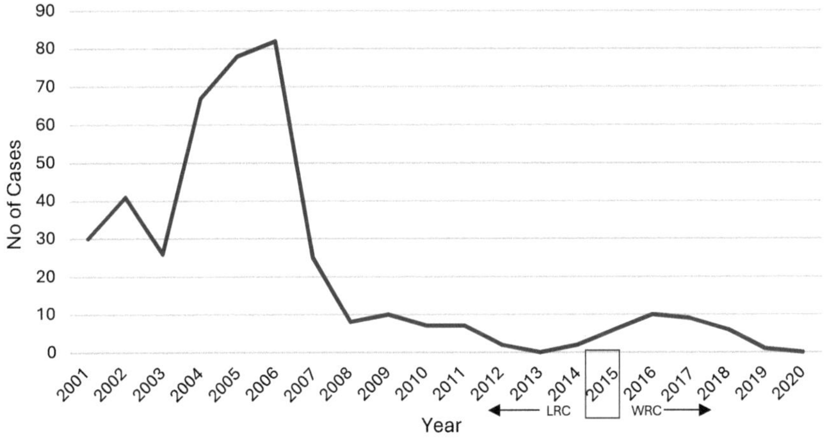

Figure 3.5 Incidence of Cases under the 'Right-to-Bargain' Procedure.

Role of LRC/WRC set in statutory instrument No. 76/2004 – 'Industrial Relations Act 1990 (Enhanced Code of Practice on Voluntary Dispute Resolution) (Declaration) Order 2004.'

Source: LRC/WRC Annual Reports.

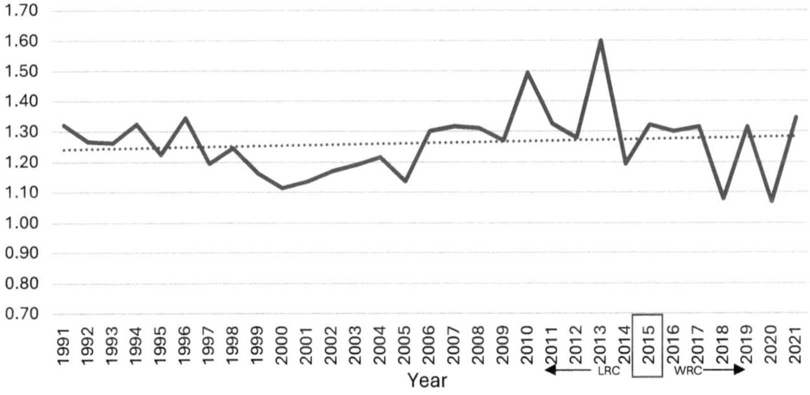

Figure 3.6 Average Number of Conciliation Conferences Per Case Referred to Conciliation.

Source: LRC/WRC Annual Reports.

deregulation and the growing prevalence of change and restructuring programmes (Mulvey 2010: 50). These developments were seen to require an increasing level of conciliation input per referral (Labour Relations Commission 2010). Figure 3.6 reveals that the number of conciliation conferences per referral rose modestly from an average of 1.3 at the outset of the LRC's life to 1.6 in the agency's penultimate year.

The LRC's conciliation service remained consistently highly effective. Over 80 per cent of all disputes referred to conciliation were resolved – a record significantly in excess of that registered when conciliation had been provided within the ambit of the Labour Court (Wallace et al. 2004: 99–100; 2013: 97). Yet it remained the case that the LRC's original core domain – providing support of various kinds to resolve or prevent collective conflict – was contracting significantly. Industrial conflict and conflict resolution support services were increasingly concentrated in declining traditional industries and the public sector (Teague et al. 2015: ch. 2). Many expanding sectors of the Irish economy, including some of the most dynamic industries, remained largely outside the domain of the LRC's collective dispute resolution services and supports. Like their unionized counterparts, non-union firms were subject to complaints with respect to employment rights legislation. But even here larger non-union firms and especially multinationals were turning to in-house ADR practices to avoid engaging with the state conflict resolution agencies (Doherty and Teague 2012). These firms were seldom subject to referrals to the LRC under the right-to-bargain laws. Brendan McGinty, an employer nominee to the board of the LRC, reflected on the deeper implications of these developments. Contributing to a symposium celebrating the 20th anniversary of the passing of the 1990 Industrial Relations Act, McGinty complained that the codes of practice developed by the LRC reflected a 'bias towards a collective ethos in the framing of employment law in Ireland'. McGinty also wrote of a need to 'acknowledge the legitimacy of employment models that are built upon the direct employment relationship' (McGinty 2010: 82).

Individual grievance resolution services

The individualization of conflict resolution, evident in Figure 3.2, began during the first decade of the LRC's operation, progressing exponentially from the early 2000s, and showing a dip only following the advent of the Great Recession, which appeared to suppress people's willingness or opportunities to pursue grievances against employers. The demand for individual grievance resolution then stabilized around a new threshold from the beginning of economic recovery around 2013. Kieran Mulvey commented on the changed character of the Commission's activity:

> While the level and extent of large-scale collective industrial action has decreased significantly in recent decades, the number of disputes referred to the various state dispute resolution bodies has continued to mount, a reflection of the fact that conflict at work has become increasingly absorbed by institutions and procedure, as well as becoming more individualized.
>
> (Labour Relations Commission 2009: 14)

Rights Commissioners provided the pivotal service for resolving individual employment grievances. Much of the rapidly growing work of Commissioners involved dealing with complaints by employees that statutory employment rights had been infringed. Already by 2010, Rights Commissioners exercised a quasi-judicial role in respect of 32 separate employment rights and regulations (Mulvey 2010: 57). The volume of claims in respect of more general employment grievances that had provided the original rationale for establishing the service had declined significantly by the end of the first decade of the millennium (Cashell 2011: 59). From 2005, a code of practice on workplace bullying, issued by the Health and Safety Authority, designated Rights Commissioners as the service for handling complaints that could not be resolved at workplace level in the case of categories of employees with access to the LRC under the 1990 Act (Health and Safety Authority 2005: 20).

As a growing number of cases before the service involved alleged violations of employment rights, Rights Commissioners developed an innovative approach to grievance resolution that combined grievance mediation with adjudication. Commissioners promoted mediated solutions to employment grievances wherever possible, resorting to adjudication only where mediated outcomes were unobtainable. In the words of one Rights Commissioner:

> If the Rights Commissioner senses that the parties are disposed to trying to settle the matter, then he/she will mediate to try and reach a settlement. If, on the other hand, there is no possibility of doing this, or if the attempt fails, then a decision/recommendation will be issued'.
>
> (Bragazzi 2012: 172)

A history of the Rights Commissioners similarly concluded that the modus of Commissioners was to 'adopt a pragmatic problem-solving approach' to grievance resolution, 'as opposed to a judicial process that enforces a right' – amounting to 'problem–solving in the shadow of the hearing' (Cashell 2011: 33, 47 and 73). In effect, the primary mode of grievance resolution provided by Rights Commissioners involved a form of mediation-arbitration or 'med-arb'. As Hann and Teague's examination of the Rights Commissioner service highlighted, Rights Commissioners possessed 'legal backbone' under a growing series of employment statures yet preferred to carry out their tasks in an 'informal manner', providing a service that was 'not too legalistic' and encouraging employers and employees to 'solve their problems by themselves in a manner consistent with the law' (Hann and Teague 2012: 633).

In responding to the demand for individual grievance resolution, the LRC also developed a workplace mediation service. Begun in 2005, as shown in Figure 3.7, this service remained modest in scale. Provided by

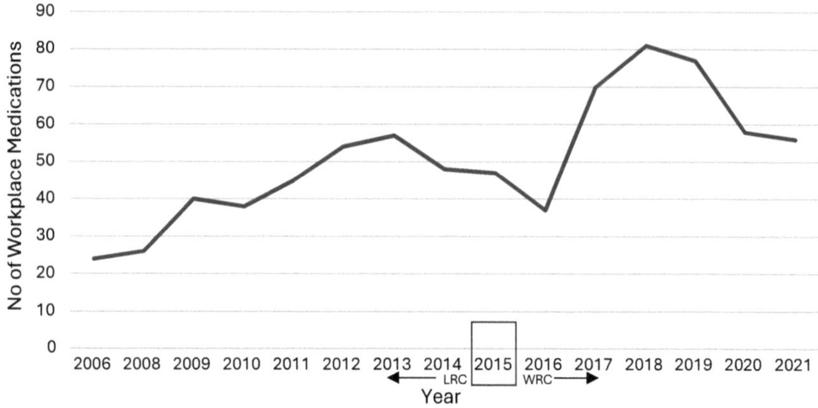

Figure 3.7 Incidence of Workplace Mediation.
Source: LRC/WRC Annual Reports.

conciliation and advisory service staff professionally trained and accredited as mediators, the mediation service supported the confidential resolution of grievances affecting individuals and small groups on an ad hoc basis. The LRC envisaged mediation in part as a means of extending its existing services to individuals and small groups without access to the LRC (in particular, public service employees) and to employees and firms where unions were not recognized (Labour Relations Commission 2011). A plan to offer an arbitration option for individuals and small groups was not proceeded with (*Industrial Relations News*, 22 July 2004). The LRC approached the provision of grievance mediation with caution, mindful that it could be resource intensive and that the agency was already stretched in delivering its range of services. In anticipation of reforms leading to the establishment of the WRC, in 2014, LRC staff became involved as 'equality mediation officers' of the Equality Tribunal.

An 'early resolution' service was also offered from 2013, having been piloted in 2012. This service again anticipated the merger of dispute resolution agencies to create the WRC and followed the format of similar services offered in the United Kingdom by Acas and in Northern Ireland by the Labour Relations Agency. The service involved case resolution officers providing mediation, initially over the telephone, to parties to cases referred to the Rights Commissioners under the employment rights legislation and to parties involved in cases at the Employment Appeals Tribunal. The purpose of the new service was to create opportunities to avoid the potential costs involved in formal hearings before either agency (Labour Relations Commission 2013: 25–26). The numbers availing of this service rose rapidly to significant levels, with a spike in the first year in which the service was formally

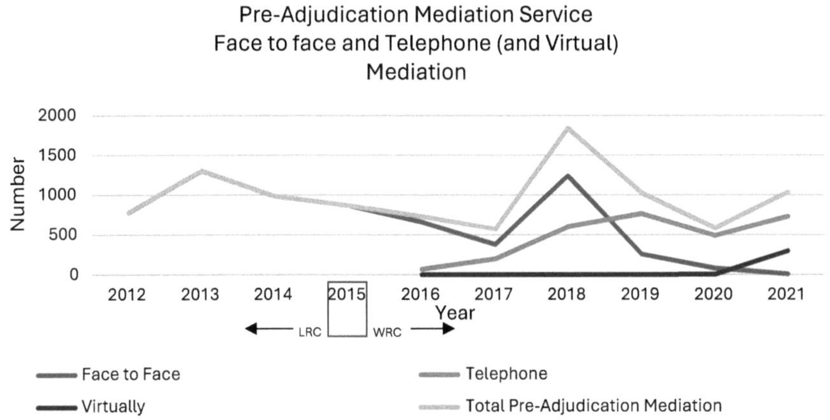

Figure 3.8 Numbers of Early Resolution Cases (Pre-Adjudication Mediation Service - Face to Face, Telephone and Virtual Mediation).

Source: LRC/WRC Annual Reports.

offered, settling down to in excess of a thousand cases during the remainder of the LRC's life as an independent agency (Figure 3.8). While an evaluation of the pilot service, introduced in 2012, concluded that a resolution rate of 60–80 per cent should be targeted, the resolution levels recorded between 2013 and 2015 varied between 36 and 44 per cent around a rising success rate. The LRC attributed the rates achieved to challenges in changing the culture of grievance and conflict resolution in favour of early mediation (Labour Relations Commission 2013: 26; and 2015: 13).

While the LRC developed alternative dispute and grievance resolution practices through its facilitation, mediation and early resolution services and through the med-arb practice of Rights Commissioners, the Commission sought little involvement in fostering the growth of ADR within workplaces. A research study examining the nature and effectiveness of emerging forms of ADR (Teague et al. 2015) was commissioned in 2013 and the Commission was well aware of the increasing role of private dispute resolution practitioners (Mulvey 2010: 55). The LRC, however, largely stood aloof from the growth of mediation in individual grievance resolution in Irish workplaces, whether provided by internal mediators or by contracted external professionals (Kenny 2019). The same stance was evident in respect of the growing incidence of the facilitation of collective bargaining by private practitioners (Roche 2015). The Commission's posture towards these developments (seen by some to be shared by the Labour Court) was described by a senior member of the Commission interviewed as one of tacit hostility, or at best ambivalence, bred in part through insecurity at what were seen as rival services. The LRC's posture was shaped as well by instances where private arrangements resulted in disputes worsening and returning to the Commission for resolution. Also informing its posture were instances where unions were seen to have supported such arrangements because they believed better deals could be obtained by avoiding the state agencies. There was also some unease that former state dispute resolution agency officers were sometimes involved in facilitating private arrangements to resolve disputes that would otherwise have been referred to the LRC and Labour Court. As early as the mid-1990s, when external developments in ADR were in their infancy, the LRC expressed unease: 'The Court and the Commission are concerned that this practice in the long term might diminish the value and effectiveness of the current dispute-settling process' (Labour Relations Commission 1996: 8).

The main employers' association, the IBEC, claimed the leading role in supporting the growth of ADR within firms. A senior IBEC official and LRC board member commented on that body's commitment to an 'extensive programme of development and capability building' in ADR and workplace dispute resolution (McGinty 2010: 83). The same organization produced the first guide to ADR for firms in Ireland (Doherty and Teague 2013). Subsequently, former IBEC officials formed the nucleus of major private providers of ADR services.

The development from the early 2000s of forms of 'private dispute resolution', involving the establishment of panels, tribunals or sole adjudicators to resolve collective disputes within firms, also occurred largely beyond the ambit of the LRC, meeting with little response from the Commission. This development, which was to continue following the creation of the WRC, had begun in the environmental waste recycling firm, Oxigen in 2004 and continued with new dispute resolution arrangements in the Dublin light rail service, Luas in 2010 and the Central Bank in 2012. By 2019, some 12 such private dispute resolution arrangements (PDRAs) had been created in 11 private sector and state companies and agencies, with more emerging in subsequent years. Most PDRAs envisage a complete break with the state dispute resolution bodies by providing for binding adjudication following internal conciliation. A minority provides for the referral of unresolved disputes to the LRC/WRC and Labour Court. While in some instances dissatisfaction with the service provided by LRC/WRC was identified as an influence on the establishment of PDRAs, in most cases, internal concerns and developments were uppermost in their creation (Roche 2021). By the closing years of the LRC's operations, the scale and diversity of individual and collective ADR practices in firms and public service organizations was such that some commentators were writing about the emergence of a 'dual dispute resolution system' in Ireland, challenging the long-established monopoly of conflict resolution by the public agencies (Roche 2015).

While the Act that created the LRC specified a clear and largely effective division of functions and activities between the agency and the Labour Court, the LRC's work was hemmed around by a growing number of agencies focused on different aspects of conflict resolution and promoting good industrial relations. The activities of these agencies are outlined in Figure 3.1. The Employment Appeals Tribunal was created in 1977 and dealt with individual grievances under a growing raft of employment statutes. The NCPP was created in 1997 by employers, unions and the state and charged with fostering partnership in workplaces. The same parties created the NIB in 2000 to resolve disputes that threatened national pay agreements or seemed likely to cause serious economic dislocation. The Equality Tribunal was created in 2004 to investigate alleged breaches of equality legislation. The National Employment Rights Authority was established in 2007 to enforce employment standards, following a series of scandals and controversies surrounding violations of employment rights.

The activities of some of these bodies overlapped the functions and activities of the LRC. The NCPP's role in fostering workplace partnership significantly overlapped with the work of the LRC in promoting good industrial relations. The work of the NIB bore centrally on the collective dispute resolution activities of the LRC (and the Labour Court), although in practice the employer and union leaders and senior civil servants who made up the NIB were careful to direct their efforts at mobilizing their respective networks to seek compliance with national pay agreements and to channel disputes to the LRC and the Labour Court (Roche and Higgins 2016). In anticipation of the merger that created the WRC, the LRC began to share services, such as early resolution and meditation, with the statutory agencies: the EAT and ET. Ultimately, as discussed in the next chapter, the proliferation of agencies and the growing complexity and cost of conflict resolution resulted in the rationalization and merger of agencies that led to the creation of the WRC and repurposing of the Labour Court in 2015.

Conclusions

The creation of the LRC reflected the effects on the State's then pivotal conflict resolution agency, the Labour Court, of decades of industrial relations upheaval marked by rising industrial conflict, a mounting industrial relations crisis and ongoing debate about the reform of industrial relations and specifically the manner in which conflict was resolved. Ironically in the decades that followed the creation of the Commission, industrial conflict and the demand for the collective conciliation service of the LRC entered a phase of long-run decline – the period from the early 1990s onwards in many respects resembling a 'golden era' of persistently low collective conflict in workplaces. At the same time, the incidence of individual grievances in workplaces, certainly as reflected in demands by employees for grievance resolution and adjudication by Rights Commissioners and other conflict resolution and adjudication agencies, increased significantly as the jurisdictions of all agencies expanded on foot of the enactment of new and revised employment rights. Parallel developments in ADR in workplaces developed apace, but drew little response from the LRC, which engaged in some ADR innovations within its own service offerings, in particular through the provision of 'facilitation' for employers and unions engaged in complex negotiations, often surrounding significant programmes of change and restructuring. The LRC was regarded as a highly effective and reliable agency and the radical reforms that were to lead to the establishment of the WRC were triggered by the growing fragmentation of a conflict resolution system comprising multiple agencies with increasingly expansive and overlapping jurisdictions.

Notes

1 A recrudescence of the 'revolving door' issue was reported in 2017, when the Labour Court announced that the protocol agreed with the LRC in 1997 was to be revisited in the light of a number of rejections of Labour Court recommendations in high profile disputes (*Industrial Relations News*, 9 March 2017).

2 The parties themselves orchestrated the negotiation of the programmes and their associated pay agreements. Central review committees and quarterly reviews were also operated by union and employer leaders and senior public servants (Roche 2007). These negotiating and monitoring mechanisms mirrored earlier institutional arrangements supporting national pay bargaining during the 1970s, when deals were negotiated and trouble-shooting undertaken by a bilateral 'employer-labour conference' (O'Brien 1980).

3 The agreement was named after the eponymous sports stadium in which the deal was negotiated – a practice continued under two successor agreements, the 'Haddington Road' and 'Lansdowne Road' agreements.

4 The Workplace Relations Commission

Introduction

The creation of the Workplace Relations Commission (WRC) in 2015 involved the most radical series of reforms in workplace conflict resolution in the history of the State. The emergence of the new agency marked the culmination of decades of debate on the need to respond to the growing fragmentation, complexity and opacity of the State's conflict resolution agencies. Yet, paradoxically while the case for reform was widely canvassed and accepted by many professionals working in the field, as well as senior public servants, ministers and politicians, for long inertia, rooted in vested interests, dominated, and few of the many reforms that were canvassed got beyond the drawing board. This pattern of inertia and the developments that finally broke it open and resulted in radical change will be examined in subsequent chapters.

The WRC, which subsumed the LRC, came into being following the passage of the Workplace Relations Act 2015. The performance of the LRC had never been a major concern of the reform debate that ensued from the early 2000s – though the Commission regularly drew attention to the growing difficulty of resourcing the Rights Commissioner service in particular. The reforms targeted rather the exploding demand, growing complexity, duplication and cost of the employment rights agencies as a whole.

The WRC was created through the merger of the LRC, Employment Appeals Tribunal (EAT), Equality Tribunal and NERA. The agency was assigned first-instance jurisdiction for all complaints involving employment rights and grievances and for collective conciliation. The Commission also became responsible for the enforcement of employment standards. In assuming the remit of the Equality Tribunal, the WRC became responsible for determining complaints of discrimination beyond the workplace under the Equal Status Acts 2005–2015.[1] The Labour Court was to become an appellate agency for WRC adjudication decisions on individual rights and

DOI: 10.4324/9781003520054-4

grievance cases and would also investigate and adjudicate on collective disputes that remained unresolved following conciliation at the WRC.

The WRC operates a single port of entry for all complaints notified, supported by an IT system. This is managed by an information and customer service centre, essentially a call centre. Since 2015, this centre has operated a dedicated anonymous telephony system known as 'Infoline'. The purpose of Infoline is to provide clear, accurate and relevant information to employers and employees and members of the public on employment rights and entitlements and industrial relations issues; information to members of the public on how to redress breaches of employment rights; and information on employment permits and on how to make an application for an employment permit. Most enquiries received are related to employment rights, employment permits, terms of employment, payment of wages, conciliation, redundancy and unfair dismissal etc. When dealing with individual calls, information officers use a network access database to record specific information related to things such as the status of the person calling (employee, employer), the region (or county), what the enquiry/complaint relates to, the sector of the activity and the type of enquiry. This information provides integrated and ready-to-hand statistics on the main issues affecting the workplace, whether employment violations are concentrated in specific sectors and/or particular parts of the country, the nature of occupations that are more likely to make calls etc.

Through a customer relations management (CRM) technology platform cases are referred to the adjudication and inspection and enforcement services. The platform facilitates the early codification and assessment of cases for adjudication. A similar technology-based procedure is being built for the processing of cases for the newly integrated conciliation, facilitation, mediation and advisory service. Senior management regards the information and customer centre as being critical to the core strategic goal of using technology to improve access to the services of the WRC. In the next few years, a new single CRM technology platform will be built to support the multiple services of the WRC, in the process leaving behind inherited technological systems of the past that were fragmentary and incomplete.

Before the creation of the WRC, the EAT and the Rights Commissioners bore the burden of the big increase in the number of individual employment rights cases. Perhaps, the most far-reaching change made by the creation of the WRC was the replacement of the Rights Commissioners with a new adjudication service. The remit of the new adjudication service is to investigate disputes, grievances and claims that individuals or small groups of workers make under employment and equality legislation, as well as employment grievances submitted under industrial relations legislation. Under a new WRC procedure, a single adjudicator hears and adjudicates on complaints concerning employment rights and grievances. Mediation is decoupled from adjudication in a reverse of the practice that prevailed under the Rights Commissioners. A two-staged process addresses complaints referred to the adjudication service. The first stage is pre-adjudication mediation – a successor to the LRC's early dispute resolution service – that can be conducted by telephone, in the case of basic complaints or face-to-face, where complaints are complex.[2] A new virtual mediation option has also been provided with as yet a very modest level of take up. Pre-adjudication mediation is voluntary, requiring the consent of the parties before it can occur. It is set up as a confidential process, although the terms of any agreement reached are legally enforceable. Designed as an early intervention, the aim of this first stage is to provide parties to the complaint with a less costly and less stressful process in which they can influence, if not own, any agreement reached. In 2015, no face-to-face mediations took place and only 201 telephone mediations were completed. By 2018, these numbers had increased drastically, to 603 and 1,241, respectively.

If the case is not settled through mediation, the case moves on to the second stage, which is adjudication. Adjudication occurs de novo: the adjudicators being unaware that the parties have undertaken mediation.[3] Both parties to adjudication are required to make submissions and an adjudication hearing is convened. An adjudication officer manages the hearing and the parties are provided with an opportunity to present their case, using any evidence considered relevant, including any witnesses or documentation. Recording of the proceedings is not permitted. Parties can be, and frequently are, accompanied and represented by a solicitor/barrister, trade union official or an acceptable lay person. Hearings are semi-judicial in character as they allow for cross-examination of witnesses and the making of legal statements. No decision is announced at the hearing, but decisions are normally issued within a six-week period. In cases that seek the vindication of employment rights, adjudication officers usually make legally binding decisions, whereas in cases that mostly involve industrial relations matters, they tend to make recommendations that are non-binding.

WRC Adjudication hearings were initially held in private and decisions were published on an anonymized basis. This was viewed as an important feature of the service that would protect the parties involved, especially employees, from adverse publicity that might affect their subsequent reputation or employment prospects. However, this practice was discontinued in 2021 following the Supreme Court judgement in the Zalewski case. Following a complaint adjudicated by the WRC Thomas Zalewski, a retail manager, mounted a constitutional challenge against sections of the 2015 Workplace Relations Act, claiming that they were incompatible with the rights to a fair trial and effective remedy enshrined in the Irish Constitution and European Convention on Human Rights. Zalewski's lawyers argued *inter alia* that there was no requirement under the 2015 Act that adjudicators should be legally qualified; evidence should be heard under oath and hearings should be conducted in private. The Supreme Court challenge was to 'the statutory provisions establishing and governing the adjudicative process for almost all individual rights disputes within the state' (Application for Leave and Notice of Appeal, Supreme Court, 7 March 2018; Supreme Court 2021). The stakes in the Zalewski case were very high for the WRC. Should the adjudication procedure have been found to be unconstitutional, the legal basis for the most widely used conflict resolution service in the public system would collapse.

The Supreme Court ruled that two aspects of the Workplace Relations Act 2021 were repugnant to the constitution: the blanket prohibition of public hearings and adjudication officers having no statutory powers to take evidence on oath or affirmation. The Court was also critical of the lack of an explicit provision for the right to cross-examine witnesses – though cross-examination was permissible in adjudication hearings (Zalewski v Adjudication Officer and WRC, Ireland and the Attorney General [2021] IESC 24; *Industrial Relations News*, 15 April 2021). Following the judgement, the WRC changed its procedures to provide for the holding of hearings in public and for the taking of evidence under oath or affirmation, other than in hearings on grievances that are not justiciable and decisions that are non-binding. False evidence is punishable. Adjudication decisions are no longer anonymized. Mediation remains private and confidential. The new procedures were given effect in the Workplace Relations (Miscellaneous Provisions) Act 2021. Adjudication cases may still be heard in private and parties to cases not identified if an adjudication officer deems it necessary to hold the hearing in private due to what the Act refers to as 'the existence of special circumstances'. The judgement posed significant immediate logistical challenges for the WRC as cases needed to be heard in public during a period when COVID-19 necessitated the holding of cases online. Cases involving a conflict of evidence that required the administration of an oath or affirmation also had to be adjourned pending changes in the law. The longer-term result of the Supreme Court ruling is that greater formality has been introduced into adjudication hearings.

The WRC's adjudication service processes between 7,000 and 8,000 cases each year. These commonly cite a number of 'specific complaints', arising around particular rights or issues, ranging from 14,000 in 2016 to a peak of 21,000 in 2019. The ratio of specific complaints to complaints provides a proxy measure of the complexity of cases. This shows a modest increase over the period from 2016 to 2020, ranging from approximately two specific complaints in the earlier years to 2.5 in 2019 and 2.3 in 2020. There were 5,000 adjudication hearings in 2019, with a steady rise in the incidence of hearings from 2016. The workforce mediation programme previously operated by the LRC was also carried over to the WRC and continues at a similar scale – the modest reach of the service described by the Commission as an 'ad hoc add on' to the work of the new conciliation, mediation and advisory service.

Collective conciliation and advisory services continue as under the LRC but are now integrated into a common service division that also involves mediation. Facilitation also continues and encompasses work assisting the classical change programmes around which the service originated, as well as support to parties in the public service without a statutory entitlement to avail of the WRC's services and to some non-union firms.

The WRC's inspection and enforcement service enforces employment standards – a function previously discharged by NERA. The Workplace Relations Act 2015 gave the new WRC powers to carry out an investigation at a place of employment in order to ensure compliance with equality and employment-related legislation. For the most part, these powers consolidate pre-existing powers under separate pieces of employment legislation and as a result labour inspection has not changed significantly with the creation of the WRC. Before the merger of the dispute resolution bodies, NERA's labour inspection service was situated in Carlow, approximately 90 km from Dublin and this remains the location of the service, resulting in the inspection and enforcement function being geographically separate from the other functions of the new agency. The Director of Inspection and Enforcement service attends virtually weekly senior management meetings and attends in person WRC board meetings. In addition, email and telephone contact between the Dublin and Carlow offices is frequent and on-going. The Carlow Office is made up of 57 labour inspectors (five of whom are Assistant Directors, effectively regional managers for separate employment enforcement teams in Carlow, Dublin, Cork, Sligo and Shannon. The Assistant Directors for Carlow and Dublin manage two teams each). A further 20 Executive Officers are employed at the site, mostly in the WRC's information and customer centre, but also in administrative support.

To encourage compliance with employment standards, the WRC uses a range of progressively more severe penalties: for milder cases of non-compliance, the WRC issues a contravention report that gives employers the details of breaches and instructions on how to rectify these, along with a time frame for compliance. For slightly more serious cases, a compliance notice is issued that outlines what the employer is not compliant with and gives them a time frame for compliance. In others cases where the non-compliance is considered to merit a financial penalty, a fixed payment notice penalty of up to €2,000 may be issued. The WRC has the power to launch formal prosecution proceedings, where employers refuse to comply with the law, fail to cooperate with the inspection process, and/or who have been found repeatedly in breach of the law. The WRC has also the authority to inform tax authorities and other agencies of any relevant breaches. In 2019, a total of 4,904 inspections were carried out, resulting in the issuing of 52 compliance notices, 12 fixed payment notices and the launching of 175 prosecutions. Overall, these figures suggest that the WRC does not operate an enforcement regime that imposes hefty penalties

The overall national conflict resolution system was further streamlined when the National Implementation Body disappeared following the collapse of social partnership and the National Centre for Partnership and Performance was abolished under cost-saving measures introduced during the period of fiscal austerity. The functions and activities of both bodies, especially the NIB, had overlapped with the LRC – the new head of the WRC observing that the NIB had served 'over time subtly to undermine the authority of the state industrial relations bodies' (Buckley 2018: 4).

Kieran Mulvey, soon to retire, was appointed as the first Director General of the WRC. He was succeeded in 2016 by a career civil servant, Oonagh Buckley, appointed to the position through open competition. She was succeeded in 2018, on the same basis, by another career civil servant, Liam Kelly, who had worked as chief operations officer and in other roles in the WRC. Existing officers of the LRC and NERA, Rights Commissioners and adjudicators who had worked in the Equality Tribunal, transferred to the new agency. New appointments to adjudication roles in the WRC are made following open competition to panels rather than, as hitherto, by the minister from nominees of employer and union bodies.[4]

The board of the WRC is an advisory board rather than the executive board that pertained under the LRC. The main functions of the board involve the submission to the Minister of triennial strategy statements and annual work plans, following consultation with the Director General. The board does not play a role in resource allocation within the Commission. Compared with the LRC board, the board of the WRC has been expanded from six to eight members; the appointment process has also changed. The minister appointed the chairman and two board members from among persons he deemed to represent respectively the interests of employers and employees. Also appointed were one member deemed to represent bodies promoting equality in the workplace and three with expertise across the areas under the remit of the WRC.[5] In numerical terms, this involved a dilution of employer and union representation as compared with the board of the LRC. These representatives, however, remain influential. Appointments to deputy chair positions at the Labour Court, hitherto based on nominations by employer and union bodies, are also now made on the basis of open competition, as is the appointment of chair of the Court, hitherto in the main rotated between employer- and union-nominated deputy chairs.[6]

Reflecting on the 2015 Act, Labour Court Chair, Kevin Duffy, commented that the statute was 'a workplace relations bill, not an industrial relations bill. Industrial relations … recognizes the centrality of collectivism. …

Workplace relations is a broader concept – one which looks at the individual in the workplace' (*Industrial Relations News*, 26 March 2015). Yet Duffy, as well as former employer representative on the LRC board, Brendan McGinty, stressed the importance of industrial relations and collective conciliation remaining central to the work of both the WRC and the Labour Court (*Industrial Relations News*, 1 October 2014; 25 March 2015).

The early work of the new agency addressed the administrative challenge of integrating the services hitherto provided by separate providers and of improving the time taken for cases to be processed. Hardly surprisingly, considering the scale of the institutional changes involved in the creation of the new agency, an early survey showed that less than a quarter of public service managers had a clear understanding of the role of adjudicators; while less than 40 per cent agreed that the new system would simplify the handling of disputes (*Industrial Relations News*, 21 October 2015). A wider survey of practitioners – most of whom were lawyers – conducted by the Employment Law Association of Ireland revealed that nearly half were dissatisfied or very dissatisfied with the new two-tier system, with 31 per cent satisfied or very satisfied. Many complaints referred to administrative processes and procedural problems (Barry 2016). The WRC's Director General admitted that the body had yet to become 'world class', though waiting times were in decline and administrative problems were being ironed out (Buckley 2016). Soon, however, surveys of HR managers pointed to general satisfaction with the service of the WRC. Six months after the agency's establishment, a sizeable independent survey of private sector firms found that most users were satisfied or extremely satisfied with the services provided and nearly seven out of ten users said that they understood the services (*Industrial Relations News*, 16 March 2016).

Surveys over subsequent years to 2019 pointed to significantly higher levels of satisfaction than dissatisfaction. Non-union companies were more likely to perceive that the services were 'pro-employee' and many expressed neutral views due to their limited engagement with the WRC (*Industrial Relations News*, 28 March 2019; 15 March 2018). A series of independent surveys of user groups, conducted in 2011 (when work had begun on integrating the agencies), in 2016 and 2019 drew responses in the main legal representatives. The surveys point to gradual improvement in overall levels of satisfaction with the new services provided by the WRC and the Labour Court. Majorities of the lawyers dominating the survey results, however, claimed that the new services as of 2019 were either no better or worse than existed prior to the creation of the WRC. Criticisms of complaints processing and adjudication focused on procedural matters, in particular the consistency of adjudication rulings. Views of mediation were largely neutral or negative (Barry 2016). A more wide-ranging survey of user groups conducted for the WRC in 2019 revealed high overall levels of satisfaction with

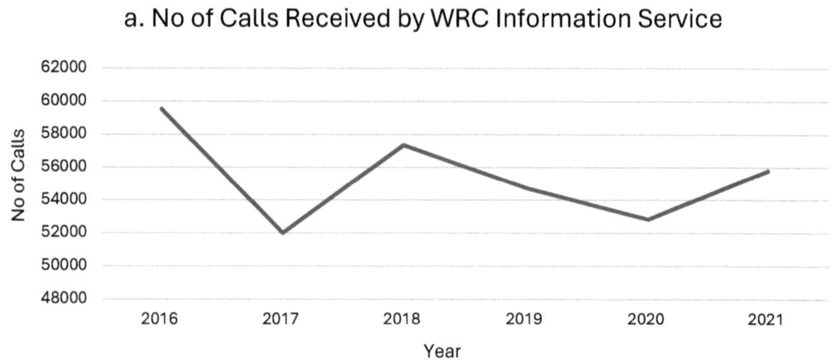
a. No of Calls Received by WRC Information Service
No of Calls
62000
60000
58000
56000
54000
52000
50000
48000
2016
2017
2018
2019
2020
2021
Year

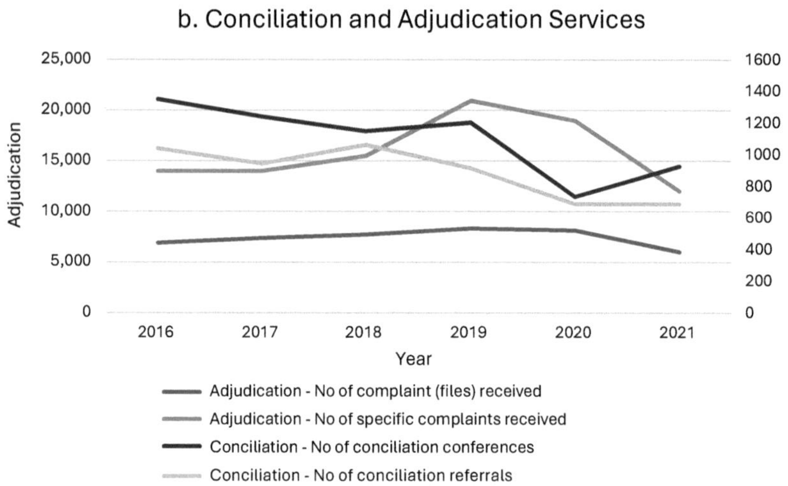
b. Conciliation and Adjudication Services
Adjudication
25,000
20,000
15,000
10,000
5,000
0
Conciliation
1600
1400
1200
1000
800
600
400
200
0
2016
2017
2018
2019
2020
2021
Year
Adjudication - No of complaint (files) received
Adjudication - No of specific complaints received
Conciliation - No of conciliation conferences
Conciliation - No of conciliation referrals

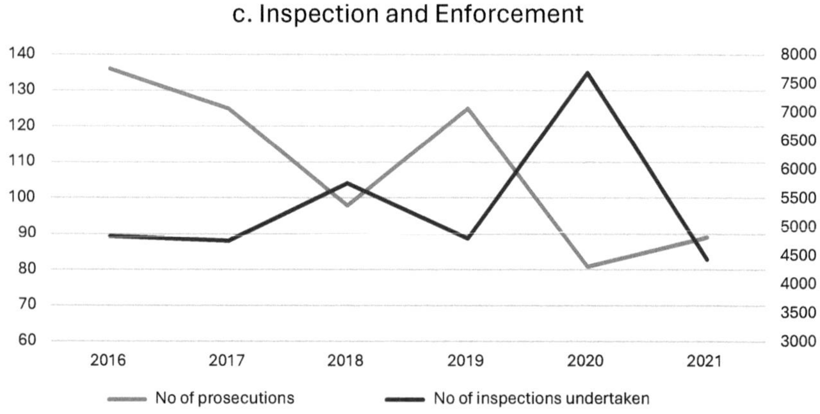
c. Inspection and Enforcement
140
130
120
110
100
90
80
70
60
8000
7500
7000
6500
6000
5500
5000
4500
4000
3500
3000
2016
2017
2018
2019
2020
2021
No of prosecutions
No of inspections undertaken

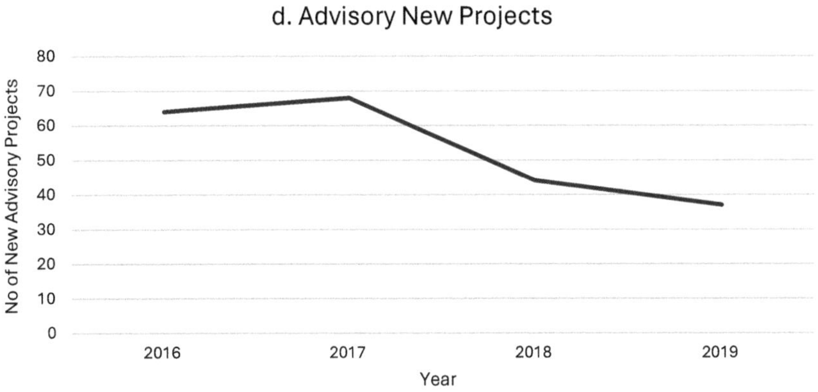

Figure 4.1 a-d Demand for Services provided by the WRC.
Source: WRC Annual Reports.

the WRC's services. The highest level of satisfaction was registered by the conciliation service but there was a low level of awareness of the advisory service. Face-to-face mediation was well regarded, but was subject to limited engagement, and concerns existed about telephone mediation (WRC 2018b).

If non-union firms, especially larger firms, in general remain determinedly beyond the reach of the WRC, plans to widen the access of public servants to both the WRC and the Labour Court will significantly increase the agencies' client base within the unionized sector. In 2016, police officers (Gardai) were granted ad hoc access to the WRC and Labour Court in a dispute over pay. They were subsequently granted formal access under the Industrial Relations (Amendment) Act 2019, effective from February 2020. Civil servants, formally excluded from the public conflict resolution agencies, had from time to time been granted ad hoc access to services of the LRC (Teague et al. 2015). As discussed above, the LRC had also played a central role in facilitating successive public service pay agreements since 2010. It has been agreed in principle that formal access to the conflict resolution services of the WRC and Labour Court will also be extended to civil servants, and there have also been calls from some politicians for access to representative associations in the defence forces (*Industrial Relations News*, 27 July 2019; *Dáil Éireann, Dáil Debates*, 18 October 2018). These developments will widen the catchment of the WRC and Labour Court and they also appear to herald the end of the remaining parallel conciliation and arbitration schemes for public servants (see Figure 4.1).

Changing patterns of demand and service delivery

Changes in services and sometimes in the way data are recorded mean that direct comparisons between the WRC and the LRC are not always possible. Trends in the volume, scope and relative significance of the services delivered by the WRC merit examination. As shown in Figure 4.1a, the volume of calls received by the WRC's information service, 'Infoline', has varied between almost 60,000 in the Commission's first full year of operation and over 55,500 in 2021. Figure 4.2 shows that the largest share of requests for information in 2021 (41 per cent) relate to work permits. Other subjects with significant shares include inquiries regarding complaints (19 per cent), with working hours (9 per cent), redundancy (7 per cent) and payment of wages (6 per cent). The rest of the calls received less than 5 per cent across a wide range of areas.

The pattern of demand for the WRC's services highlights the extent to which conflict resolution is now dominated by individual employment grievances, mainly surrounding employment rights. Figure 4.1b shows that over the period from the first full year of the WRC's operations to 2019, the number of complaints received claiming refractions of employment rights and other employment grievances ranged from just under 6,000 to

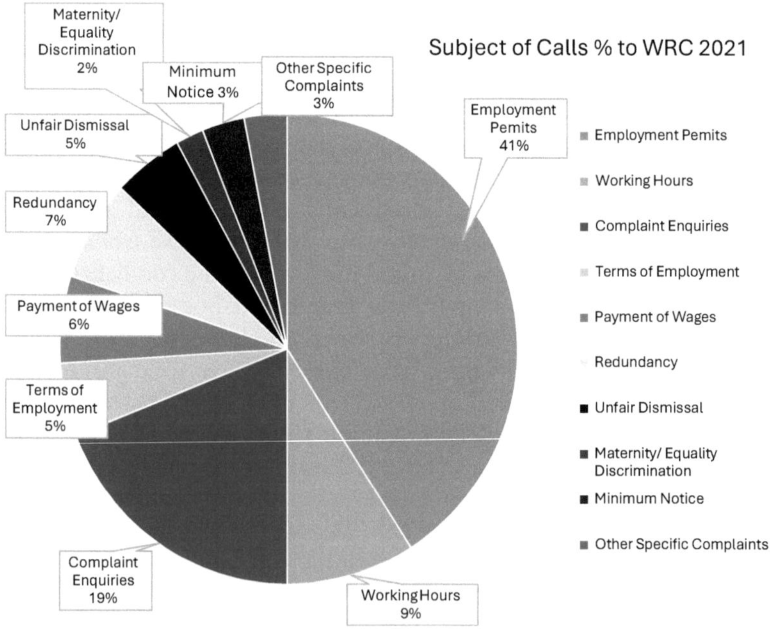

Figure 4.2 Subject of Calls to the WRC (2021b).

Source: WRC Annual Report 2021.

over 8,000. As many complaints claim alleged infractions under more than one area of legislation, the number of 'specific complaints' ranged between 12,000 and 21,000. Both indicators are trending upwards until 2020, but dip following the onset of the COVID-19 pandemic. Figure 4.3 for 2021 shows how complaints are distributed across issues. Complaints about pay represent the largest single area at 25 per cent of all claims. Hours of work, discrimination/equality and unfair dismissal are also significant, ranging from between 12 and 14 per cent. The rest of the complaints received are spread across a broad range of areas, including workplace grievances and disputes other than concerning employment rights at 10 per cent. Considering how this pattern compares to previous years, the distribution of issues appears volatile year-on-year but with areas of Discrimination/Equality, Hours of Work, Pay and Unfair Dismissal consistently claiming a greater proportion of total complaints. Spikes in redundancy-related complaints in 2020 and a significant decrease in Hours of Work complaints in 2020 and 2021 are noted, and both can be explained by labour market uncertainties and variations in working patterns throughout the COVID-19 pandemic.[7]

As an indication of individual grievance resolution, Figure 4.4 reveals a rising trend of adjudication complaints and modest increase in workplace mediation until 2019, thereafter dipping in 2020 and 2021, which is more than likely explained by COVID-19 disruptions. The incidence of pre-adjudication mediation reveals a spike in cases in 2018 (see Figure 3.8 in Chapter 3), seemingly due to a significant number of face-to-face 'class

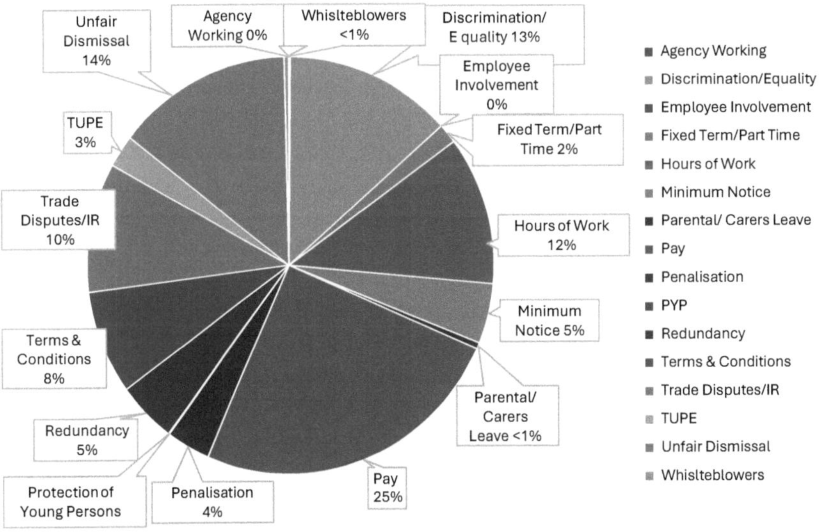

Figure 4.3 Issues Involved in Specific Complaints for Adjudication 2021.

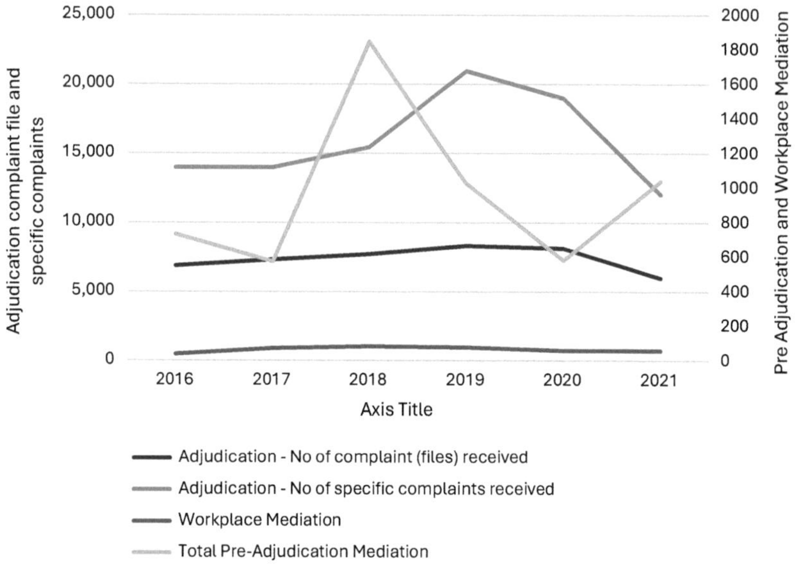

Figure 4.4 Indicators of Individual Grievance Resolution.

Source: WRC annual Report.

mediations' (WRC 2018a: 6). The success rate of pre-adjudication mediation ranged from 40 to 64 per cent and although this rate has fluctuated since 2016, the success rate has improved since the inception of the service in 2012 under the LRC. The WRC's workplace mediation service remains modest in scale (see also Figure 3.7 in Chapter 3). The level of activity surrounding the policing of employment rights conducted by the inspection and enforcement service (Figure 4.1c) also rose substantially over the period; the number of resulting prosecutions has declined, while the prosecution rate remains low at between 2 and 3 per cent of inspections.

The scale of the WRC's individual dispute resolution and inspection services is greatly in excess of the incidence of activity focused on the resolution or prevention of collective disputes. Figure 3.2 reported in Chapter 3 and Figure 4.1b reveal a continuation of the long-run decline in the incidence of collective conciliation that was evident under the LRC. The reach of this service can, however, be very significant: in 2019, WRC conciliation conferences covered disputes involving 1.3 million workers (WRC 2019b: 17). The success rate of the service remains high, with over 80 per cent of disputes settled at conciliation. The facilitation services provided by the WRC's advisory staff, including work carried out chairing joint working parties and conducting industrial relations reviews, also remains modest in scale and the volume of activity has declined (see Figure 3.4a).

Reflecting the changing patterns of demand for the services of the WRC, by 2021 more than 42 adjudicators worked for the WRC; the majority were newly appointed from panels established to augment the service (*Industrial Relations News*, 3 October 2019; 16 March 2016). The Commission has sought to maintain a balance between the professional backgrounds of the parties appointed as adjudicators. As well as a significant group of public servants (transferred from the Equality Authority), adjudicators comprise Rights Commissioners transferred from the LRC and people newly recruited to the role. Adjudicators thus include public servants, people with HR backgrounds, former officials and officials of employer bodies and people with training and experience as solicitors or barristers. The panel of adjudicators provides the WRC with the flexibility to respond to changes in the volume of complaints, in complaints originating in different regions and in complaints of different types.

As conflict resolution surrounding employment rights has come to dominate the work of the WRC – as had also progressively been the case in the LRC and the Labour Court – the competencies required of adjudicators have changed. Considerable effort has been devoted to providing formal training for WRC adjudicators – a much less prominent feature of the LRC. Shared learning between adjudicators is also promoted through regular plenary conferences at which experiences are discussed. Labour Court members also increasingly possess or acquire training in employment law (*Industrial Relations News*, 7 October 2015). In this sense, the two main public dispute resolution agencies have changed from relying nearly exclusively on industrial relations knowledge to knowledge of the law; a level of legal knowledge is probably a prerequisite for staff providing a range of services.[8]

The juridical scope afforded to WRC adjudicators has also changed following a decision by the Court of Justice of the European Union in 2019. In the case of Minister for Justice and Equality, Commissioner of a Gardaí v Workplace Relations Commission – the Boyle case – the ECJ ruled that the WRC and Labour Court could 'disapply' Irish law where it conflicted with European law. The decision arose from a compliant of age discrimination in recruitment to the police force (Gardai) originally lodged with the Equality Tribunal. An upper recruitment limit of 35 years had been fixed in secondary legislation and the Irish Courts had taken the view that the Equality Tribunal/WRC could not dis-apply Irish law by hearing the case. The decision by the ECJ reverses this position. This is seen by some legal commentators as a 'radical change to the Irish legal framework for the resolution of employment disputes' that has significantly expanded the jurisdiction of WRC adjudication, with important consequences for the training burden for members of the service who may not often hold formal legal qualifications (McDermott 2019). The WRC is less concerned about the direct effects of the Boyle judgement, regarding this in essence as highlighting a legal principle that has long been part of Irish law.[9]

Resort by organizations and unions to various forms of individual and collective ADR has continued to grow. The WRC's position is to support internal conflict resolution arrangements that contribute to industrial peace and good employment relations – provided that any role assigned to the Commission in such arrangements is agreed in advance, and the parties give consideration to what follows if such arrangements fail to function (Perry 2018). The WRC like the LRC has provided independent chairs for some private dispute resolution arrangements. The Commission has experience of assisting firms and unions where private dispute resolution has malfunctioned and has found that conflict resolution in these instances is made more difficult by the failure of such arrangements. The incidence of ADR in firms is also seen as limited and the Commission does not view ADR initiated by firms or unions, or the private parties who facilitate new arrangements, as competitors. At the same time, the WRC does not as a matter of strategy or policy proactively promote private dispute resolution.

Conclusions

The creation of the WRC as the primary agency and port of first call for resolving all instances of collective conflict and individual employment grievances and for policing employment standards marked a radical break with the pattern of fragmentation and inertia that had long dominated the provision of state conflict resolution services. Long-run trends apparent prior to the creation of the WRC continued to affect the pattern of demand for the services: in particular, the decline in the incidence of collective conciliation and the growth of the demand for the adjudication of employment grievances and complaints. Adjudication soon became the pivotal and most heavily resourced service provided by the WRC. Pre-existing ADR services were maintained and the WRC continued to provide facilitation and to provide mediation services both to individuals and groups engaged in workplace conflict and in the context of a pre-adjudication option for complainants and respondents. The WRC continues the posture adopted by the LRC to external developments in ADR – largely remaining aloof from such developments; welcoming them if they are seen to contribute to good relations in employment but envisaging no evident role in proactively encouraging the wider uptake of ADR. The Zalewski case represented an existential challenge to the core adjudication service of the agency. Ultimately, the Supreme Court judgement resulted in the holding of hearings in public, unless adjudicators have compelling reasons for holding cases in private, and a significant legal formalization or 'juridification' of the processes involved in hearings. Following some early turbulence in the views of stakeholders regarding the effectiveness of services provided by the new agency, the WRC has grown to enjoy high levels of confidence on the part of users.

Notes

1 Such complaints, arising for example, where people were denied services for discriminatory reasons make up a small proportion of overall complaints. In 2008, complaints under the Equal Status acts represented 7.7 per cent of complaints notified to the WRC (WRC 2018c: 21). In such cases, appeals of adjudication decisions are made to the civil courts.

2 Mediation is not offered in redundancy cases where statutory entitlements exist, or in industrial relations cases, where conciliation is undertaken.

3 This is one of a series of 'Chinese walls' maintained between individual service providers within the WRC. Another arises between the adjudication service and the WRC's inspection and enforcement service.

4 Panel members selected for adjudication positions are paid on a per diem basis.

5 All appointees applied under the standard public appointments process.

6 In 2004, one deputy chair appointment by open competition had been secured by a senior officer of the LRC.

7 For 2019, the *Annual Report for 2019* noted that specific complaints in relation to hours of work are by far the most prevalent at 6,266 which is over three times the number of complaints (2,026) received in 2018. The number of claims in relation to terms and conditions at 1,435 represented an 18 per cent increase. There was also a sizable increase in claims relating to pay at 5,214 specific complaints, which is up 20 per cent on 2018. Some 2,166 complaints were lodged relating to unfair dismissal, which is comparable with 2018 figures, and 1,827 in relation to discrimination and equality, which is down 14 per cent on 2018 figures.

8 A similar fate has befallen the Labour Court. The juridification of the Labour Court (Kerr 2014) began with the Anti-Discrimination (Pay) Act 1974 and the Employment Equality Act 1977, which charged the Court with an explicitly legal role in adjudicating on statutory rights to equal pay and the prohibition of sexual and marital discrimination. The process was to intensify following a raft of employment legislation during the 1990s granting the Court an appellate role in respect of Rights Commissioner decisions. By the time the WRC was created, the then Chair of the Labour Court noted that the Court's caseload had shifted from the vast bulk of its work having been in the industrial relations sphere to 42 per cent now involving employment rights cases. These cases consumed significantly more than that proportion of the Court's resources (*Industrial Relations News*, 25 March 2015; Duffy 2010: 68). The juridification of collective dispute resolution by the Court also gathered pace. In 2007 the case of the low-cost airline Ryanair successfully challenged a Court ruling on the 'right-to-bargain' procedure contained in the Industrial Relations Amendment Act 2001 and the Industrial Relations (Miscellaneous Provisions) Act 2004. Successful constitutional challenges were also taken in 2011, 2013 and 2021 with respect to the Court's role in fixing pay and conditions under the Joint Labour Committee system in low-pay industries and the registered employment agreements system in a number of sectors, especially construction and electrical contracting. Changes in the law intended to restore the right-to-bargain procedure, introduced in the

2015 Industrial Relations Amendment Act 2015, have also resulted in juridical rigorous and legally contested cases at the Labour Court (*Industrial Relations News*, 19 July 2018).

9 At issue here was an adjudication by the WRC that a driver was an employee of the company and not, as maintained by the employer, self-employed. The company described the judgement as having 'potentially enormous commercial and financial implications' and sought a judicial review in the High Court on the basis that adjudication officers have powers not compatible with the Irish constitution and the European Convention for the Protection of Human Rights and Fundamental Freedoms. Echoing Zalewski, Brennan's submitted that the adjudication officer's lack of a legal qualification was 'manifest and led to errors of law and of fact' (*Industrial Relations News*, 5 March 2020).

5 Pressures for the reform of conflict resolution agencies

Introduction

A series of external pressures beyond the borders of the Labour Court were instrumental in the creation of the Labour Relations Commission (LRC) and in the subsequent dissolution of that agency and other conflict resolution and adjudication agencies and creation of the Workplace Relations Commission (WRC). These pressures worked in tandem with radical reform proposals emanating from within the LRC and the National Employment Rights Authority to lead to the wholesale reconfiguration of conflict resolution agencies represented by the creation of the WRC. The emergence of radical reform proposals was discordant with a long-established pattern involving inertia in the positions and relations of different agencies within the overall conflict resolution system and, at best, cautious incremental change in service provision within agencies. The critical driver of change was a common vision of a new dispensation for conflict resolution on the part of two senior conflict resolution professionals and the space opened up for reform by the economic and fiscal crisis that followed the global financial crisis.

This chapter examines pressures for the reform of conflict resolution that led first to the creation of the LRC and to the subsequent wholesale reconfiguration of conflict resolution involved in the creation of the WRC.

Changing patterns of workplace conflict

The establishment of the LRC in 1991 was a response to a series of pressures on the Labour Court and the wider system of industrial relations – some longstanding. Reviews of the operation of the Labour Court had begun in the late 1950s and early 1960s, triggered by refusals of parties to accept recommendations in high-profile industrial disputes, by delays and by a decline in the success of the Court's conciliation service (Cashell 2011: 8–10; Wallace et al. 2004: 99). Behind these developments, as evident in Figure 5.1,

DOI: 10.4324/9781003520054-5

Figure 5.1 a and b Long-Run Trend of Collective Conflict at Work.

Source: Central Statistics Office.

were rising levels of industrial conflict. A rolling series of reform proposals extended from there up to the creation of the LRC in 1991. The various reform packages that emerged sought to address how best to configure state conflict resolution services against the background of changes in the pattern of industrial conflict and the growing significance of employment rights legislation.

The primary initiators of reform proposals were senior civil servants and the major players in the reform process were unions, employer bodies and conflict resolution agencies. The established reform process involved searching for consensus, especially among employer and union bodies. Debates on institutional reforms in the Irish Parliament focused in the main on technical issues, with few evident clashes of political ideologies or politically inspired reform programmes.[1]

Some radical changes were mooted, such as making Labour Court decisions binding and requiring the Court to take account of the 'national interest in the economic field' (Owens 1996: 10).[2] However, the Rights Commissioner service created in 1970 was the sole major institutional development up to the founding of the LRC in 1991. The new service was a serendipitous outcome of abortive debates surrounding more radical changes to collective dispute resolution. Commissioners were intended to provide a rapid and private grievance resolution service that could prevent minor issues devoid of knock-on consequences for wider groups of employees from becoming major disputes or from evolving into strikes (Cashell 2011: ch. 1). A further objective was to lighten the workload of the Labour Court by removing issues that affected individuals or small groups from the more formal process of Court hearings (Bragazzi 2012: 167; Murphy 1997: 295).

A Commission of Inquiry on Industrial Relations was established in 1978 against the background of a further sharp escalation in industrial conflict. The Commission returned to the operation of the Labour Court and other conflict resolution agencies. The Commission's report envisaged the creation of a two-tier system by merging and reorganizing a number of existing agencies and services. A Labour Relations Board was to be responsible for the provision of conciliation, the investigation of disputes of a non-legal character and the preparation of codes of practice. A Labour Relations Court was to play an appellate role in respect of recommendations by the Labour Relations Board and was also to be assigned a remit, inter alia, to investigate disputes and grievances in respect of employment statutes. The EAT was to be abolished and its functions subsumed into the Labour Relations Court (Commission of Inquiry on Industrial Relations 1981). The Commission's report was quietly shelved, but its lineage to the reconfiguration of the dispute resolution agencies is recognized (see Mulvey 2010: 46).[3]

A further package of reform proposals in 1988 led directly to the creation of the LRC. The reforms to conflict resolution institutions proposed in 1988 mirrored earlier packages of reform measures proposed in 1986, 1985 and 1983. In effect, the original 1983 proposals evolved on the basis of ongoing dialogue and consensus-seeking with employers and unions. The reforms leading to the creation of the LRC were unveiled and further developed by Labour Party ministers in a series of coalition governments with the liberal right-leaning Fine Gael Party. A centrist Fianna Fáil minority government passed the 1990 Industrial Relations Act that created the LRC. The changing political complexions of governments from 1983 to 1991 had little effect on the manner in which the reforms evolved. Debates surrounding the proposed changes were focused on reforms of the law governing the conduct of industrial disputes. Reforms of the conflict resolution institutions attracted little controversy (Wallace 2010). The main opposition to the creation of the LRC came from the Labour Court, which resisted its dismemberment by unbundling conciliation into the new agency (Labour Court 1989: 108; Owens 1996: 23–24).

The background to the quickening pace of reform activity was a continuation into the 1980s of the historically high levels of industrial action that had emerged during the 1970s. This contributed to an explosion in the demand for the conciliation and adjudication services of the Labour Court, while the effectiveness of the Court's conciliation service declined significantly (Murphy 1997: 354–357; Wallace 2010: 35–36). Industrial disputes were also seen to have become more complicated and more difficult to resolve (Ahern 2010: 1–2; Horgan 1987: 171–173; Murphy 1997: 297 and 301–307; Teague et al. 2015: ch. 2). Growing resort to the Labour Court was also influenced by developments in conflict resolution procedures. A series of nine national pay agreements that spanned the 1970s into the early 1980s contained dispute resolution procedures requiring the referral of disputes over issues covered in the agreements to the Labour Court (Bonner 1989: 266; Horgan 1987: 172; O'Brien 1980). A reform document noted that this development resulted in the Court being 'subject to severe pressure and strain' (Department of Labour 1983: 3). The more general diffusion of grievance and dispute procedures as an offshoot of the professionalization of industrial relations management also contributed to normalizing referral to the Labour Court where grievances or disputes could not be resolved within workplaces (Roche 2016b: 63–65).

More than in earlier reform initiatives, the focus was on the provision of conciliation. The excessive burden of adjudication endured by the Labour Court was attributed to 'access to the Court proper of minor and trivial issues and of disputes which should properly be settled at conciliation level'. The result was that a body intended as a Court of 'last resort' had developed over time into a 'court of first resort' (Department of Labour 1983: 4). Kevin Bonner, the senior civil servant responsible for framing the Act, endorsed the view of Labour Court chairman, John Horgan that 'negotiators were losing the art of compromise' and had become subject to a 'vastly increased reluctance ... to reach sensible solutions themselves' (Bonner 1989: 266 quoting Horgan 1987: 172). Compounding this problem was what was referred to as the 'revolving door', discussed above, whereby Labour Court recommendations – intended as terminal dispute resolution proposals – were becoming subject to further negotiation and requests for conciliation. The medicine prescribed was to separate out the conciliation service from the Court and prevent the fast tracking of some disputes from conciliation to full Court investigation and adjudication – and possibly back again to conciliation via the revolving door. The reforms that created the LRC also focused on a further concern: the difficulty that had faced the Labour Court in fostering good industrial relations, while at the same time avoiding pronouncements that might impede its primary role in resolving disputes (Bonner 1989: 265–266; Horgan 1987: 174; McCarthy 1978).

Kevin Bonner noted the irony that the 1990 reforms came into effect when strikes had reached an all-time low level (Bonner 1989: 262). As Figure 5.1 shows the incidence and volume of collective conflict continued to fall over the subsequent two decades, influencing the decline in the demand for collective conciliation at the LRC and subsequently the WRC. Reductions in trade union density (from 48 per cent in 1992 to 25 per cent in 2015); a decline in the proportion of the workforce employed in strike-prone sectors; the stability provided by social partnership agreements;

the growing openness of the Irish economy, and possibly also sociological change in members' views on how unions should best engage with employers, contributed to these developments (Teague et al. 2015: ch. 2).

The overall incidence of individual employment grievances, on the other hand, as reflected in cases referred to the various state conflict resolution agencies, including the Labour Court, rose significantly and sometimes exponentially, as evident in Figure 5.2. The exception was the trend in

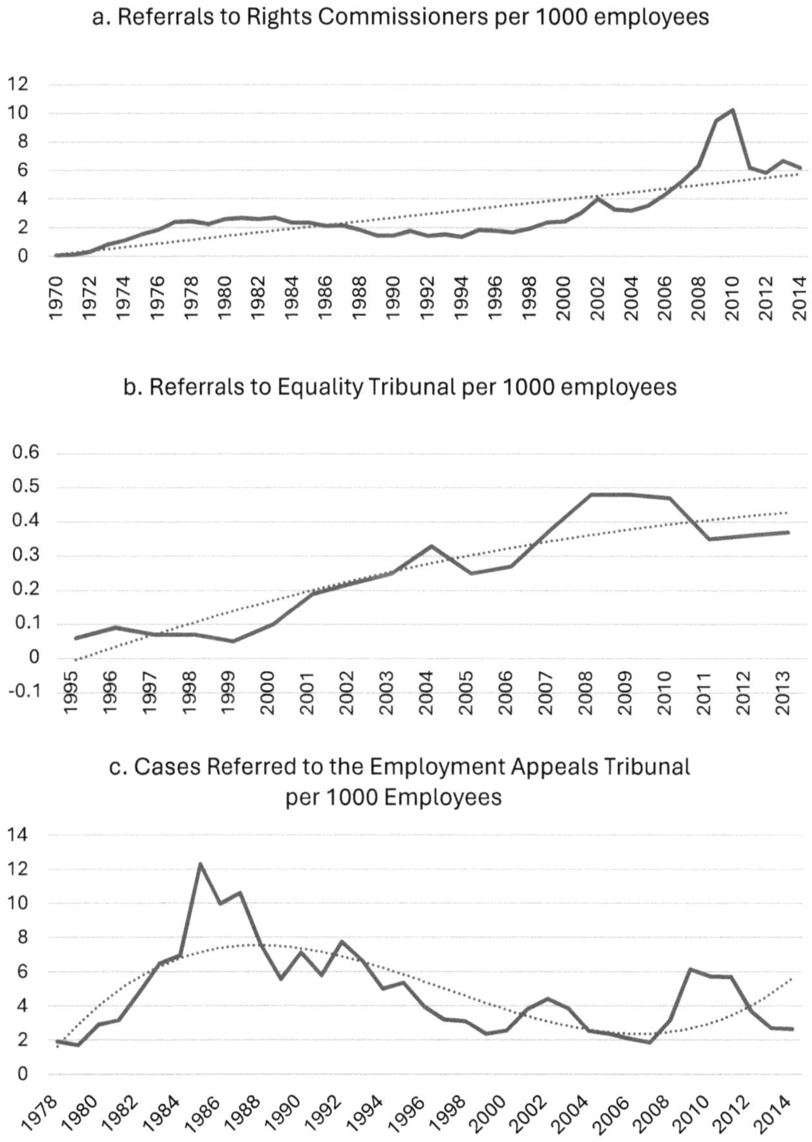

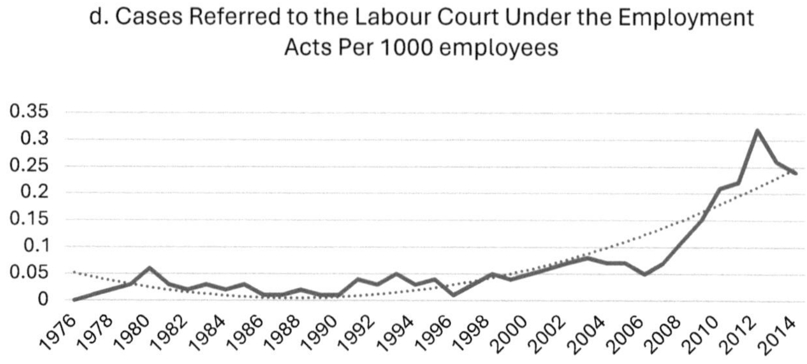

Figure 5.2 a,b,c,d Long-Run Trend in Individual Employment Grievance.
Source: Annual reports from LRC, Labour Court and Equility Tribunal.

complaints to the EAT, where grievances mainly involving claims of unfair dismissal and disputes over redundancy payments displayed a stronger pro-cyclical pattern. The individualization of workplace conflict evident in these trends contributed significantly to the growing demand for the LRC's Rights Commissioner service. They also primed individual alternative dispute resolution (ADR) innovations by the Commission and led to growing demands on other conflict resolution agencies. Of course in Ireland as elsewhere grievances or complaints referred to the state agencies represent only a fraction of all instances of workplace conflict involving individual employees. Official statistics for 2019 indicated that 10 per cent of people at work had experienced discrimination in the workplace or looking for work over the previous 2 years (CSO 2019a: 4). A 2018 survey of employees showed that 37 per cent had experienced what they regarded as 'unreasonable management'; 31 per cent had experienced incivility or disrespect and 3 per cent had experienced violence (Hodgins et al. 2018: 16). In the same year, those lodging single or multiple complaints with the WRC represented 0.4 per cent of employees at work (WRC 2018; CSO 2018 (Q4).[4] No reliable time series data are available to track trends in conflict at workplace level.

The expansion of employment rights

The more individualized pattern of workplace conflict was in turn influenced by a major expansion of employment rights from the 1990s. Figure 5.3 shows the growing incidence of statutes granting employees new rights or enhancements to existing employment rights. The most salient

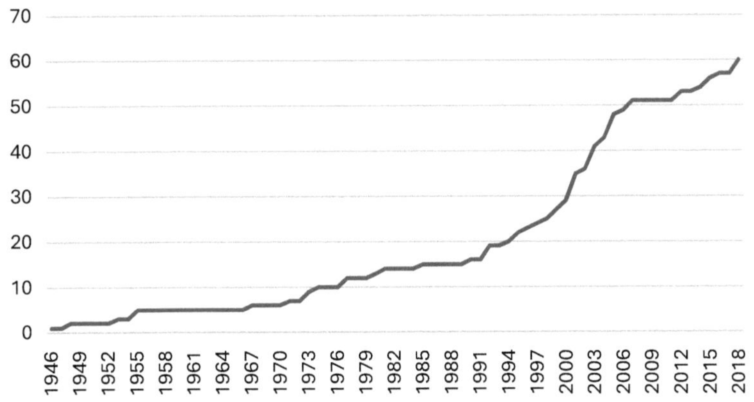

Figure 5.3 Cumulative index of employment statutes in Ireland.

Note: The graph measures the cumulative body of employment statutes enacted from 1946 granting employees general new or enhanced employment rights in the areas of pay and working conditions, employment security, equality and participation. Laws pertaining only to particular categories or industries (e.g. mining, maritime workers, employees in chemical firms, employees working in health and public service agencies) are excluded. Laws granting employees in general protection when informing of unlawful practices (e.g. restriction of competition) or providing protective disclosures are included.

Sources: Multiple sources were used to compile the index.

development was the dramatic expansion in employment rights during the 1990s. A broad array of rights were obtained by employees: spanning such areas as employment equality, enhanced protection against unfair dismissal, leave for parents and carers, maternity protection, enhanced rights for part-time workers, regulations on working time and minimum wages. Many of the new employment rights resulted from the transposition of European Union Directives into domestic Irish law. Excluding secondary legislation (statutory instruments), between 1990 and the abolition of the LRC in 2015, some 41 pieces of legislation conferred new or enhanced rights on employees. The growth of employment rights affected all conflict resolution institutions. The LRC was affected directly through the explosion in cases dealt with by the Rights Commissioner service – Rights Commissioners having being granted first-instance jurisdiction under the bulk of employment rights legislation, subject to agreement between disputing parties (Cashell 2011: 55–56; Duffy 2010: 70).[5]The expanding body of employment law resulted – following a lag – in what was referred to as an 'unprecedented avalanche of complaints by workers who sought vindication of their rights', leading to a growth in the complexity of the cases dealt with by Rights Commissioners (Cashell 2011: 58). The LRC was also to be affected indirectly by the expanding corpus of employment rights: the burgeoning demand for rights-based services strained the resources of all conflict resolution agencies and contributed to pressure to reform and rationalize the entire conflict resolution system.

Growing workforce diversity

Growing workforce diversity contributed to the rise in demand for the Rights Commissioner service. When the LRC was established, the Irish workforce was mono-ethnic and mono-cultural, and even up until the early 2000s, the share of the workforce born outside Ireland was less than 3 per cent. Strong economic growth from the early 1990s and the expansion of the EU in 2004, when 15 member states expanded to 27 and then 28, dramatically altered the composition of the workforce. Responding to full employment and labour shortages, Ireland was one of a small number of EU countries to allow unrestricted labour market access to people from the new member states. The result was a sharp rise in the number of migrant workers in the workforce, which expanded to about 16 per cent prior to the advent of the Great Recession (Glynn and O'Connell 2017: 295). The recession led to a significant outflow of non-Irish workers, but the migrant share of the workforce returned to pre-recession levels with economic recovery (CSO 2019b).

Survey-based studies have reported consistently higher rates of workplace discrimination among groups of migrant workers: white EU-Eastern countries were 1.5 times more likely and black non-Irish workers 2.7 times more likely to have experienced discrimination than their white Irish counterparts (McGinnity et al. 2018: 62).[6] Asian workers in Ireland were reported as nearly eight times more likely to have experienced violence at work (Hodgins et al. 2018: 14). While little data are available on the national origins of people referring cases to the Rights Commissioners, or subsequently to WRC adjudicators, data for 2018 made available by the WRC show that 27 per cent of complaints to the WRC adjudication service were by non-Irish workers.[7] This means that migrant workers were 1.7 times more prevalent among the pool of complainants to the WRC than they were in the wider workforce. Earlier data on the incidence of claims presented to the Rights Commissioners and on the outcomes of cases during one year indicated that non-Irish workers were also 1.7 times more likely to present claims than Irish workers and that claims by non-Irish workers were 1.3 more likely to be successful than by Irish-born workers (Hann and Teague 2008a: 31).[8] The incidence of race-related discrimination claims at the ET more than quadrupled during the 2000s to peak in 2008 when the Great Recession significantly choked off referrals.[9] The disproportionate share of complaints among migrant workers and the more egregious rights infringements suggested by their higher success rate were subject to comment at various points by the LRC (see Labour Relations Commission 2008 for example). The main focus of migrant workers' complaints concerned the Payment of Wages Act, which covered such basic entitlements as the correct payment of wages, holiday pay and pay for working premium hours (Cashell 2011: 61). Public scandals and controversies surrounding the exploitation of migrant workers led directly to the creation of NERA in 2007.

Between 1992 and 2015, female participation in the Irish workforce of women aged between 20 and 64 years rose from 48 to 68 per cent (Bercholz and Fitzgerald 2016: 16). In 2021, Ireland's female participation rate across all age categories reached a historic high of 60 per cent (Central Bank 2021: 65–66). A number of studies reported that, other things being equal, female employees are between 1.5 and 1.8 times more likely to have reported experiencing discrimination at the workplace than their male counterparts (McGinnity et al. 2018: 32; 2017: 62).[10] While little data are available on the gender composition of claims of different types referred to the public conflict resolution agencies, the available data suggest that this gender-based differential in experience of discrimination at the workplace may not have translated into higher rates of complaints by women at the Rights Commissioners, EAT or Equality Tribunal.[11] Data on the incidence of gender discrimination at the Equality Tribunal points to a sharp rise from the early 2000s to 2008 with a decline thereafter – influenced by the advent of the Great Recession (Equality Tribunal 2005 to 2013). Gender-related employment cases referred for adjudication to the WRC point to a rise again to levels evident prior to the recession.[12] Notwithstanding apparently lower rates of referral of discrimination and grievances by women to state agencies than they report experiencing in workplaces, rising female involvement in the workforce, allied with an expansion in the scope of employment equality legislation, contributed to the growth in the volume of complaints referred to the equality service of the LRC (and subsequently to the Equality Tribunal, when the service was transferred to that agency). This trend again contributed to pressure for the rationalization of all dispute agencies that led to the creation of the WRC.

Over the period from 1998 to 2018, the number of older workers (aged 55 years or older) rose sharply and their share of the workforce increased from 10 to 20 per cent (Privalko et al. 2018: 16). Available data on levels of age-related discrimination referred to the Equality Tribunal under the Employment Equality Acts 1998 during the 2000s, however, reveal no upward trend.[13] Studies of the incidence of discrimination at work, or by those seeking work, reported by older workers (45–64 years and 65 years or older) also show no upward trend over the period 2004–2014 (McGinnity et al. 2018: 43). Yet, data reported by the WRC show a very sharp rise in the incidence of age discrimination complaints in 2018 compared with earlier years: age-related complaints for that year far exceeding numbers of complaints citing discrimination on grounds of gender, race and disability (WRC 2018a: 22). This trend appears to have been sustained into 2019 (WRC 2019a).[14]

While the reasons for the sharp recent rise in the incidence of age-related employment discrimination remain unclear, age-related discrimination has gained growing media and public attention – as have WRC adjudication decisions on age discrimination complaints. The age at which the state pension is paid changed in 2014 from 65 to 66 years and might increase to 68 in 2028. The mandatory retirement age for public servants was also increased in 2019 from 65 to 70 years. While no mandatory retirement age exists in the private sector, employment contracts generally stipulate 65 years as the normal age of retirement. Changes to the state pension age, the higher retirement age in the public service and increased life expectancy, may well increase the incidence of complaints alleging age discrimination, and indeed, recent changes in the state pension age and the growing public salience of older workers in the world of work may have contributed to the recent spike in age discrimination complaints to the WRC.

The fragmentation of grievance resolution

As early as 2000, even before the sharp escalation in the number of cases referred to Rights Commissioners and the Equality Tribunal and a resurgence in cases dealt with by the EAT, senior public servants were concerned that the incremental piecemeal evolution of employment legislation had resulted in a conflict resolution system that was complex and costly, involving a duplication of functions and a divergence in procedures and remedies (Cashell 2011: 67). This was to remain the animating concern of successive reform proposals that eventually led to the creation of the WRC in 2015. Throughout, reform initiatives were concerned in the main with the operation of the EAT. While resourcing the growing caseload of the Rights Commissioner service and mounting delays and backlogs also received attention, the operation and services of the LRC were never a major concern: reform proposals from 2000 were mainly focused on the fragmentation and cost of the conflict resolution system in total rather than on issues pertaining to the LRC.

The Programme for Government agreed by the incoming coalition of the centrist Fianna Fáil Party and the neoliberal Progressive Democrats in 2002 announced a fundamental review of the functions of the employment rights bodies (Government of Ireland 2002: 9). This was undertaken by an interdepartmental review group (of civil servants), which reported in 2004 (DETE 2004). The review proposed merging the services of the EAT and the Labour Court. The number of divisions of the EAT, whose members were part-time, had grown rapidly in response to the explosion in employment statutes, giving rise to concerns about the consistency of decisions across divisions and over time. It was proposed to make Rights Commissioners the first-instance body for all employment rights cases, other than equality cases. A greater role for mediation was envisaged – although, as discussed above, mediation was in fact woven into the routine delivery of the Rights Commissioner service. The complexity and procedural diversity of the incrementally expanded system of employment statutes were to be tackled by consolidating employment law into a single employment rights statute (DETE 2004). To proceed with the reform programme, a number of agency-focused working groups were established. While one of these focused on Rights Commissioners, none was concerned with the LRC as a whole. Observing that appointments to the EAT had been viewed as a channel of political patronage, commentators remained sceptical that the agency would be abolished (*Industrial Relations News*, 26 July 2004). Patronage extended beyond the EAT, however, as many former trade union, HR and employer figures were among nominees as Rights Commissioner.

Kevin Bonner, the now-retired senior civil servant who had spearheaded the reforms that led to the creation of the LRC, was tasked with reviewing the reform proposals in consultation with employers and unions. This review led to the dropping of the earlier proposal to merge the EAT and the Labour Court. Concern had been expressed, especially by employer bodies, that were this merger to proceed the legalistic approach that characterized the EAT would damage the greater informality of Labour Court proceedings (*Industrial Relations News*, 9 September 2004). Reforms were instead to focus on streamlining the EAT (DETE 2005).

Plans to assign Rights Commissioners first-instance jurisdiction – opposed by IBEC, citing the risk of 'overload' – remained under consideration (*Industrial Relations News*, 3 February 2005; 24 May 2005; 3 October 2006). Employers also expressed opposition to expanding the role of mediation in the Rights Commissioner service (*Industrial Relations News*, 9 September 2004). While the Taoiseach (Prime Minister) called for the simplification of the 'maze of employment rights laws and bodies' (*Industrial Relations News*, 18 November 2004), observers feared that matters would be 'allowed to drift' and noted that the reform debate was entirely driven by public servants rather than ministers (*Industrial Relations News*, 24 May 2005). In the event, a new employment rights group was established as an implementation body and given 18 months to complete its work, while work was also to begin on consolidating employment law (*Industrial Relations News*, 26 May 2005). The reform process and the work of the employment rights group next interacted with the social partnership agreement concluded in 2016, leading to the creation of NERA. The agreement included a comprehensive set of employment rights compliance measures. These included the establishment of a new statutory office of director of employment rights compliance. The proposal to assign first-instance jurisdiction to Rights Commissioners in cases other than unfair dismissals and industrial relations laws reappeared. Resources and staffing of the employment rights bodies were to be increased to accelerate the processing of cases (Government of Ireland 2006: ch. 7).

Notwithstanding, the litany of reform initiatives and proposals from the early 2000s momentum for reform of the overall conflict resolution system seemed to have been all but lost, the focus now confined to streamlining procedures at the EAT to expedite hearings and upskill Tribunal members (DETE 2008).[15]

The global financial crisis, austerity and pressure for public sector reform

The advent of the 'Great Recession' triggered by the global financial crisis was a game changer. During 2009, GDP contracted by 10 per cent and unemployment rose sharply. The economic crisis triggered a profound fiscal crisis. Prior to the recession, the Irish state had one of the lowest ratios of public debt to GDP in the European Union. The public finances, however, had become increasingly dependent on taxes related to property transactions. With the acute downturn in economic activity, collapse of the property market and restrictions on the availability of money in international markets, the Irish financial system reached the point of near disintegration. The state effectively brought the domestic banks into national ownership. With the support of the European Central Bank, huge sums of public money were injected to recapitalize the Irish pillar banks. By the end of 2010, this auto-austerity had reached its limits and Ireland was forced to accept a financial rescue package from the Troika of the European Central Bank, the EU Commission and the International Monetary Fund (Roche et al. 2017: ch. 1). By 2013, the debt to GDP ratio had climbed to 124 per cent from the pre-recession level of 25 per cent.

The economic and fiscal crisis led to a programme of measures designed to cut public spending, reduce public service numbers and restructure public agencies (Government of Ireland 2010). Among the early austerity initiatives was a review of public service numbers and expenditure, which extended to proposals to restructure public agencies. The review proposed merging the LRC and the Labour Court; discontinuing the LRC's advisory and workplace mediation services, merging NERA and the Health and Safety Authority; merging the Equality Tribunal into the new 'rationalized IR structure' and abolishing the National Implementation Body (NIB). Other reform proposals focused on achieving administrative savings by redistributing activities across the various agencies (Department of Finance 2009: Vol. 2: 85). The proposals were criticized by industrial relations observers as crude and ill informed (Sheehan 2009; Teague and Doherty 2009b; Wallace 2010). The memorandum of understanding agreed with the Troika as silent on reforms of industrial relations institutions other than institutions for fixing minimum pay rates in some low-pay sectors (IMF 2010).

The incumbent Fianna Fáil-Green Party government continued to recite the problems besetting the conflict resolution system but appeared disinclined to tackle these decisively.[16] At a conference celebrating 20 years since the Industrial Relations Act 1990, the Minister of State for Labour Affairs repeated the now familiar policy refrain:

> The incremental evolution of employment rights legislation over the past 20 years has resulted in a complicated system, which is both confusing and costly. The duplication of functions within the fragmented architecture of industrial relations and employment rights is reflected in needless divergences in procedures and remedies.
>
> (Calleary 2010: 12–13)

The Minister announced the establishment of a departmental working group on the LRC to streamline the channels through which grievances could be pursued, 'short of re-engineering the entire framework through legislation' (*Industrial Relations News*, 21 August 2010). Pronouncements by employer figures also stuck to familiar concerns and proposals – fragmentation, duplication and the cost of resolving conflict (*Industrial Relations News*, 18 March 2009). Unions were focused on problems in collective labour law, in particular, the stalled 'right-to-bargain' procedure and the enforcement of minimum employment standards (see O'Connor 2010).

Matters changed significantly in 2011 when a new Fine Gael-Labour Party coalition government gained the largest parliamentary majority in the history of the state. The government was elected on a platform that included radical political and administrative reforms (MacCarthaigh 2017: 60). The new government pledged to reform the public service, cut the number of agencies and reduce costs. Following the election, the Department of Enterprise, Jobs and Innovation sought proposals for reform from the Department's agencies. The substantive case for the reform of the conflict resolution agencies had been made in numerous reviews stretching over a decade. What was missing was a strong political impetus for reform and a compelling vision of what a reformed conflict resolution system might look like.

Beyond incrementalism and inertia

Up to that point, the conflict management agencies showed a disinclination to disrupt the inertia that had built up in the multi-agency conflict resolution system. With the Irish public dispute resolution system becoming so fragmented, agencies remained cocooned and focused on their own remits and concerns. The strategies and activities of each agency were more or less developed separately: no overarching or cross-cutting organizational imperative or dynamic appeared to bind together the four dispute resolution agencies at any time. Each body had its own organizational peculiarities, set organizational priorities in isolation and responded to pressures for change in distinctive ways. Thus, for example, the strong organizational impulse of the LRC was consistently to preserve its mainstay service, conciliation. New services were provided for or developed, such as the advisory division or new mediation programme, but these did not detract from the LRC's focus on the resolution of collective employment disputes, the widely accepted original *raison d'etre* of the organization. For sure, the LRC was open to innovation, but the unwritten rule was that any change would be evolutionary and piecemeal and would be introduced in a manner that did not compromise its core activity.

Over the course of its institutional life, the LRC continued to follow a course consistent with its founding mission. A succession of Strategy Plans produced over the lifetime of the LRC reveals a continuous preoccupation with three key themes. One was to create a stable industrial relations environment relatively free from workplace conflict and when problems at work occurred that these be identified early and resolved speedily. A second was to ensure that the work of the Commission was fully aligned with the dominant trends in Irish industrial relations. Thus, during the social partnership years, emphasis was placed on the Commission doing everything that it was called upon to support this regime. In the aftermath of the Great Recession, the WRC put a priority of promoting policies that protected jobs and encouraged socially responsible organizational restructuring. A third was to review continuously the internal organizational structure of the Commission to ensure that it was delivering effective and efficient services. Thus, recruitment and retention policies were frequently reviewed and modified to maintain a high level of the right skills and capabilities inside the organization. Technology and management processes were also continuously upgraded so that constituent parts of the Commission could operate to the highest quality.

Board members and senior professional staff identified no major disjunctures or turning points in the strategic objectives or priorities of the LRC during the life of the agency. It remained very much a case of 'steady as it goes'. The decision of the CEO to make the case for and subsequently to broker engagement between the government and public service unions following the financial crash and fiscal crisis represents the exception. This initiative had not emanated from the LRC's board, where it met resistance. Internal influences on strategy and priorities reflected efforts to respond to well-defined external pressures: especially the growth of individual employment rights cases. The expanding remit and increased number of Rights Commissioners brought with them the challenge of resourcing the service and managing the work of an increasingly key group, who worked within the LRC, but continued to provide a statutorily independent service and guarded their autonomy.

No evidence emerged of any strong 'endogenous' pressures for change reflecting members' views or ideologies, or the views or ideologies of the bodies they represented, or any vision emanating from senior management. In effect, the board seemed wedded to the framework of principles that informed conflict resolution since the foundation of the Labour Court and subsequent creation of the LRC. In retrospect, some board members considered that the LRC (like the Labour Court) was out of touch and 'cut off' from outside developments in areas such as new direct engagement models of employment relations and developments in ADR within organizations, which the agency regarded with what one senior figure described as 'thinly disguised antipathy'.

The organizational logic pursued inside the other major and expanding conflict resolution agency, the Employment Appeals Tribunal emphasized that people should 'have their day in Court'. This became the organizing principle of the agency, to the point that it became its abiding core feature. As a result, the agency was quite content to ignore new developments emerging nationally and internationally in ADR (Employment Appeals Tribunal 2011). Because ADR practices sought to settle disputes before reaching a formal judicial hearing, they represented a direct challenge to the Tribunal's preferred way of working. Unsurprisingly, therefore, ADR-style reform was never seriously countenanced by the Tribunal. But by repudiating the notion of settling disputes informally, the Tribunal narrowed its room for reform and modernization. Embedding 'having your day in court' as an unwavering principle meant that the Tribunal would be unable to alter substantially its heavy legalistic character. Little wonder that the EAT came to be seen by many industrial relations practitioners and policy makers as a conservative organization, unwilling, and in the end unable, to enact new ways of working – a feature that became more pronounced and subject to increasing external criticism as the institution evolved. By way of contrast, the Equality Tribunal had introduced (by its own estimation) a successful pre-adjudication mediation programme but EAT remained disinclined to adopt a similar innovation.

Probably, the characteristic that the five dispute resolution agencies had in common was a strong motivation to defend their own organizational territories: each agency coveted its own statutory role: any encroachment by any of the other dispute resolution agencies, whether deliberate or not, was met with hostility. As a result, the tendency was for the agencies to be respectful of each other's bailiwicks, and conscious efforts were made by each agency to stay within their own portfolios of activities: each agency focused on advancing its own objectives and priorities in isolation from the others. An important exception was NERA, where the Director soon formed the view that an agency established to regulate employment and enforce standards was not fit for purpose in the absence of a reconfiguration of the entire conflict resolution system. This view was aired with peers in other agencies but received little traction. The dysfunctions of the conflict resolution system were also highly salient to the LRC's CEO, Kieran Mulvey. Mulvey, however, made no public programmatic pronouncements on the need for reform until 2011 when fiscal crisis placed public service reform front and centre of Irish politics and government policy.

Of course, each agency defending its own turf minimized the risk of inter-agency rivalry or conflict. At the same time, it effectively closed off the possibility of cross-agency collaborative initiatives. Joined-up or coordinated activity across agencies to address an identified problem simply did not occur, at least not in any meaningful way. Perhaps, the only exception was the interaction between the LRC and the Labour Court: these two organizations maintained a high level of organizational 'tick-tacking' over the years, but even in this case, the level of cooperation should not be overplayed and focused in the main around responding to the 'revolving door' problem, especially during the early years of the LRC.

The single-minded focus of each agency on ploughing its own narrow organizational furrow had the effect of dampening pressures for systematic change: if an agency was working full throttle to accomplish its core statutory objectives, why should it consider championing change that was far reaching in nature? Ironically, however, the more each agency went about accomplishing its own mission, the more apparent became the overall fragmentation of the public dispute resolution regime. In a sense, a curious dynamic emerged whereby the shortcomings of the dispute resolution system were external to individual agencies, but internal to the regime as a whole (Teague and Doherty 2009b). Putting right the structure of the dispute resolution system was never really going to emerge from within the system – short of a major external shock – even as the growing problem of fragmentation was clear to all.

Equilibrium within the dysfunctional conflict resolution system was also preserved by political stasis and the absence of cleavages or fresh thinking within the political system. No new paradigm for delivering the state conflict resolution service emerged and cross-party consensus remained on the principles informing public policy since the establishment of the Labour Court in 1946.

The Mulvey-Deering proposals

In early March 2011, LRC CEO, Kieran Mulvey, canvassed a radical proposal for the reconfiguration of the conflict resolution agencies in a public lecture. Seeking to contribute to the debate on public service reform in the aftermath of the recent general election, Mulvey called for the creation of an 'Employment Relations Authority', combining the roles of the employment rights agencies and the LRC. Appeals of decisions in employment rights cases to be made by the authority's 'deciding officers' were to be referred to the Labour Court. It was envisaged that the Court would retain its existing role in investigating collective disputes unresolved following conciliation. Collective conciliation was now to be provided by the Employment Rights Authority (Mulvey 2011).[17] Following the general election, the Department of Enterprise, Jobs and Innovation's called for reform proposals from agencies under its remit. In response to the call the Director of NERA, Ger Deering, drafted a paper outlining proposals for merging the dispute resolution and employment rights agencies. Deering proposed the creation of a single body of 'first instance' subsuming the roles of the EAT, Equality Authority, NERA, Rights Commissioners and the LRC and an 'appellate body' that would adjudicate all individual rights cases and collective disputes unresolved at the body of first instance (Deering 2011).[18] Deering's radical and detailed proposals met with little evident enthusiasm from senior civil servants in the Department of Enterprise, Jobs and Innovation. The proposals presented were viewed as more visionary than as providing a practical set of reforms for an incoming minister. Others subsequently involved in the reform process had a similar perception of the Department's posture.[19] Deering responded by retitling his document, which now became 'Vision for a World Class Equality, Employment Rights and Industrial Relations System'. Seeking an alternative pathway to gain traction for his proposals, Deering made informal contact in early March with prospective government ministers and then engaged in negotiating a programme for government, explaining that a major opportunity now existed to reform the agencies.

The Programme for Government agreed between the Fine Gael and Labour Coalition contained commitments to reform public sector agencies but made no specific mention of the dispute resolution and employment rights agencies (Government of Ireland 2011: 18–31). Deering forwarded his reform document to the new Minister with responsibility for the conflict resolution agencies, Richard Bruton, and opened dialogue with the Minister's Senior Advisor, Patrick Cluskey. The new Minister disavowed an incremental approach to reform and supported a visionary and ambitious plan. Informal soundings were taken by Cluskey with Kieran Mulvey, whose reform proposals had attracted media attention.

In July, following formal dialogue with the dispute resolution and employment rights agencies, the minister announced his intention to reform the conflict resolution agencies (Bruton 2011). The proposed reforms followed the principles set down in the Mulvey-Deering proposals. The reforms were welcomed by the board of the LRC. It noted that the Commission had advocated such an approach for some time and reiterated its support for structural reform of the dispute resolution system in its recent strategy document (*Industrial Relations News*, 27 July 2011; Labour Relations Commission 2011: 22–23).

The Minister issued a detailed consultative document setting out the objective of creating a 'world-class workplace relations service' and employment rights framework (DJEI 2011a). The document identified the familiar litany of defects and dysfunctions of existing arrangements. The conflict resolution system was described as too complex and onerous, taking too long to navigate and costing too much (DJEI 2011a: 2). The agencies created to safeguard employment rights had different operating procedures. Delays were endemic. Different channels of appeal existed: under some statutes Rights Commissioners' judgements could be appealed to the Labour Court and under other statutes to the EAT. The same complaints could be referred to different agencies (particularly Rights Commissioners or the EAT in the case of unfair dismissals). Grievances could also be parcelled into multiple claims under different statutes and presented to different agencies, leading to 'forum shopping' by complainants and their representatives. Different facets of complaints could be submitted to several agencies through multiple claims. Many complainants felt the need for legal representation; the EAT in particular had become overly legalistic. Services were fragmented and under-resourced. Irrational and inequitable variations existed in how compensation was determined and in the remedies available. The Rights Commissioners and Labour Court services needed to be promoted to non-union employees. The system was now so complex that even practitioners found it difficult to navigate. Many other defects were listed – none differed from previous reviews or commentaries by observers (DJEI 2011a: 16, see also Bruton 2011: 2).

While the litany of problems was familiar, the proposed reforms were very much more radical than hitherto. Five agencies were to be consolidated into two institutions. A new agency was to be created by merging the LRC, the EAT, the Equality Authority and NERA. The agency would be assigned first-instance jurisdiction over all individual employment grievances and complaints and would assume the collective conciliation and advisory functions of the LRC. The new agency would also take over the compliance function of NERA. A second appellate agency would adjudicate appeals of decisions by the first-instance agency and investigate and adjudicate collective disputes unresolved by conciliation at the first-instance agency (DJEI

2011a). This two-agency two-tier model would involve a radical streamlining of the conflict resolution system.

Bruton appointed Ger Deering to lead a reform implementation group within the Department of Jobs, Enterprise and Innovation. The Minister chaired a steering group comprising the heads of all the agencies involved, senior departmental officials and Patrick Cluskey. Kieran Mulvey was appointed head of NERA and continued as CEO of the LRC. From here, the reform process followed the established model of consultation with stakeholders with two major differences. First, consultation periods would be short. Second, work on merging administrative IT processes and the agencies was to begin immediately. Legislation would follow. Union and employer bodies responded positively to the reform proposals and endorsed the two-tier model; their comments were focused largely on technical issues and matters of detail (IBEC 2011; ICTU 2011). The Employment Bar Association (EBA), representing employment lawyers, endorsed the two-tier model but warned that the European Convention on Human Rights entitled parties to cases involving employment rights to a public hearing. The EBA's preferred form of adjudication was the EAT model of three-person panels presided over by a trained lawyer. Ominously, the EBA hinted that the model of adjudication proposed by the Government may give rise to large numbers of appeals or applications to the High Court for judicial review (EBA 2011: 10). The EAT opposed its own abolition for similar reasons (EAT 2011).

Four months after the publication of the reform proposals, the Department confirmed the direction of travel in a summary and analysis of the consultative process (DJEI 2011b). Six months later, the Department set out its detailed blueprint for delivering a 'world-class workplace relations service' involving the two-tier structure comprising the WRC and the Labour Court (DJEI 2012a). Stakeholders were invited to provide further feedback on the blueprint. Another submission by the EBA claimed that the objections originally made had been 'dismissed in their entirety', and the body repeated its legal objections to the operation of the new institutions, particularly the proposed adjudication service, and reiterated its earlier warnings (DJEI 2012a: 199–201; *Industrial Relations News*, 4 July 2013). The EAT advanced similar objections (DJEI 2012a: 161–166).

Work on legislation proceeded while the various agencies prepared for the new structures (DJEI 2012b). These preparations culminated in the 2015 Workplace Relations Act, which established the statutory basis for the new conflict resolution arrangements. Debates among practitioners surrounding the Bill, published in July 2014, focused on a claim that the WRC was overly concerned with rights-based disputes to the neglect of the interest-based disputes, collective conciliation and conventional industrial relations. Employment lawyers, led by the chair of the EBA, Peter Ward, continued their criticism of the new WRC adjudication procedure (*Industrial Relations News*, 1 October 2014; 12 November 2014). The first head of the WRC, Kieran Mulvey, later responded defiantly that 'threats of judicial review' and 'constitutional challenges' belied what the reforms sought to achieve – a 'user-friendly and non-legally confrontational first instance adjudication service' (*Industrial Relations* News, 30 September 2015). Others expressed concern that under the proposed governance arrangements which provided for an advisory board the WRC would cease to be an independent statutory body and would fall under the remit of the parent government department (*Industrial Relations News*, 1 October 2014). Debate on the Bill in the Dail raised the issue of civil servants being granted access to the WRC – something that had been mooted by the Department of Public Expenditure and Reform but had not received the support of all civil service unions (*Industrial Relations News*, 5 November 2014).

The Workplace Relations Bill met with a wide measure of support from across the political spectrum – parliamentary debate focused largely on technical issues. The main provisions of the Bill met with no political opposition although small parties on the left and some independents were critical of the protections afforded to workers in employment law and with the inadequate enforcement of employment standards (*Dail Éireann Debates*, 8 October, 12 November 2014; 21 January, 12 and 13 May 2015). Commentators hailed the reforms as 'profound and revolutionary' and a 'revolution in Irish employment law' (*Industrial Relations News*, 24 June 2015; 19 November 2014).

While the reforms radically reconfigured agencies and services, they were not marked by any ideological or philosophical disjuncture with previous public dispute resolution services, or with earlier reform proposals. No major conflict resolution services were withdrawn, and few new services were added – the early resolution service being the exception. Employer and union bodies continued to be represented in the governance of the WRC (albeit with a diluted share of board membership, as will be discussed below,). No consideration was given to incentivizing those involved in individual or collective conflict to avail of private service providers. All services continued to be free to users at the point of use – although the 2015 Act allows for fees to be charged. While resolving conflict as close as possible to the point of origin was stated as a major strategic reform objective, little effort was directed towards measures to configure or reconfigure workplace grievance and dispute procedures. Improvements at this level were expected to result from the provision of information on options available to resolve conflict, through the provision of pro forma letters to complainants advising them first to raise matters directly with their employers, and through codes of practice (DJEI 2012a: 13–14). There would be no general requirement that workplace procedures should be exhausted prior to the referral of grievances or disputes to the WRC (Teague and Doherty 2012: 183–191). Views were canvassed as to whether scope existed for forging positive connections between the public dispute resolution system and external experts (DJEI 2011a: 9). The responses received were mainly positive but very general and varied and they resulted in no initiatives or innovations (DJEI 2012c: 42–43).

Conclusions

A series of reform proposals focused on the Labour Court emerged over the decades since the Court was established. The case for reform was spurred by the escalating industrial relations conflict and wider industrial relations crisis of the 1970s. The key substantive reform leading to the creation of the LRC in 1991 echoed a long-standing concern that the Court was no longer an effective court of last resort and that the Court's conciliation service had, in effect, become a turnstile to full Court investigations and the issuing of recommendations. The growing sense of the inadequacy of conciliation, as then configured, reflected the apparent impotence of conflict resolution procedures in successive national pay agreements throughout the 1970s in the wider context of rising price and wage inflation. The splitting off of conciliation from investigation through the creation of the LRC provoked little political controversy or debate.

Growing concerns about conflict resolution from the 1990s were rooted in the fragmentation of workplace conflict across multiple overlapping agencies and the advent of new agencies within an already costly, opaque and dysfunctional system. This problem was compounded by a sharp rise in employment statutes from the 1990s, introducing new or extended employment rights for people at work. The growth of workforce diversity, in particular brought about by a sharp rise in workers born outside Ireland, increased the number of cases of alleged infringement of employment rights. As in the case of proffered reforms of the Labour Court in earlier decades, various reviews identified change priorities, but these were met by and large by inertia as each agency protected its own patch. The LRC retained its practice of making incremental changes to its services.

The global financial crisis and accompanying fiscal crisis were game changers in propelling the case for public service reform and the consolidation of public service agencies. As reform became a political priority, Kieran Mulvey and Ger Deering seized the opportunity to press the case for a radical reconfiguration of the conflict resolution system through the creation of the WRC and the repurposing of the Labour Court. Improbable, if not inconceivable, in the years before 2008, this was to become the most significant reform programme for workplace conflict resolution in the history of the State.

Notes

1 See Cashell's (2011: ch. 1) account of the reform process and parliamentary debates surrounding radical proposals to reform the Labour Court contained in the 1969 Industrial Relations Bill.
2 The 1946 Industrial Relations Act had obliged the Court when investigating industrial disputes and issuing recommendations to set forth its opinion on the merits of disputes and the terms on which 'in the public interest and with a view to industrial peace' they could be settled (Owens 1996: 7). Pronouncements in the early 1950s by the Labour Court's chair, Roland Mortished, against a general increase in wages in the economic conditions that prevailed, landed the Court in controversy; something repeated during the 1970s (McCarthy 1978: 5–6; O'Mahony 1965: 19–20). The original 1946 Act obligation to have regard for the public interest was rescinded in 1969.
3 The Commission was dealt a fatal blow when its trade union members withdrew in a dispute over extending immunities under the laws regulating industrial conflict to public sector workers.
4 Data on complainants to the WRC as a proportion of estimated numbers of employees at work. Of those people who had experienced any kind of discrimination (work-related or otherwise), only 3 per cent reported that they had made complaints to the WRC or other public agencies (CSO 2019a: 13).
5 If any of the parties objected to referral to Rights Commissioners, grievances were referred to the Employment Appeals tribunal.
6 Minority black and Asian Irish workers also reported significantly higher levels of workplace discrimination than their white Irish counterparts (McGinnity et al. 2018).
7 A caveat is that 22 per cent of complainants fail to provide details of their national origin.
8 Data on outcomes from the study was kindly made available by Deborah Hann. The same pattern, however, was not apparent in a sample of claimants at the EAT in 2008, where for every claim by an Irish worker, non-Irish workers presented 0.73 claims (Hann and Teague 2008b: 22 and CSO, *Quarterly National Household Survey, Quarter 2 2008*).
9 *Annual Reports of the Equality Tribunal.*
10 Gender differences are not, however, always found to be significant in studies of workplace, violence, incivility and unreasonable management expectations (Hodgins et al. 2018: 24).
11 Hann and Teague's (2008a: 29–30) analysis of large samples of cases at the Rights Commissioners during 2008 suggest that claims by women made up 40.4 per cent of claims whereas claims by men made up 58.5 per cent. A similar analysis of claims at the EAT (Hann and Teague 2008b: 19–20) suggested that claims by women made up 33.8 per cent of all claims whereas claims by men, 65.9 per cent. These proportions are broadly in line with the gender composition of the workforce in 2008 (CSO, *Quarterly National Household Survey, Quarter 2 2008*).
12 Data from *Annual Reports of the Equality Tribunal.* These data exclude significant numbers of claims citing multiple grounds for discrimination under the Employment Equality Acts. Data from period from 2016 (the first full year of operations by the WRC) are from *Annual Reports of the Workplace Relations Commission.* These data are not directly comparable to data in ET annual reports in that they appear to include *all* instances where gender discrimination is cited, including as part of claims citing multiple grounds.

13 Annual Reports of the Equality Tribunal, 2005–2013. A problem that arises in assessing the trend is that ET annual reports only systematically report data on cases where age discrimination is cited as the sole ground for complaints. Age however is also cited in larger numbers of cases citing multiple grounds for discrimination (see *Annual Report 2006*, Appendix 6), but these data are not regularly reported.

14 A large-scale survey of discrimination conducted in 2019 reported that of people in the workforce who had experienced discrimination at work, nearly 26 per cent cited age discrimination, while age-discrimination looking for work was cited by just over 35 per cent – by far the highest grounds reported (CSO 2019a).

15 The Tribunal now comprised 115 part-time members: 35 legally trained vice chairs were ministerial appointees and 36 members were each nominated by trade unions and employer bodies (*Industrial Relations News*, 30 January 2017). Research reported that legal procedure and argument at the EAT had become more rigorous and that lawyers had intensified their grip on the Tribunal (*Industrial Relations News*, 30 October 2007).

16 Besides its preoccupation with the banking crisis and the growing problem of raising funds on bond markets, the government was becoming increasingly beleaguered and unstable. From November 2009 the Fianna Fáil-Green Party government was supported by independents. From January 2010, when the Green Party withdrew from the cabinet, a minority Fianna Fáil administration carried on until defeated in a general election in 2011.

17 Mulvey's proposal (2011: 12) envisaged responsibility for health and safety, discharged by the Health and Safety Authority, also being assumed by the Employment Relations Authority – a function that was not assigned to the Workplace Relations Authority that emerged from the reform proposals.

18 Deering envisaged that the new first instance body would also subsume the then Equality Authority, a state advocacy and advisory agency charged with progressing all dimensions of equality (Deering 2011). This was not proceeded with.

19 This posture was reported as being consistent with the prevailing outlook of senior staff of most of the existing conflict resolution agencies pre-crisis, who saw little prospect of radical change.

6 The new organizational character of conflict resolution

Introduction

The organizational restructuring of the dispute resolution service resulting from the creation of the Workplace Relations Commission (WRC) was far reaching in its impact. Five bodies that had all been taking decisions on employment matters, spanning workplace conflict, dismissals, discrimination and an array of expanding employment rights were merged into one new organization. Motivating the creation of a single integrated agency was the desire to deliver a higher quality service and faster outcomes for parties involved in employment disputes. The underlying changes in patterns of workplace conflict and other pressures that had animated the creation of the WRC and that resulted in new service delivery and priorities also brought with them significant changes in the skills required of many professionals involved in service delivery and in the organizational character of conflict resolution. These changes went hand in hand with other changes in leadership, board composition and corporate governance, which also affected the work of the new agency. This chapter examines the changes that have occurred in the manner in which the public conflict resolution service provided by the WRC is now delivered.

The organization and management of the WRC

The architecture of the WRC's new public dispute resolution regime is set out in Figure 6.1. There was much talk about creating a 'world-class' service, about effectiveness and efficiency being maximized, about building organizational procedures that were accountable and transparent.

Figure 6.1 shows the four constituent services of the new WRC: inspection and enforcement; adjudication; voluntary dispute resolution; and information and customer services. These separate functional activities are supported by a shared, centralized corporate and legal team. Combining these diverse functional activities within one organization was certainly

DOI: 10.4324/9781003520054-6

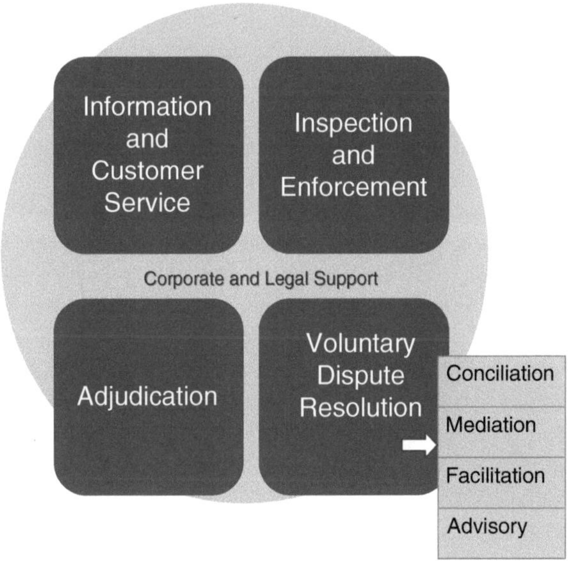

Figure 6.1 Services of the WRC.

innovative and challenging. Traditionally, across the Anglo-American world, these types of functional activities have been kept separate from one another. Because the WRC is such a bold institutional departure, it begs a host of questions. Has the housing of these previously separate services within one organization led to new forms of joint working? Has the Agency been successful in creating an overarching organizational mission or set of core organizational values to bind together the different services and skill sets of service providers? Or does each constituent part of the organization operate autonomously from each other, suggesting ***plus ça change, plus c'est la meme chose***? It will be shown below that the setting up of the WRC should be considered a far-reaching development, with significant implications, not all of which were foreseen at the time of its creation.

Since the outset, the WRC senior management team has been heavily preoccupied with developing an appropriate organizational infrastructure to allow it to operate effectively and with promulgating a new set of internal values and modes of behaviour to secure staff buy-in. These tasks are particularly challenging for an organization that was created largely as a result of the merger of pre-existing organizations and charged with the administration of a body of employment and industrial relations legislation that remains unconsolidated and fragmented. Much organizational memory and many pre-existing organizational routines needed discarding so that plans for the new organization were not thwarted by legacy issues or by employees failing to adapt to their new organizational circumstances. For the most part, the senior management team has been successful in establishing an effective internal organizational structure, securing staff buy-in for the organization and adopting a work programme aligned with its core mission. It has done so by pursuing a corporate strategy that simultaneously promotes organizational integration and differentiation.

Setting up a single agency charged with delivering workplace conflict management services and the inspection and enforcement of employment standards effectively ruled out from day one the WRC being a fully integrated homogeneous organization. Internal differentiation was always going to be a core organizing principle for the new body as quite different skill sets and methods of working are required to accomplish the wide-ranging designated tasks set for the WRC: conducting proper and thorough labour inspections, for example, demands different expertise than navigating a collective workplace dispute to a successful settlement, or adjudicating on alleged breaches of employment rights. Thus, from very early on, it was recognized that the three core services of the WRC – inspection and enforcement, adjudication and collective dispute resolution – would have to operate fairly autonomously.

In some instances, separation between some of the core services was considered an organizational imperative. Thus, from day one, the WRC proclaimed a 'Chinese Wall' would exist between its enforcement and adjudication services. The rationale being that if the enforcement service alleged an organization was not complying with some employment standards, it would be improper for it to be involved in any way, or to inform, an adjudication process to determine the merits or otherwise of cases of alleged breaches of employment rights. Core principles of procedural justice would otherwise be violated (Weil 2008). But, the erection of 'Chinese Walls' did not solely involve enforcement and adjudication. A rigid demarcation was also introduced between mediation and adjudication to ensure that mediators who had tried to settle a case informally would not become involved in adjudicating its merits or otherwise, and that adjudicators would decide cases without knowing about mediation efforts. The ethical case for this demarcation is not as obvious in this instance. A common practice across dispute resolution bodies is to combine mediation and adjudication together in a single service – usually referred to as med-arb. But, the key point is that to secure legitimacy for delivering simultaneously effective services in its three core functional areas meant that the new WRC had to design its internal organizational structures in quite deft ways. It also meant that it could not replicate the LRC in seeking – at least initially – to foster a single, overarching organizational identity of being a key institutional enabler of collective industrial relations in Ireland. The WRC defined its organizational mission in more multi-dimensional terms, which really reflected the multi-dimensional nature of its work.

Yet, recognizing that differentiation had to be a core organizational design feature ran the danger of the WRC operating like a holding company, consisting of largely independent divisions with minimal overarching integration. Senior management has made sustained efforts to avoid this happening. Firstly, the devolution of decision-making to the core divisions has been constrained. Whether it is conciliation, labour enforcement or adjudication, key strategic and operational decisions are taken by the senior management team collectively. Secondly, a series of measures have been taken to tie the separate functional areas to the new organization as a whole. In the WRC, the organizational status of the corporate support team has been greatly increased. Under the leadership of the Director General, the corporate support team has developed comprehensive yet customized training and skill development programmes for each division, a task that was done in a piecemeal manner in the past. At the same time, to enhance internal organizational flexibility, it also provides a level of cross-functional training. Conciliators, for example, who are normally involved in collective industrial relations disputes are given the opportunity to acquire mediation skills so that they can get involved in the settlement of (mostly) individual employment rights cases.

Thirdly, the corporate support team also monitors continuously progress made by each division of the organization towards reaching the goals and targets set for it by the senior management team in conjunction with the advisory board. The corporate support team also ensures that each functional area follows HR policies that are in line with those set down for the Civil Service generally – for example, it ensures that performance management procedures are conducted consistently and regularly across the organization and it insists that each area completes a workforce planning exercise to ensure that staff shortages do not arise due to people leaving or retiring. All in all, the corporate team creates the internal organizational web that connects the separate functional areas of the WRC.

Fourthly, a communications strategy has been developed for the organization that simultaneously seeks to transmit a set of core values for the WRC yet allows promotional and information activity to be tailored to the needs of users of each functional area of the organization. In all its publicity material, including the development of a user-friendly website, a focused effort is made to highlight, consistent with its core values, that the WRC provides services that are free, impartial, confidential and readily available and delivered to the highest standards of integrity and probity. This is the generic brand that the organization seeks to promote for itself. Yet, there is a recognition that different groups of employees and consumers are more likely to use a particular service or perhaps more in need of a particular service and as a result customized communication strategies are developed for identified segments of the workforce and user groups. Considerable outreach effort, including the use of multiple forms of social media, is made to raise the profile of the organization amongst particular groups of people – for example, young employees, women and migrant workers who are less likely to be aware of the WRC. The objective is to increase the overall visibility of the WRC, but in a manner that improves user access to services that they are likely to need the most.

Maximizing the use of technology is another core overarching goal for the WRC, although it is recognized that different parts of the organization will roll out any innovation in a distinctive manner. Thus, in the area of adjudication, a case management system has been put in place, whereas in the area of employment enforcement, inspectors are now using secure mobile devices that permit them to interrogate data from a range of sources and to input information into other databases. These innovations emerge from planned and concerted efforts from the centre of the organization and are not left to the discretion of functional areas. As a result, the effectiveness of each constituent part of the organization once again is dependent on the organization operating effectively as a whole.

Lastly, a battery of initiatives has been implemented to integrate people working for the organization. The key purpose is to socialize people into working in the organization, to leave behind the organizational values and routines of their old organizations and to internalize the new brand being fostered by senior managers. A number of communication schemes have been put in place to keep staff informed of key developments. Team briefings include inputs from senior managers so that discussion is not exclusively about the immediate concerns of the division in which employees work. Interviews suggest that the WRC has been able to constitute itself with minimal disruption to employees: most have transitioned to the new organization smoothly and readily identify and are supportive of the WRC being an entirely new public body for workplace conflict management and employment standard-setting. Building a stable and fully operational organizational architecture for the WRC has been time-consuming and challenging for the senior management team. Overall, the team has successfully created an organizational system that blends differentiation and integration: an overarching identity is being fostered for the WRC, but at the same time, each functional area has secured the autonomy required to fulfil its mandate successfully.

Beyond enabling collective industrial relations – a multi-purpose professional agency

The setting up of the WRC was a landmark event. Its creation represented a shift away from the notion of a public dispute resolution body (mostly) functioning as an institutional enabler of collective industrial relations in Ireland. In the past, the LRC, mainly through the activities of the conciliation service, performed this role in a thorough going manner and was unabashed about doing so. In concrete terms, there were three key elements to this institutional enabling role. One was fire-fighting: the LRC was seen as the key organization that could bring high-profile, sometimes embittered, disputes to a successful resolution. Government ministers and politicians were repeatedly grateful to the LRC for carrying out this role as it ensured contentious, awkward-to-solve disputes could be shunted into the public dispute resolution arena to be managed in a procedural manner, thereby reducing the risk of negative political fallout. The wider public came to regard the organization as reliable as it invariably succeeded in taking the heat out of big employer-trade union conflicts by steering them towards a settlement pathway.

A second dimension to this institutional enabler role was orchestration. Developing and sustaining interactions between trade union officials, HR managers of large private and public sector organizations as well as other members of the industrial relations community was an important role of the LRC. These interactions were used to etch out the boundaries between acceptable and unacceptable pay demands, promote particular approaches to employment relations issues – for example, how pension reform should be managed and how union recognition issues should be addressed. Informal orchestration activity of this kind was seen as instrumental to creating an orderly, stable collective industrial relations environment.

A third role was agenda-setting. Over the years, the LRC performed the important role of advocating change to collective bargaining arrangements or broader industrial relations processes. More often than not when the LRC called for a new departure to some industrial relation practice or process, the result was decisive action. A vivid example of this influence was when the Government introduced a swinging public sector retrenchment programme in 2009 involving large reductions in numbers employed and significant pay cuts in response to the global financial crisis. At the time, it was uncertain whether public sector unions would follow their counterparts in countries like Spain, Greece and Portugal and initiate large-scale strike action. To avoid widespread public sector unrest, the CEO of the LRC intervened and called for talks between all public sector unions and the Government to conclude an overarching agreement that would ensure that retrenchment policies would be negotiated first with relevant trade unions and then implemented through agreed processes. Very quickly, talks were convened and in a fairly short period of time, the landmark Croke Park Agreement 2010–2014 was concluded, which ensured that public sector restructuring occurred in an orderly manner. Subsequent public service agreements were also brokered by the LRC and latterly the WRC. Through performing its agenda-setting role, accompanied by credibility and deep experience in facilitating complex negotiations, the LRC successfully ensured that a consensus-orientated approach was adopted to managing economic adjustment to the financial crash in Ireland and latterly to restoring public service pay and brokering deals on pay rises as the economy and the public finances recovered.

In combination these three roles explain why the LRC enjoyed political and public legitimacy as the institutional enabler for collective industrial relations in the country. The overwhelming public view was that the organization performed a necessary and positive role in the Irish economy. As a result of the LRC having a high level of organizational legitimacy, collective industrial relations was broadly accepted as a feature of Irish economic and social life: there has been no attempt to assail trade unions or collective bargaining in Ireland in a manner that has occurred in other Anglo-American countries (Roche and Teague 2015). For the most part, the reliability of the LRC to address effectively on-going collective industrial relations challenges was rooted in its organizational make up – its role as an institutional enabler of collective industrial relations, governed in the main by social partner organizations, was baked into the structure and conduct of the organization. Fulfilling this role made an indelible imprint on the organizational characteristics of the LRC – the way it trained its staff; the manner in which staff were given discretion to customize settlements or agreements that were sensitive to the peculiar circumstances of the disputing parties; and the importance attached to engaging continuously with external stakeholders to maintain its organizational identity as the country's main public employment dispute resolution body. These three tasks were the key organizational imperatives for the LRC from the beginning in a manner that is not so pressing for the WRC, given its wider remit, the precipitous decline in trade union density, the narrowing coverage of collective bargaining and the low level of collective conflict.

The reputation of the LRC was predicated on its ability to solve collective industrial relations yet a challenge it constantly faced was the absence of specialized skills on the external market from which to recruit appropriate staff. Most public agencies that conduct high-grade tasks or deliver complex services employ highly skilled professionals. Normally professionals acquire their skills through a formal instructional curriculum in which teaching and learning goals, practices, and outcomes are clearly defined and accredited by a recognized professional body. The LRC could never really use this type of professional status framework to recruit staff because there was no widely recognized accreditation body able to organize conciliators, facilitators and others involved in the resolution of mostly collective industrial disputes into a tightly delineated occupational group. What compounded the problem was recruitment was initially confined to civil servants working for the LRC's parent department, although it was subsequently widened to include the whole public sector. The only positive thing that could be said about having such a restrictive recruitment pool was that public servants were more likely to possess – and be seen to possess – the ethos of impartiality that was so central to the work of the LRC.

So the skills – and probably as important – the status of conciliators, facilitators and others as highly skilled and respected problem-solvers had to be fostered after staff were recruited from within the ranks of the civil service, usually at a relatively junior level. To this end, the new recruits acquired knowledge and expertise of conflict management processes through a process of on-the-job learning and reflection gained by working closely with mentors on real disputes backed up by engaging in various associated organizational activities and administrative tasks. An integral part of this informal training programme was role socialization that involved the acculturation of recruits into the LRC's normative and performance expectations. The purpose was to initiate the new recruits into a 'community of practice' dedicated to solving (mostly) collective industrial relations disputes: new recruits would acquire a new 'professional' identity that involved internalizing the values, norms and relationships appropriate to the LRC's methods of problem-solving collective employment disputes.

To enable this informal knowledge generation process to work effectively and to allow conciliators and others to devise bespoke solutions to workplace disputes, the LRC had to possess a decentralized organizational structure that granted considerable decision-making discretion to conciliators. They would decide, for example, whether or not negotiations should be conducted face-to-face, if they should be intensive or whether a cooling-off period would be appropriate. Thus, rather than following a hierarchically determined set of prescribed rules and processes, LRC staff used techniques such as conciliation and facilitation in an adaptive way. Although emphasis was placed on the need to be pragmatic and experimental, sight was never lost of the main goal of crafting a solution that was acceptable to all the involved parties.

These officials were also embedded within a dense and active, yet informal and discrete, network of collective industrial relations specialists that extended beyond the organizational boundaries of the LRC. For the most part, this network was made up of senior representatives of employer organizations and trade unions as well as senior HR managers in large organizations. The network had multiple purposes. One was to maintain a near-continuous conversation about unfolding developments in Irish industrial relations and to assess whether any new action may be required. Another was to provide intelligence about the nature of particular disputes, the informal dynamics driving the strife, the nature of the personalities involved in the dispute and so on. Another was to engage in persuasion and deliberation. Trade unions and employers might be engaged with each other in an effort to effect change to their respective positions on pay or some other collective bargaining demand. Feedback might be provided to the LRC on the strengths and weaknesses of settling a dispute in a particular way. In a nutshell, the purpose of the network was to ensure that stable and orderly collective industrial relations institutions were not left to serendipity.

The conciliation service of the WRC retains its longstanding features and its gilt-edged reputation continues for being highly professional and effective. In recent years, for example, the conciliation service has been to the fore in brokering a series of public service-wide pay agreements and in resolving high-profile disputes in the public sector involving Gardai, transport workers, nurses and healthcare assistants. New recruits to the service continue to be trained along 'sitting-by-nellie' principles and an informal network of collective industrial relations experts still exists, although its strength has been diminished by the main Irish employers' organization stepping back from collective industrial relations activity. While, as one senior figure put it: 'politically the WRC *is* conciliation', the Commission is positioned as an agency delivering multiple services. Conciliation, though remaining central to public and political perceptions of the effectiveness of the WRC, no longer constitutes the agency's main service in the manner that long pertained in the LRC. The large and growing volume of complaints dealt with by the adjudication service and the dramatically increased numbers of staff involved in the delivery of the service are salient features of patterns of demand and resource allocation, not to mention the significant numbers involved in inspection and enforcement. Conciliating collective industrial relations, while central to the work of the WRC, is no longer the primary determinant of the organizational character of the agency in the way that it was in the LRC.

The growing cadre of Rights Commissioners in the LRC dealt in the main with conflicts surrounding employment rights and acquired an increasingly pronounced and legally circumscribed judicial role, like conciliation officers they enjoyed considerable latitude to craft bespoke solutions to resolve conflicts. As discussed above, they enjoyed the discretion to decide whether mediation or adjudication – or both in sequence – were optimal in the circumstances of particular cases. Reflecting their professional backgrounds as former union officials and HR managers, the knowledge they brought to bear in their work derived mainly from domain expertise in employment relations rather than from knowledge of juridical procedure or expertise in the law. While the skills and knowledge required by adjudicators continue to draw on domain expertise in human resource management and employment relations, knowledge of juridical procedures and the law are now of considerably greater importance and seems likely to become even more so as conflict resolution becomes increasingly juridified.

Another dimension of the changing organizational character of public dispute resolution concerns leadership and governance. Kieran Mulvey, the CEO of the LRC, was a public service outsider and adopted a very hands-on approach to dispute resolution. Mulvey enjoyed a high public and media profile, and actively engaged in public debate and sometimes in public controversies surrounding employment issues and industrial disputes. For example, he was publicly critical of the treatment of migrant workers and domestic au pairs. In 2010, as industrial conflict threatened public service delivery following pay cuts, he called for rapprochement between the government and public service unions without any evident appetite for such a course on the part of the principals and with no settled view among the LRC board. In 2012, during a bitter dispute involving Dublin light rail (Luas) workers that disrupted transport in the city, he publicly criticized the scale of the pay claim lodged by Luas workers, leading to a call for his resignation by the leader of Ireland's largest union, SIPTU. Under Mulvey's leadership, the LRC maintained a high profile, leading to it being frequently in the news.

Mulvey's hands-on and high-profile leadership was a source of tension within the board of the LRC during the Commission's early life. The controversy was aired during meetings between the board and the Minister. Ultimately Mulvey prevailed and a new chair was appointed to lead the board. The CEO enjoyed the confidence of his senior staff and set about making appointments to key positions in the LRC. Some centrally involved in the agency's work formed the view that there was a resolve within the public service that the WRC should be led in a different manner. Since Kieran Mulvey's retirement, two career civil servants have led the WRC – the first of these making it clear publicly that they would not seek to emulate the outgoing Director General (Walsh 2017). The main focus of WRC leaders post-Mulvey has been their concern with integrating and streamlining the services of the new agency and to that end engaging in dialogue with external stakeholders.

Governance arrangements have also changed. The LRC was governed by an executive board, where board members were responsible for making and reviewing strategy and also engaged in decisions over resource allocation and lobbied for additional resources. The pivotal board members were senior officials of the major trade unions and of the employers' body IBEC. These same people were also centrally involved in negotiating a series of tripartite national social partnership agreements and so were highly influential in the world of employment relations and in broader macroeconomic governance. The first chair of the LRC's board was a former leader of the main employers' body active in industrial relations, and Kieran Mulvey had held a high-profile role as head of one of the teachers' unions.

The WRC is governed by an advisory board, which, while responsible for proposing strategic priorities to the Minister, substantially works to support the Director General and plays no direct role in resource allocation or management. The oversight group that had guided the creation of the WRC presented a range of alternative governance arrangements to the WRC's parent department. The department opted for an advisory board.[1] In the view of the Commission, the advisory board in no way compromises its independence and there has been no external interference in its work.[2] The board receives regular reports from senior managers of the Commission's divisions and monitors and reviews associated workflow metrics. The board has a primarily operational focus and its deliberations to date reflect the priorities and work of senior management in integrating and streamlining the Commission's services. Union and employer association board members are numerically less prominent in the new board than in the LRC. Since the collapse of social partnership, they no longer occupy such an influential role in economy-wide pay bargaining or macroeconomic governance. The 'social partner' board members remain influential, however, and their views are listened to by management both at board level and in other ways.

Finally, as highlighted earlier, the WRC has adopted a more formalized series of management processes and systems. Greater formalization in part results from organizational scale and complexity: in 2018, the WRC employed 210 people, as compared with 43 people who worked for the LRC in 2013. It also, however, results from the drive to integrate and streamline services. Management formalization encompasses policy formulation and review by senior officers, as well as target setting, financial management, data harvesting and training and development. As a result of these changes in service priorities and resourcing, in leadership, governance and management processes, the organizational character of public dispute resolution has changed significantly.

Conclusions

The WRC was created to address two problems. One was to end the institutional fragmentation that had crept, largely by stealth, into the delivery of public services to resolve workplace conflict. Institutional fragmentation had resulted in these services being delivered inefficiently. The other was a concern that the public policy regime for workplace conflict resolution was not fully aligned with the changing nature of conflict at work. With its strong ethos of collective industrial relations, the LRC, the dominant public agency concerned with workplace conflict, was not seen as fully in step with the strongly individualized nature of most contemporary employment problems. A solution to these two problems was seen as involving not only the creation of a single, overarching agency, but also one with an entirely new organizational culture and *modus operandi*. Creating the WRC was thus seen as a way of bringing greater institutional coherence to public conflict resolution services and establishing a new rhythm between what the public conflict resolution regime does and the unfolding dynamics of conflict emerging in organizations.

This chapter explains the distinctive organizational character of the WRC. It argues that far from being a spontaneous process, the building of WRC's organizational structure and methods of working required strong and creative leadership to address a series of internal and external challenges. These challenges have been successfully weathered and the WRC is now functioning in a manner of the new organization envisioned by the senior management team: even though it is a multi-purpose agency providing a range of employment-related services that are hardly compatible with each other, the WRC is widely viewed as operating as a cohesive, single agency. A unity has been secured between organizational integration and differentiation largely by introducing greater formalization into managerial and operating processes. There are frequent scheduled meetings not only at senior management level, but also within teams to review work progress and performance. An emphasis is placed on identifying and meeting client-related outcomes. There is a continuous concern with building the visibility of the WRC across different segments of the workforce as the go-to agency for employees with problems at work. Feedback and other forms of surveys are constantly used not only to gauge how the organization is doing in terms of satisfactorily meeting the needs of clients, but also to identify what more needs to be done to provide services that are simultaneously comprehensive and customized.

The strong external focus on identifying and meeting the needs of clients has heavily shaped internal workings. Each part of the organization engages in objective and target setting so that purpose and direction is introduced into their work and a measurement baseline is created to assess the performance. A systematic approach has been adopted to training and skill development across the organization, but particularly in relation to adjudication: there is an acute realization that client needs can hardly be met if their fate is to be determined by adjudicators with rudimentary knowledge and skills of not only the law and legal processes, but also of how quasi-judicial hearings should be conducted. To sustain the focus on client and organizational outcomes, greater formalization has been introduced into some organizational processes. The corporate service unit now performs a lynchpin role in the organization, it seeks a full and reasoned explanation from each division as to why it has set particular objectives and targets and reviews whether these have been met. It operates like an organization pivot to reconcile the competing demands of differentiation and integration inside the WRC. Other organizational processes such as HR have become formalized: performance management is used in a more thorough-going manner and a systematic approach is taken to workplace planning. All in all, the greater rationalization and formalization that has been introduced into the working of the WRC marks it off from previous public conflict management agencies. In standing apart from the past, the WRC has moved decisively closer to other mainstream public agencies. Of course, making this transition in no way guarantees that the work of the WRC will be smooth and problem-free. The next chapter shows that nothing could be further from the reality as it highlights the strategic challenges looming ever larger on the horizon for the WRC.

Notes

1 The Secretary General of the parent government department is the designated accounting officer (accountable public servant) for the WRC, as was the case for the LRC. One view is that such an arrangement when combined with an executive board renders a secretary general accountable for the financial activities of the agency without the commensurate authority to ensure that the agency's financial affairs are soundly managed.

2 The WRC's adjudication service has found against a minister of state (junior minister) in its parent department in a complaint over gender inequality in an appointment to a public service position (RTE 2017).

7 COVID-19 and the delivery of conflict resolution services

Introduction

The COVID-19 pandemic has had a profound impact on economic and social life almost everywhere. Debates continue about the long-term consequences of the pandemic on macroeconomic management, on the well-being of young people, and so on. One interesting line of argument that gained traction during the crisis was that businesses would use the pandemic as an opportunity to adopt radical, highly disruptive organizational strategies (Autor and Reynolds 2020). By and large, this argument had two subparts. One was that the emergency shift to remote working that occurred in most countries in response to the virus is likely to mutate into a permanent feature of working life because the experience of most businesses with remote working has been better than expected. The other is that an unintended consequence of the pandemic has been the adoption of automation-forcing innovation strategies by businesses with far-reaching implications for work and employment. In this view, either to facilitate remote working or reduce the demand for labour, organizations have sunk substantial investments in physical and human capital that most will be reluctant to write off. If we add to the mix the apparent growing acceptability, relative to pre-pandemic times, of remote working and a reluctance by many employees to return to pre-pandemic ways of working, then the assumption is that COVID-19 will pave the way for a far-reaching reordering of working life.

The starting point of this chapter is that much can be learned about the argument by looking at how the pandemic affected the work of the WRC. An examination of this type provides insight into the extent to which the WRC was obliged to introduce new forms of work as a result of COVID-19 and assess whether those adjustments are likely to be permanent. It also permits an analysis of the extent to which the WRC invested in new technologies and digital capabilities to address the challenges introduced by the pandemic – in other words, did COVID-19 have an 'automation-forcing' effect on the work of the public dispute

DOI: 10.4324/9781003520054-7

resolution service? For example, did the crisis accelerate the implementation of technologies that digitally enabled the delivery of services such as online mediation, conciliation or adjudication and, if so, are those innovations likely to be permanent? Finally, this chapter assesses the degree to which COVID-19 affected the nature and scale of employment disputes. On paper, the potential for a significant increase in employment disputes appeared high. Large-scale redundancies, the freezing (if not reduction) of pay and bonuses and the rush to introduce new flexible work practices unilaterally – all fertile ground for workplace conflict – emerged very quickly as real possibilities at the start of the pandemic. Thus, it is useful to gain some sense of whether the WRC experienced a spike in disputes arising from employers finding themselves unable (or unwilling) to comply with existing employment contracts, employment standards, or collective agreements because of COVID-19.

This chapter is organized as follows. First, an overview is presented of the impact of COVID-19 on employment and work patterns in Ireland. After this assessment, an examination is made of how the pandemic affected the work of the WRC, not only as an organization overall but also in the three critical areas of adjudication, conciliation and enforcement of employment rights. After that, this chapter addresses the question whether the pandemic gave rise to new or peculiar forms of workplace conflict. The penultimate section provides insight into patterns of private forms of workplace conflict resolution to ascertain whether any patterns emerged that were at odds with the WRC experience. The conclusions bring together the argument of the chapter.

COVID 19 and work patterns

The Irish Government did not hesitate in its response to COVID-19, imposing what amounted to one of the most restrictive lockdown regimes in the EU. On 12 March 2020, the Taoiseach (Prime Minister), Leo Varadkar, announced that schools, colleges, cultural institutions and childcare facilities would close. Restrictions were imposed on indoor and outdoor mass gatherings. Where possible, people were advised to work from home. Working times and break times were to be staggered. Shops, public transport and hospitality continued to operate. Later that month a de facto two-week lockdown was introduced, with only essential work exempted. Lockdown measures were further intensified during the spring, to be eased in summer 2020. Restrictions were tightened again later that year, loosened in the run up to Christmas and soon re-imposed as a wave of infections caused by the Alpha variant of the virus developed. For much of 2021, tight restrictions remained in force. These were relaxed again in summer 2022. Some restrictions were re-imposed later in the year as the Omicron variant threatened public health. The purpose of this chapter is to review the impact of the pandemic on the activities of the WRC. But first, a brief assessment is made of the impact of COVID-19 on work patterns.

The measures implemented to counter COVID-19 had a major impact on the labour market, collective bargaining and work patterns. Unemployment climbed to 25 per cent in January 2021. The Government introduced a series of measures to support businesses and people who had lost their jobs due to the pandemic. An employment wage subsidy scheme was introduced to support the retention of staff in firms where turnover or orders had declined by 30 per cent or more due to the effects of the pandemic. By early 2021, more than half a million workers in 45,000 employments had received wage supports. Overall growth in the economy continued to be strong. A 3.4 per cent GDP growth rate in 2020 and projected growth of 14.6 per cent for 2021 were buoyed by the strong performance of multinational firms in the trading sectors of the economy. When restrictions were eased in the summer of 2021, the economy and employment rebounded quickly and strongly: unemployment declining to 6.9 per cent in November 2021.

The effects of the pandemic restrictions on collective bargaining were significant but uneven. In sectors heavily impacted, such as transport, non-essential retailing and hospitality, retrenchment programmes and concession bargaining returned. In other areas of the economy and in particular in the multinational sector, collective bargaining continued to focus on improvements in pay and conditions. However, the incidence of newly negotiated collective agreements declined significantly compared with the years preceding the advent of COVID. The median of basic pay increases in 2020 was 2.5 per cent – on par with the pattern for 2019. Some existing agreements were renegotiated and some agreed pay rises were deferred. During the first nine months of 2021, the incidence of pay settlements increased and pay rises averaged between 2 and 2.5 per cent (*Industrial Relations News*, 21 October 2021).

The pandemic restrictions had a significant effect on work patterns. Surveys in April–May 2020 found that 69 per cent of firms had implemented remote working (CSO 2020a). A CIPD survey in June indicated that 52 per cent of employers had more than 75 per cent of their employees working remotely. 70 per cent of employers said that they would facilitate more employees to work remotely when the COVID-19 crisis ended (CIPD 2020). A July-August survey by the Central Statistics Office found that 23 per cent of firms planned to make remote working a permanent part of their operations (CSO 2020b). A survey by the employers' organization, IBEC, in October 2020 found that remote and hybrid working were 'high priorities' for 45–51 per cent of member firms (IBEC 2020).

Surveys of employees also revealed a consistent picture of significant change in work practices and priorities. A large online survey found that

68 per cent of employees were working remotely in October 2020. More than nine out of ten said that they wanted to work remotely some or all of the time when the COVID-19 crisis ended and most expressed a preference for hybrid working (National University Galway and Western Development Commission 2020). A large national online survey conducted by the Central Statistics Office in November 2021 revealed consistent results showing that of those who could work remotely, 88 per cent said they would like to work that way all or some of the time when all pandemic restrictions were lifted (CSO 2021a). A survey of members of the largest public service union, Fórsa, found that 86 per cent were interested in working remotely in future and most preferred a hybrid model (Fórsa 2020). In the autumn of 2021 as COVID-19 restrictions were relaxed, employers and the Government began a phased and staggered return to workplaces. A survey of IBEC members in the spring of 2021, examining employers' intentions around returning to work, showed that just over eight out of ten employers expected some form of hybrid working in their organizations post COVID (IBEC 2021a). A subsequent IBEC Survey of members' priorities for 2022 showed that 62 per cent expected that some or all employers would operate a hybrid working week (IBEC 2021b). A survey by the Institute of Directors in 2022, however, suggested that businesses may have rowed back on earlier positive assessments of remote working. Opinion was split between those who viewed it too soon to judge the success or otherwise of hybrid working in their organizations: 36 per cent of directors and CEOs agreeing and 26 per cent disagreeing; most of the remainder stating that the issue was 'under review' (IOD 2022).

The extent to which the work patterns and preferences following the advent of the pandemic may continue post-pandemic will be influenced by public policy, legislation and collective agreements, Fórsa (2021) . The Government launched a National Remote Work Strategy in 2021, announcing legislation to provide a 'right to request remote work' from employers (Government of Ireland 2021). A Right to Request Remote Work Bill 2021 was subsequently published and entered the legislative process. The Bill envisaged a right by employees to request remote working. Employers may refuse such requests on 'business grounds'. In all, ten such grounds (not intended as exhaustive) are stated in the Bill. The Bill attracted heavy criticism from the ICTU, which viewed the arrangements envisaged as 'fatally flawed' and tantamount to an employers' charter for refusing employees' requests for remote work. The Bill provided for the referral of grievances for adjudication by the WRC and Labour Court, but only on procedural grounds, for example where employers failed to respond to employees' requests within the period stipulated. IBEC viewed the establishment of the proposed right as premature (Dail Eireann 2022). The Bill was later subsumed into a broader Work Life Balance and Miscellaneous Provisions Act 2023, which still envisaged largely restricting the role of the WRC (and on appeal the Labour Court) to adjudicating complaints on procedural grounds. However, if an employer is found to be in breach on procedural grounds of an employee's right to request remote working, then the employee is entitled to make a claim before the WRC which could attract potential damages, or a direction by the WRC to comply with the requirements of the Act. The WRC was also charged with drafting a Code of Practice on the right to request remote working, which will be placed on a statutory footing and will be admissible to cases at the WRC, Labour Court, courts and tribunals (*Industrial Relations News*, 16 February 2023).

The National Remote Work Strategy contained a pledge by the Government to facilitate 20 per cent of public servants to work remotely by the end of 2021. A 'right to disconnect' was also provided for, guided by a code of practice developed by the WRC (WRC 2021a). The Code envisages unresolved grievances being referred to the WRC for resolution or adjudication. Fórsa announced its intention to negotiate a collective agreement on remote and hybrid working across the public service. In July 2021, the Government, unions and employers developed a COVID-19 Return to Work Safely Protocol, which assigned a role to the WRC in conjunction with other agencies in carrying out workplace inspections to provide guidance for employers regarding their obligations under the protocol (DETE, 2021).

The WRC did not put forward a view on whether changes in work patterns caused by the pandemic are likely to be permanent, nor commented on their implications for dispute resolution. The Commission, however, anticipated that there would be more cases presented relating to unfair dismissals, redundancies and hours of work due to COVID-related changes in employment and work patterns and observed that these had already become evident towards the end of 2020 (*Industrial Relations News*, 12 November 2020).

The effects of COVID-19 on the delivery of dispute resolution services

The scale of the restrictive country-wide lockdown regime announced in March 2020 by the Taoiseach (Prime Minister), Leo Varadkar, was not initially fully anticipated by the senior management team of the WRC. But they quickly realized that the impact on the WRC's work programme would be far reaching. A crisis management mode of working kicked-in almost instantaneously. At a hastily convened staff meeting, senior management announced to staff that everyone would be working from home with immediate effect apart from a few exceptions where office attendance was considered essential. All face-to-face adjudication hearings and conciliation conferences as well as other planned meetings were suspended. Staff were told that they would be provided with laptops, mobile phones and other technical equipment so that they could work from home effectively.

Maintaining the WRC website and the telephone service that provided information, advice and guidance on employment rights amongst other things was identified as a priority for the organization. As it was likely that, in the context of the lockdown, large numbers of employers and employees would be reaching out for advice on multiple employment rights matters, keeping these services in operation was considered important, particularly as none, on paper at least, required any, or very minimal, face-to-face contact. However, the ability of the WRC to deliver these information services digitally by staff working from home faced one big problem – it did not possess the necessary phones and supporting telephony equipment. In the words of one senior official of the organization, 'a mad scramble' ensued to source the appropriate devices and technology. After several days of near round-the-clock efforts, an old telephony system was secured from its sister organization in Northern Ireland, the Labour Relations Agency. Within a week, the WRC was in a position to reboot its full information and advice service via homeworking.

This episode encapsulates the focused, problem-solving approach that the WRC adopted throughout the COVID crisis. Some important, long planned for organizational changes such as the opening of regional offices were mothballed so that the emphasis could be squarely placed on identifying the immediate pandemic-related challenges faced by the organization and then designing feasible solutions. Thus, after the move to working from home was secured, attention switched to working out how the organization could best function and remain coherent in the absence of face-to-face interactions between staff. To this end, each division was asked to develop procedures and safeguards to ensure that orderly and comprehensive filing systems were maintained during the period of home working. Each division was also asked to explore alternative ways of delivering services for which it was responsible. Senior management recognized that any type of virtual or digital delivery of services would require a comprehensive learning and training programme to make staff proficient in the use of the enabling technology. No effort was spared on this front. Those who operated the information service from home were trained in the telephony machinery that had been acquired. When the adjudication division started to offer virtual hearings all relevant staff were trained in the digital platform – WebX – that the WRC had to adopt to deliver these meetings.

Faced with staff working remotely, the senior team also considered it important to develop a substantive engagement and communication strategy to maintain not only staff morale and collegiality, but also the cooperative, integrated organizational culture that had been so assiduously cultivated in the years preceding the pandemic. Online organization-wide staff meetings were held to communicate developments and provide staff with the opportunity to ask questions. These gatherings were complemented by regular (usually weekly or bi-weekly) divisional staff meetings. A weekly news email was sent to all staff. A battery of online events was organized for staff. Virtual staff seminars usually lasting 1½ hours were organized, covering a wide range of issues. One set of seminars involved linking up with the main dispute resolution agencies in other Anglo-American countries to discuss and compare how each was responding to the pandemic. Others involved connecting with external bodies such as Deloitte to explore how workplace conflict was addressed in countries like Vietnam. Yet, others addressed matters such as well-being in the context of remote working. Various social events, online quizzes for example, were also organized for staff. All in all, a dedicated effort was made to ensure that people continued to believe that they belonged to a supportive, purposeful organization even if they had to work alone at home.

Once the organization's home-working regime was fully established, each division set about exploring how it could deliver services in a manner that did not require face-to-face interactions. This challenge was more burdensome for some parts of the WRC than others.

Adjudication

When the lockdown was announced in March 2020, the WRC had no option but suspend face-to-face adjudication hearings (*Industrial Relations News*, 23 April 2020). However, the prospect of not addressing any adjudication cases during the lockdown filled the team with foreboding: about 300/400 hearings would go unheard each month, which would no doubt cause disaffection amongst those involved in cases and lead to the reputation of the WRC being damaged; in the end, up to 2,000 hearings could not proceed due to COVID-19 restrictions in 2020. Thus, it was seen as an imperative that a strategy was devised to deliver some type of adjudication during the pandemic. A four-pronged strategy was quickly developed. First, a concerted push was made to encourage – at times it came close to exhorting – the parties involved in cases to reach a settlement through telephone mediation. To enhance the attractiveness of this option, which all those lodging an adjudication case are offered, efforts were put in train to deliver mediation virtually (*Industrial Relations News*, 21 May 2020). In 1,600 cases filed for adjudication, the WRC contacted the parties to determine their willingness to accept virtual mediation. Most opted to wait for adjudication or for face-to-face mediation, with 36 per cent proceeding to mediation: 85 per cent of these were conducted by telephone, 14 per cent face-to-face and the remaining tiny number virtually (*Industrial Relations News*, 29 April 2021).

Second, the team explored the possibility of using 'written procedures adjudication', where adjudication was conducted without a hearing, based on evidence supplied. A number of different pieces of employment legislation were viewed as providing the statutory basis for this resolution method: cases related to the payment of wages, holiday entitlements, terms and conditions of employment were considered suitable for this method of adjudication, while unfair dismissals and equality cases were not. Overall, the 'written procedure' method of adjudication was found to have worked well for less complex cases, although it has to be said that the legal profession was more welcoming of the procedure than employees or employers involved in cases. (*Industrial Relations News*, 29 April 2021).

Third, conducting adjudication hearings by way of videoconferencing – virtual hearings – was considered another possible option, although it was recognized from the very start that a lot of preparation would be needed to make this adjudication method a realistic alternative. The WRC did not possess the enabling technology to conduct virtual hearings and as none of the adjudication officers had previous experience of this resolution method it was very much a step into the dark for them. More pressingly, although the WRC was satisfied that it had the powers to conduct hearings remotely, there was no explicit statutory basis for this adjudication method in any piece of employment law. As a result, it was questionable whether an adjudication officer could seek to resolve a case virtually without the consent of the participating parties. And finally the great unknown was how the legal profession, employers and trade unions, as well as those involved in cases would respond to the prospect of virtual hearings. Thus, the WRC had a job of work to do to make virtual hearings a viable option.

The first step taken by the adjudication team was to hold a consultation exercise to gather people's reactions and concerns about conducting adjudication virtually. Less than a month after lockdown, the consultation exercise, which was to last three months, was up and running. As the consultation exercise was proceeding, the WRC, with the help of its parent department, the Department of Enterprise, Trade and Employment, installed the technology platform WebX, to conduct the proposed virtual hearings. Adjudication officers as well as administrative support staff were trained intensively in how to operate the technology. By the time the consultation period ended, the WRC was technically proficient to operate virtual hearings. But, the 50 submissions to the consultation exercise checked the ambition of the adjudication team to launch fully this option. Overall, the submissions provided only lukewarm support for virtual hearings, with the biggest concern expressed being the danger of procedural justice being compromised. A further view emerging from the submissions was that it would be preferable to establish clearer statutory grounds for the WRC to engage in remote adjudication. In these circumstances, the WRC considered it prudent only to proceed with virtual hearings on a pilot basis, focusing on what were perceived to be relatively straightforward cases and where the involved parties had provided their consent.

Even then it was difficult to get parties to take up the offer of using remote adjudication to settle their cases. The adjudication team estimates that 85 per cent of offers for virtual hearings were rejected: evidently, people considered the option as too innovative and without proper legal foundations. But, some virtual hearings did go ahead and the issue that surprised the WRC the most was the labour-intensive nature of the entire process. Conducting virtual hearings was seen as involving 25 additional tasks compared with doing face-to-face hearings. Organizing hearings was more cumbersome and operating the virtual hearings more burdensome. For example, staff had to be assigned to each party as well as to the adjudication officer to troubleshoot if connections were lost or some other technical glitch occurred. To address this problem, the WRC set up a dedicated concierge system so that administrative support was provided for virtual hearings – six additional staff were provided by the Department of Enterprise, Trade and Employment to operate the system. Alongside these efforts to establish smooth running virtual hearings, the WRC engaged with Government legal counsel to provide the organization with unambiguous legal authority to conduct virtual hearings.

In September 2020, just six months after the lockdown announcement, a new statutory instrument came into effect that provided this authority: parties could no longer refuse virtual hearings unless these would be 'contrary to the interests of justice' (Industrial Relations News, 12 November 2020). Where parties raised issues in relation to fair procedure in remote hearings the presiding adjudication officer could take any steps they deemed necessary, including adjourning cases to permit face-to-face hearings to take place (Industrial Relations News, 23 November 2020). In the first three months of the operation of the new statutory powers, some 100 objections to virtual hearings were lodged – some citing IT-related problems and others the complexity of cases – and 60 per cent of objections were successful (Industrial Relations News, 29 April 2021).

The senior management team recognized that no matter how successful the organization was in getting cases resolved through telephone mediation or by way of a written adjudication process or via virtual hearings, there would always be complex cases requiring face-to-face hearings. So the last leg of its four-pronged strategy was to continue with a limited number of face-to-face hearings to address cases that were considered difficult-to-resolve. These hearings were organized extremely carefully to comply fully with the Government's lockdown restrictions. Thus, for example, face-to-face hearings were restricted to 2.5 hours and limitations were imposed on the numbers allowed to attend per party (Industrial Relations News, 23 August 2020). The WRC considered it important to maintain restricted in-person hearings largely to uphold its reputation as being responsive and effective in addressing all kinds of employment-related disputes. But, after the Government was obliged to tighten COVID-19 restrictions in the autumn of 2020, face-to-face hearings were postponed. Although these hearings returned for a short time in late November, they were once again postponed in December. The level of consent to virtual hearings was described as disappointing, with less than 20 per cent agreeing to virtual hearings.

Getting virtual hearings up and running as well as generally adjusting to the pandemic was challenging for the adjudication service. For example, the pandemic exacerbated tensions between the WRC and some adjudication officers employed on contract who complained about lack of communication and loss of work and income caused by constraints on holding hearings (Industrial Relations News, 4 March 2021; 23 July 2020). Yet, by the start of 2021, conducting virtual hearings was the mainstay of the adjudication service. Adjudication officers as well as the back-up administrative team by this stage had become accustomed to hearing cases remotely. A tight scheduling regime, which involved timetabling cases both to start earlier in the day and later in the evening, alongside resolving cases expeditiously, led to the virtual hearing service becoming very efficient. An additional contributing factor was that the nature of the cases that were being heard were more or less the same as those being heard before the pandemic.

If COVID-19 had given rise to significantly different cases, then inevitably hearings would have been more protracted and thus the overall regime less efficient. Impressively, the adjudication team was able to address and conclude more cases under the virtual hearings regime than when they were using face-to-face hearings. So proficient had the adjudication service become in operating virtual hearings, it was able in the first nine months of 2021 to make significant inroads into the backlog of cases that had built up in 2020. A colossal amount of hard work over a sustained period of time plus considerable adaptability by all members of the adjudication team were considered to be the key factors lying behind this success. As the adjudication team slowly emerged from the pandemic, no fixed view was formed on the desirability of continuing with virtual hearings. The team expressed an interest in operating some type of hybrid model that would involve introducing some virtual element into face-to-face hearings. Such a hybrid system was seen as making the deliberations in cases more comprehensive and thorough-going. Currently, some 30 per cent of adjudication hearings are either conducted digitally or involve some online input. However, it is unlikely that services will be redesigned in any far-reaching way to switch completely to virtual forms of conflict resolution. A cautious, evolutionary approach is likely to be adopted to all matters digital.

Conciliation

Over the years, the conciliation service has prided itself on being a tightly integrated team with the ability to respond in a calm and professional manner to unanticipated external events. The make-up of the team has changed little in nearly two decades and previous difficult times such as managing the fall out of the 2008 financial crisis was seen as solidifying internal cohesion. Thus, when it was announced that the team would be obliged to work remotely due to lockdown restrictions, there was a steely steadfastness to adjust the service to the new challenging times. After a quick transition to homeworking, the team set about organizing a virtual conciliation service. From the start, the team was under no illusion that when delivering virtual conciliation it was operating in a second-best world. Face-to-face meetings were seen as a much better way of doing conciliation as they enable the conciliation team to foster closer relationships between disputing parties, assess more accurately the depth of animosities involved in a dispute and gauge more precisely the possibilities for a settlement (Industrial Relations News, 29 April 2021).

In setting up the virtual conciliation service, the team experienced a number of fairly predictable challenges. For example, some team members unaccustomed with the software packages used to conduct virtual meetings had to receive extensive training. Like their colleagues in adjudication, the conciliation team quickly found that setting up and conducting virtual meetings was a labour-intensive business. Operating virtual conciliation sessions initially was not easy as participants were both hesitant and nervous about engaging with one another online. Thus, for example, some trade union representatives were uncomfortable with using online break-out rooms as they were suspicious that confidentiality would be compromised. After a period of time, these problems eased without being eliminated fully. Overall, the team views the operation of the virtual conciliation regime as a success. No backlog of cases built up as a result of doing online conciliation conferences and the success rate for the service remained high at over 80 per cent. But, the team were confident that virtual conciliation would not become a permanent feature of the work of the WRC and anticipated a full transition back to face-to-face engagements once the pandemic abated.

Information, inspection and enforcement

As highlighted earlier, the information, inspection and enforcement services of the WRC operated out of separate offices in Carlow, about 90 km from the main WRC site in Dublin. We have already seen how enlightened improvisation allowed the information service, which before the pandemic operated via a call centre at the Carlow offices, to be delivered virtually.

After an initial period of intensified learning and adaptation, the information service operated online throughout the COVID-19 crisis in an unencumbered and broadly efficient manner. The same smooth transition to remote delivery cannot be said of the inspection and enforcement services. After the lockdown announcement, onsite WRC inspections ceased for a number of months – largely because organizations that had been targeted for inspections were themselves closed. Instead, the inspection team busied itself reducing the large backup of inspection 'files' that had mounted up.

Once the backlog had been reduced, the work of the team got dispersed over a range of different activities. As a result of the Government, unions and employer bodies agreeing a 'return to work safely' protocol, some members of the inspection team linked up with the Health & Safety Authority to conduct inspections to ensure that businesses were creating safe workplaces for their employees. This involved the WRC inspectors receiving extensive training on such matters as how to verify that any personal protective equipment (PPE) being used by organizations was not damaged in any way and provided the intended full protection. Other members of the team started doing 'desktop' inspections, which involved requesting businesses to provide relevant files in relation to such things as the payment of the minimum wage and the existence of work permits for the employment of migrant workers. This method of inspection was not considered satisfactory as it only proved effective with larger firms who possessed the administrative capacity to keep well-managed files. But, of course, it is larger firms that are the more likely to be fully compliant with these employment standards. Desktop inspection is a crude procedure to reach the type of organizations that are more likely to violate employment rules.

Still other members of the team devoted much of their time to trying to devise smarter and more targeted ways of doing inspections once there was a return to 'normal' business life after the pandemic. Thus, new procedures such as the design of online questionnaires and the adoption of new technologies were developed to improve inspections. The team was confident that a return to normal service would see it implementing its sectoral enforcement strategies, which had to be mothballed during COVID-19, in a more rigorous and effective manner. Overall, although the team was satisfied that they could not have adopted any better to the COVID-19 crisis, they did feel the pandemic had an adverse effect on their work. The consensus view was that the team would revert fully back to established ways of working after the pandemic ended.

COVID-19 and patterns of demand for conflict resolution

Some policy and legislative changes introduced in the wake of COVID-19 have permanently extended the mandate of the WRC: the introduction of a right to request remote work and a right to disconnect. Workplace inspections under the Return to Work Safely Protocol also involve an extension to the Commission's mandate while the protocol remains in place. New initiatives, such as the right to request remote work, the right to disconnect, may take some time to affect workplace grievances. Changes to workplace regimes may also take time to solidify. A survey of private sector firms by Industrial Relations News and the CIPD found that the incidence of grievances in workplaces remained largely unchanged during the pandemic, while the incidence of bullying and harassment had declined – a development possibly associated with the advent of remote working (Industrial Relations News, 8 July 2021).

Adjudication and mediation

The volume of calls to the WRC's Infoline fell in 2020 by 3.5 per cent on the previous year, but this was a slower rate of decline than registered in 2018. Levels of demand for other WRC services in 2020 are consistent with a chilling effect influencing employees' behaviour. There was a marginal fall in 2020 in complaints referred for adjudication – the first time this had occurred since 2016. The incidence of support for mediation in workplaces also declined from a low base. Reflecting the reluctance of disputants often to opt for pre-adjudication, even where the pandemic had caused significant scheduling backlogs for adjudication hearings, the incidence of mediation declined. The rate of decline however was less than that recorded in 2019 – reflecting perhaps the efforts of the WRC to gain acceptance for pre-hearing mediation under pandemic constraints.

In assessing any impact the pandemic may have had on issues submitted for adjudication, some fluidity in baseline pre-COVID patterns of 'specific complaints' referred for adjudication needs to be borne in mind. For example, comparing 2018 and 2019 specific complaints ranked highest varied to some extent, with changes in rank order largely attributed to multiple complaints by groups of employees working for small numbers of employers (WRC 2019a: 23). Nonetheless, a number of areas dominated pre-pandemic patterns of complaints: these were pay, hours of work, unfair dismissals, discrimination, terms and conditions of employment and industrial relations/trade disputes. The pattern for 2020 was broadly consistent with the pre-COVID-19 pattern of complaints, with the exception of a sharp rise in the share of hitherto marginal redundancy-related complaints and a sharp fall in the share of equality and discrimination complaints. The rising share of redundancy-related complaints was largely attributable to a sizeable number of complaints by the employees of one employer, the retail multiple Debenhams Ireland (WRC 2021b: 20). Some 1,400 workers at Debenhams were issued with redundancy notices following the company's liquidation in April 2020. In addition to undertaking industrial action in protest at the closure and the redundancy terms on offer – enhanced terms in a collective agreement with the Mandate union having been voided when the company went into liquidation – the workers' union submitted multiple complaints to the WRC. The complaints sought compensation for the company's failure to provide information and to engage in consultation, as required under the law governing collective redundancies (Mandate 2020). A fall in discrimination and equality complaints may reflect a chilling effect of the pandemic on such claims in circumstances where remote working had become widespread.

Conciliation and facilitation

The pattern of demand for collective dispute resolution services can first be examined against the backdrop of trends in industrial conflict in the economy. The 21,700 working days lost in 2020 is significantly below the levels recorded most years since the economy recovered from the Great Recession, while working days lost in 2021 were the lowest on record (CSO 2021b). Thus, the pandemic appears to have chilled or suppressed industrial conflict. The number of disputes referred to conciliation at the WRC in 2020 shows a sharp fall of just under 25 per cent compared with 2019 and with the general pattern of recent years. In fact, the figure for 2020 represents the lowest number of disputes referred for conciliation for some 50 years.

The issues involved in conciliation during 2020 were little different to the pre-COVID pattern. Pay, organizational issues and industrial relations continued to rank highest and ranked well above all other issues referred for conciliation (WRC 2020). Redundancy-related issues remained a small share (3 per cent) of issues in dispute between the parties to conciliation – reflecting in part, perhaps, the wage supports introduced for companies affected by sizeable falls in revenue and orders. The low incidence of redundancy-related disputes may also have been affected by the introduction in March 2020 of a special emergency measure that suspended an employee's right to seek redundancy if they had been laid off or put on short-time work due to the measures required to limit the spread of COVID-19.

The number of facilitation meetings chaired by the WRC increased marginally on 2019 –facilitation activity during 2019 and 2020 included the Commission's work in brokering a new public service pay agreement.

Inspection and enforcement

Unlike the other services examined, inspection and enforcement activity is determined in the main by the WRC, although complaints influence inspections. The incidence of workplace inspections rose significantly in 2020 due to the WRC's role in supporting the Return to Work Safely Protocol that came into force in May. Of all inspections carried out, 68 per cent occurred under the protocol (WRC 2020: 17). The number of prosecutions for breaches of employment legislation declined during that year.

The overall picture of patterns of workplace conflict during the pandemic is that they seemed broadly similar to pre-pandemic patterns. Post-pandemic patterns may depend in large measure on the extent of remote working and on the eventual effect of the right to request remote and flexible working. However, there appears little reason to believe that the pandemic and its effects on work and employment patterns will prove transformative for levels or types of demand for workplace conflict resolution services.

The WRC and COVID-19: a strategy of batten down the hatches

To summarize the work of the WRC during the pandemic, it would not be credible to suggest that the WRC pursued radical transformative strategies. No concerted effort was made to use the COVID-19 crisis to accelerate the introduction of new technological processes or to reshape important features of its work operations. For the most part, the posture adopted by the organization can be best characterized as adaptation, problem solving and consolidation. On the one hand, the pandemic was viewed as an unforeseen organizational shock which required an immediate and systemic response from the organization. The focus was almost exclusively on devising solutions to problems and challenges generated by the COVID-19 crisis in a manner that would allow the organization to deliver the best possible service and maintain its internal cohesion and integrity. On the other hand, the senior management team considered themselves operating in an external environment replete with pervasive uncertainty. In these circumstances, the team viewed it as appropriate to adopt a risk-averse strategy and consolidate the organization around established corporate objectives without launching any new initiatives. This posture is also reflected in the WRC's Strategy Statement 2022–2024, launched as pandemic restrictions were being wound down. The medium-term strategy recognized that the pandemic and associated changes in work and employment may have lasting effects, and committed the WRC to providing an 'appropriate mix of remote, hybrid and in-person services' (WRC 2022b: 4). Yet, the overall feature of the strategy is that it maintains a steady course focused on 'resilience and continuity' (WRC 2022b: 3).

Indicative of this cautious approach was how the organization retreated from aspirations to develop HR policies and working methods that were at least semi-independent from the Civil Service employment model. Thus, for example, the senior management team stated that the WRC intended to remain fully aligned with the Civil Service's policies and practices in relation to transitioning out of the COVID-19 and a return to 'normal' working. It also stated that there would be no deviation from the wider Civil Service's policy towards home and hybrid working after the pandemic had subsided. In the past, for example, the senior management team had expressed an eagerness to introduce an open recruitment policy that would allow vacant positions to be filled from outside the civil service. But this eagerness appears to have fallen away largely as a result of the organization's desire to remain inside the civil service's internal labour market. Being part and parcel of this internal labour market was seen as insulating the organization from people management risks and uncertainties caused by COVID-19.

Beneath the surface of the risk-averse, cautious approach is a preference inside the WRC for face-to-face methods of conflict resolution. Across the organization, whether it is adjudication, inspection and enforcement or conciliation, there is consensus that resolving conflict virtually is often a second-best alternative to in-person problem-solving and dispute resolution. The pandemic will not prove transformative in relation to how the WRC works and delivers its services.

Private conflict resolution during the pandemic

In examining the impact of the pandemic on private mediation, we sought to distinguish between providers of mediation in individual employment grievances and interpersonal conflicts and providers of collective dispute resolution, although some providers offer services in both areas.

No longer 'sceptics of the screen': private mediation in individual employment grievances and interpersonal conflicts

A profile of developments in general mediation practice, which includes employment mediation, based on data collected from 13 mediators suggests that a small decline (7 per cent) in the incidence of mediation had occurred during the period from March 2020 to March 2021 (Kenny 2021: 9). In-person mediation could not be conducted in the early stages of the pandemic due to public health restrictions. A sharp rise was reported in telephone and subsequently in online mediation. The main challenges reported by mediators concerned people's familiarity with technology and access to broadband; meditators striving to maintain a balance of power between participants by supporting parties to present themselves appropriately online; difficulties assessing the dynamics and reactions of persons participating in online mediation, and maintaining confidentiality. In general, mediators nevertheless reported positive experiences of online mediation and also reported similar feedback by mediation participants (Kenny 2021).

Data on workplace mediation was also obtained from a mediator with an extensive professional network and deep involvement in the main professional body in the field. The experience reported draws on the activities of established mediators and is broadly in line with that reported for mediation more generally. Regarding the demand for workplace mediation, little activity occurred during the early months of the pandemic. However, demand thereafter is seen to have quickly returned to pre-pandemic levels. While conflicts that had 'smouldered on' from before the pandemic again came into play, a new pattern was evident. This involved a concentration of mediation among workers in essential industries and services concerning pandemic-related issues such as workplace safety, vaccination status and issues surrounding people returning to work following work from home. Established experienced mediators sometimes saw a growth in demand for services among essential workers involving these issues. Mediation commonly involved a combination of telephone and online activity, with online preparatory work supporting in-person meetings where public health regulations permitted. The experience both of mediators and parties to mediation was again reported to have been generally positive. Ease of scheduling and less need for travel were seen as significant advantages for mediators and some parties. While mediators may have found it more difficult to gauge the dynamics between the parties, for some the online environment muted the negative emotions that might have risen from face-to-face encounters, especially in cases involving bullying and related problems. The durability of mediation agreements reached online was also seen as less assured, as conflicts between parties might be triggered anew when they returned to working side-by-side.

The expectation was that various forms hybrid workplace mediation would continue post-pandemic and indeed become the norm in private practice. As virtually no online mediation occurred prior to the pandemic – other than pre-adjudication mediation conducted by telephone by the WRC – this would represent a remarkable transformation of mediation practice. A study of online dispute resolution (ODR) in Ireland in 2015, drawing on a survey of 214 mediators, described practitioners as 'sceptics of the screen'. Very few had used online technologies in their work and a popular sentiment among practitioners was that online conflict resolution was not superior to face-to-face meetings (Boehme 2015).

Anticipating a full return to face-to-face processes: private collective dispute resolution

To augment discussions with the WRC and the private sector meditator, an experienced conflict management professional working in a large and prominent consultancy providing organizations with advice, guidance and support for workplace conflict management was interviewed. In relation, to the consultancy's advisory activities, they were adamant that COVID had no real impact: providing information and guidance proved to be as effectively done virtually as in person. However, they said that the pandemic adversely affected, and heavily so, the representative and advocacy roles of the consulting body, which involves directly helping firms address collective disputes or problems. Throughout the pandemic, nearly all forms of collective dispute resolution switched to being online. This method of conflict resolution was considered inferior to face-to-face engagement for three reasons. First of all, virtual forms of collective dispute resolution were viewed as excessively cumbersome. Unlike face-to-face problem-solving, seeking to resolve disputes digitally required many more formal meetings, particularly lengthy meetings before and after formal sessions to address problems. Moreover, the adjournment of meetings and the need to reconvene sessions increased significantly under virtual collective dispute resolution. The comments of the WRC's conciliation team about online forms of engagement being challenging for both employers and trade unions were also echoed. It took considerable time for both parties not only to become technologically competent, but also to gain the confidence and trust to negotiate online.

Secondly, the actual process of deal-making or problem-solving was seen as being more difficult online. It was stressed that the human contact that comes from cross-the-table, face-to-face engagements immeasurably improves the chances of settling a dispute or problem successfully. Virtual collective dispute resolution was seen as depriving negotiators of these social interactions and as a result engagement remained cold and stilted. As well as not being conducive to fostering meaningful, affective relationships, online platforms were viewed as squeezing out flexibility and informality from the dispute resolution process. It was 'hard to read the room' virtually and the inability to hold 'corridor' conversations during online negotiating sessions with trade unions was lamented. Constraining the space for informal dispute resolution activity, often the elixir of successful deal-making, was considered a major shortcoming of virtual forms of collective dispute resolution – virtual conflict resolution was viewed as having a 'process deficit'. In this context, it is interesting to note that although private dispute resolution arrangements in ten firms and public service agencies, served by independently sourced panels and sole practitioners, continued to function during the pandemic, only the three-person Internal Resolution Council at the Dublin Airport Authority concluded an agreement that addressed changes in pay, conditions and work practices resulting from the collapse of airline traffic (DAA and Fórsa 2020).

Thirdly, securing the formal acceptance of a proposed settlement to a dispute was considered more difficult under online collective dispute resolution. For the most part, the problem of 'getting disputes over the line' was attributed to trade union officials and representatives finding it harder to maintain internal order and coherence amongst members. When engaging in any form of workplace conflict or unrest, trade unions place a premium on being tightly organized and disciplined internally. Not only do these attributes allow the union to project a united front to employers, but they also better positioned union officials to sell a proposed agreement to rank and file members. Virtual collective dispute resolution was seen as compromising the ability of trade unions to maintain internal organizational cohesion in conflict situations. In particular, because the pandemic required all interactions and communications between union representatives and rank-and-file members to be online, the opportunities to 'disfigure' or 'contaminate' these interactions were seen to have increased dramatically. With the skilful use of social media platforms, specific groups or factions, normally opposed in one way or another to the union leadership, could discredit attempts at securing membership endorsement for a proposed agreement to a dispute.

An example was provided of a dispute involving Dublin Bus. After extensive online engagement, management and trade union representatives reached a proposed agreement to an on-going dispute. All trade union representatives recommended that the membership accept the proposed deal, but their efforts were thwarted by a sustained and concerted social media campaign against the recommendation. In the end, the membership voted to reject the agreement. In other words, orderly forms of collective dispute resolution require centrifugal pressures on internal trade union organizational cohesion to be minimal. Online collective dispute resolution, however, created an environment for these centrifugal pressures to flourish. Overall, the view was that while employers and trade unions did their best to cope with the exigencies thrown up by COVID-19, when the pandemic subsided, there would be a full return to traditional forms of face-to-face collective dispute resolution processes.

Conclusions

An influential argument was that COVID-19 would have a transformative effect on the labour market, with no return to pre-pandemic patterns of employment and ways of working. In particular, it was argued that the pandemic had released automation-inducing IT innovations and orchestrated a radical shift to remote working to the point that there would be no return to traditional forms of business or working life (Barrero, Bloom, and Davis 2021). Our assessment of how the WRC responded to the pandemic found little evidence of such influences at play. No part of the WRC viewed the pandemic as causing a permanent shift to new digital or technological conflict resolution procedures. Moreover, across the organization, a strong preference was expressed for a return to conventional face-to-face dispute resolution. Furthermore, the consensus view was that the pandemic would not result in a massive increase in remote working at the WRC itself. All in all, the considered view was that the organization was likely to revert to established ways of working, but with a significant volume of adjudication claims now involving some digital input. This is not to say that the longer-term impact of COVID-19 will not impact the activities of the WRC. For example, as the pandemic subsided, the dark clouds of inflation were beginning to hover over many economies, including Ireland's. Rising prices threatened a resurgence in robust collective bargaining as trade unions demanded high-pay settlements to maintain their members' standards of living. Far from seeing this as a threat to its steady-state organizational equilibrium, the WRC viewed it as a challenge requiring the use of tried-and-tested conciliation methods.

8 Lessons on the road to the Workplace Relations Commission

Introduction

The changes marked by the creation first of the LRC and then by the WRC represent significant developments in the configuration of public agencies delivering workplace conflict management services. The creation of the WRC was by any standards a remarkable initiative in merging and repurposing five hitherto independent bodies in a conflict resolution system rendered dysfunctional by a combination of uncoordinated changes in the law, incremental agency creation and turf protection by the multiple agencies that were created. This chapter summarizes the main findings of this book, highlights key insights arising from the analysis and examines a series of strategic challenges faced by the WRC. The world of work and employment around which the WRC and its predecessor bodies were created is changing in ways that could scarcely have been foreseen as recently as 2015 when the WRC's current suite of services was developed. Thus, the task of remaining aligned to fast-changing labour markets remains unrelenting.

Staging posts on the road to the Workplace Relations Commission

The changes that have occurred in public dispute resolution in Ireland over the last 25 years have been substantial and significant. In the wake of rising collective conflict over three decades, the LRC was spun off from the Labour Court in 1991 in response to growing concerns that the Court was becoming overloaded as employers and unions increasingly eschewed the Court's conciliation service in favour of formal investigations. Ironically, following the creation of the new agency industrial conflict fell to its lowest level in the history of the state, ushering in a golden age of industrial peace that has continued to the present. The demand for collective conciliation – the core service of the LRC at its inception – followed strike activity downwards.

DOI: 10.4324/9781003520054-8

The LRC became the pivotal institution for conflict resolution in Irish employment relations. The agency's collective conciliation service dominated the Commission's work and was the mainstay of its public reputation and legitimacy in the eyes of governments. As statutory employment rights expanded dramatically from the 1990s, demand grew for grievance resolution by Rights Commissioners – initially a modest service assigned at its inception to the LRC.

As collective conflict reached historically low levels from the 1990s, demand for individual grievance resolution by Rights Commissioners began to outstrip and then dwarf the demand for collective conciliation and allied services. The LRC was becoming transformed into an organization that dealt mainly with grievances over individual employment rights. The rise of conflict over employment rights affected not alone the LRC but also the Equality Tribunal and crucially the Employment Appeals Tribunal. The EAT became subject to long delays and extended formal legal procedure. Even experienced practitioners found it difficult to navigate the increasingly complex, fragmented and overlapping jurisdictions of the state's core conflict resolution agencies. The conflict resolution system became further fragmented as new agencies were created under social partnership agreements concluded between employers, unions and the state. These included the National Implementation Body, active in the resolution of disputes that threatened social partnership pay agreements, the National Centre for Partnership and Performance, which shared jurisdiction over the promotion of good employment relations (via workplace partnerships) with the LRC, and the National Employment Rights Authority.

External pressures for reform arose from the sharp rise in the incidence and reach of individual employment rights throughout the 1990s, as EU Directives were transposed into Irish employment law, either extending pre-existing employment rights or setting down new employment rights. The sharp rise in the migrant workforce, particularly following EU enlargement to Eastern and Central Europe in 2004, added to a rise in the rate of grievances and complaints addressed by the LRC and other conflict resolution agencies. Migrant workers both disproportionately experienced discrimination at work and referred a range of grievances to Rights Commissioners. The expansion in the female participation rate also contributed to an absolute rise in grievances and complaints referred to conflict resolution agencies, although the limited data available do not show that female workers have disproportionately referred complaints to the state agencies.

By the early 2000s, the case for the reform and consolidation of the conflict resolution system was evident to policy makers, unions and employers. Yet, little was done to disturb the uneasy equilibrium between the existing agencies. Internal pressure for change within the agencies was little in evidence, although some board members of the LRC were critical of what they saw as the Commission's failure to recognize and accommodate the growing diversity of employment relations arrangements in Ireland, especially the rising incidence of models based on direct employee involvement and a preference by many employers for direct relations with their employees, unmediated by union representation. Within the LRC, change was cautious and incremental, involving catering for a rising but still modest demand for mediation by Commission staff and responding to a growing need for 'facilitation' as distinct from conventional conciliation in circumstances marked by complex change programmes and restructuring. Significant external developments such as the growth of workplace partnership, private mediation and private dispute resolution evoked little response from the LRC. The posture towards such innovations was what one senior figure described as 'thinly disguised antipathy'. Others portrayed these innovations in less starkly negative terms, expressing a concern that they commonly failed and when they did, the work of the LRC in picking up the pieces was more complex than it otherwise needed to be.

The uneasy stasis in the conflict resolution system as a whole and the cautious incrementalism of the LRC were to change with the advent of the global financial crisis, the resulting Great Recession and the attendant fiscal crisis. Following a decade of timid and abortive proposals for reform of the conflict resolution agencies, two leaders of dispute resolution agencies seized the opportunity provided by a new minister and an electoral programme that pledged to consolidate public agencies to promote systemic reform.

The LRC's Chief Executive, Kieran Mulvey, and the Director of the National Employment Rights Authority, Ger Deering, formulated what was to be the blueprint for the consolidation of conflict resolution agencies. The Mulvey-Deering blueprint for a single agency of first resort, allied to an appellate role for the Labour Court, quickly gained strong political support. Deering and Mulvey also played key operational roles in integrating four agencies to create the WRC and repurposing the Labour Court. Mulvey had been privately critical of the increasingly fragmented and dysfunctional conflict resolution system and Deering had quickly formed the view that NERA's mission was highly constrained within a wider conflict resolution system that lacked coherence and purpose.

One constant over the period as a whole from the establishment of the LRC to the creation of the WRC was the absence of significant political and ideological schism over public dispute resolution. While politicians have fronted and won government support for reform programmes at critical junctures, conflict resolution has never been politicized in Ireland. The major reform initiatives have been formulated and implemented by public servants and leaders of conflict resolution agencies. Politicians have supported reform programmes to reduce overload, tackle needless complexity, fragmentation and service duplication and to cut costs. Otherwise, neither politicians nor governments have sought to shift the paradigm for public dispute resolution inherited at the foundation of the State and institutionalized by foundation of the Labour Court in 1946.

The non-politicization of workplace conflict resolution reflects the wider non-politicization of industrial relations in Ireland. Some differences have long been evident between the postures of the political parties towards the conduct of industrial relations. Fianna Fail has a legacy of supporting corporatist engagement between unions, employers and the state that stretches back to Sean Lemass's post-war vision for industrial relations. Lemass was the most politically engaged politician and minister with respect to industrial relations and conflict resolution in the State's history. He was the architect of the Labour Court as well as a series of tripartite bodies. His original corporatist vision intended the Court to be the fulcrum for aligning wage determination with macroeconomic management. This met with opposition from trade unions, and the Court ultimately emerged as a neutral facilitator of free collective bargaining. However Lemass's industrial relations reform measures met with little political opposition. Fine Gael has shown a marked scepticism of corporatist pay bargaining and social partnership. When in the government the Party has nevertheless supported prevailing centralized tripartite bargaining arrangements. The Labour Party and other parties of the left when participating in coalition governments have accommodated prevailing and varying pay and industrial relations arrangements. What marks Ireland out is that no sharp political divisions, contrasting visions or opposing blueprints or reform plans for industrial relations or workplace conflict resolution have existed among the main political parties. It was a Fianna Fail Minister, Bertie Ahern, who steered through the reforms that led to the creation of the LRC and a Fine Gael Minister, Richard Bruton, who legislated for the reforms leading to the creation of the WRC. Neither set of reforms was framed as a challenge to the prevailing paradigm of state support for voluntary conflict resolution, or as seeking to reverse reform programmes introduced by political competitors. This reform tradition has left change largely in the hands of senior public servants and conflict resolution professionals.

Ireland's reform legacy sharply contrasts with other Anglo-American countries. In the United States, deep political differences over labour policies separating the Democrats and Republican Parties have spilled over into lobbying groups, stymieing changes in labour relations and conflict resolution. In the United Kingdom, shifts in the postures of both the Labour and Conservative Parties have shaped the role of ACAS in collective conflict resolution. In Australia and New Zealand, politically driven acute changes of direction and focus have disrupted the priorities and activities of state conflict resolution agencies. Similar though less acute pressures have been evident in Canada, particularly in the most populous province, Ontario.

Politicians and government ministers have benefitted considerably from Ireland's legacy of political consensus on conflict resolution. For one thing, they have been able to rely time and again on professionally managed and staffed agencies, acting on the basis of agreed, consistent and abiding ground rules. This has facilitated the work of state agencies in repeatedly resolving major disputes with significant economic and political implications. Politicians and ministers have been able to avoid being drawn openly into disputes by declaring dispute resolution to be the preserve of state agencies and their independent and neutral professional staff.

While this legacy abides, the WRC is a different body to the LRC. The latter was established as a niche agency concerned in the main with resolving collective disputes, but increasingly drawn into the resolution of individual employment conflict. The WRC is a composite provider of multiple employment-related services encompassing the provision of collective conciliation and facilitation, information on employment rights, individual conflict resolution and the enforcement of employment standards. Besides changes in mission and remit, the organizational character of public dispute resolution has also changed significantly in response to changes in patterns of workplace conflict, new demands for conflict resolution services and the reconfiguration of conflict resolution agencies. The LRC was governed by an executive board dominated by high-profile leaders of major unions and employer bodies – figures deeply involved in the conduct of employment relations – through social partnership – and highly influential in macroeconomic governance.

The Commission was led by a public service outsider, with a strong public and media profile and a hands-on approach to resolving conflict. Kieran Mulvey campaigned and commented on key developments in employment relations – engaged in controversies and even at times admonished parties involved in major disputes. The culture and skill base of the LRC were formed around the primacy of collective conflict resolution and by the recruitment of staff from within the public service who were trained on-the-job. Rights Commissioners were recruited from the ranks of practitioners and deployed professional skills and experience drawn from previous careers as HR managers, employer representatives and union officials. Their strength as professional service providers resided in the practice of med-arb that had evolved over the life of the LRC. The default approach of Rights Commissioners was to mediate solutions to employment grievances, drawing on their extensive experience as practitioners, only engaging in adjudication when mediation had failed. In short, dispute resolution processes within the LRC largely eschewed the application of law and relied on knowledge and experience acquired on-the-job by civil servants or in previous roles by Rights Commissioners.

The WRC is a larger, more complex and diverse organization and possesses a different organizational character and skill set. The adjudication and to a lesser degree mediation of individual grievances surrounding employment rights is now definitively the main service provided by the agency both in terms of client demand and resource allocation. Irish and European law is increasingly framing and circumscribing the work of adjudicators. Adjudication is now decoupled from mediation. While the LRC was an independent statutory agency, strongly influenced by leaders of employers and unions, the WRC is an agency more directly aligned with its parent government department. The Commission is governed by an advisory board. The board is not directly involved in decision-making about resource allocation or lobbying but advises senior management and assists in the preparation of three-yearly strategy statements. Resource allocation is now the preserve of senior management.

To accommodate other stakeholders in the governance of the WRC, the relative number of board positions occupied by unions and employer bodies has been reduced. Union and employer bodies' influence on public policy and wider macro-governance has declined following the collapse of social partnership. The WRC has been led since 2016 by two experienced and respected public servants, whose focus was on integrating and streamlining the services previously provided by separate agencies. The agency is significantly larger than the LRC and management processes and systems have been formalized. Collective conciliation continues to be provided by career public servants. The service remains highly effective and has been least affected by the creation of the WRC. The conciliation service conducts important work, affects large numbers of people at work and bolsters the legitimacy and appeal of the WRC in the eyes of governments and politicians. The professional backgrounds of many adjudicators remain as before, but legal practitioners now play a more prominent role in the work of the WRC. Recruitment to adjudication positions has been formalized and is now subject to open competition, and off-the-job training, including training in the law and juridical procedure, has become essential and mandatory. The statutory autonomy enjoyed by Rights Commissioners with the LRC has not extended to adjudication in the WRC.

The character of the WRC reflects the passing of a world in which the governance of dispute resolution as well as careers in some areas of service delivery had been effectively monopolized by employer and union organizations. The demise of collective conflict, the growing importance of conflict surrounding employment rights and the enforcement of employment standards have opened up the public delivery of conflict resolution to other stakeholders. Service delivery now requires a wider array of professional skills. More open and transparent modes of recruitment and more formalized training have been put in place. The State's principal agency for resolving workplace conflict has evolved from a niche organization concerned in the main with 'labour relations' into a provider of multiple services spanning the spectrum of 'workplace relations'. Governance arrangements and management processes have evolved in lockstep with the new mission and suite of services. Career civil servants have occupied leadership and many senior management positions and the outspoken and campaigning styles of leadership that had characterized the LRC are no longer in evidence.

Not surprisingly given the scale of the challenge involved in integrating four existing agencies and repurposing the fifth, the early years of the WRC have been marked by controversy over the effectiveness of the new body (see above and RTE, 1 October and 30 September 2016; *Industrial Relations News*, 21 October and 30 September 2015). Much of this was focused around new processes for accessing services and details of the operation of the adjudication service. The decision of a number of major client organizations and their unions to establish various forms of private dispute resolution panels or tribunals was also attributed by some, at least in part, to concerns about the status of conciliation in the new agency (Roche 2021). Facing external scrutiny, the priority of the WRC has been to streamline access to and increase the operational effectiveness of its core services, engaging stakeholders in ongoing dialogue to this end (WRC 2016b). The objectives of establishing the WRC's 'brand', improving the effectiveness of its customer-interface and increasing the efficiency of internal processes are highlighted in its annual reports, work programmes and medium-term strategy statements (WRC 2015, 2016a; 2016b; 2017; 2018a; 2018c; 2022a). External and internal assessments by clients and stakeholder point to continuing improvements across these areas, as overall service demand continues to grow. The current combined operating costs of the WRC and the Labour Court are lower than the total nominal costs of all rights and dispute resolution agencies in 2012, pointing to significant real cost gains.[1]

Service delivery in the early years of the WRC reveals a series of salient and contrasting trends. As outlined earlier, the number of conciliation conferences has continued its long-term decline. After a slow start, the number of adjudication cases increased, though not in a linear manner. The number of inspections carried out by the labour enforcement team has increased significantly, yet the number of prosecutions for the non-compliance with employment standards has fallen off. The level of activity by the advisory team has been declining. Although the number of calls received by the WRC has increased, a sizable number of these relate to people seeking work permits.

The WRC is now adjudged by stakeholders to be a highly effective public agency, performing a key role within the economy and society with competence, professionalism and efficiency. Early complaints over access to services and their operation have abated, while the continuing success of the conciliation and mediation service in resolving disputes – highlighted by its brokerage of an extended public service pay agreement in 2022, against a challenging background involving sharply rising inflation and growing restiveness by public service unions and their members.

The approach the WRC adopted to the COVID pandemic is emblematic of the pragmatism that has long been a core feature of Ireland's workplace conflict resolution bodies. During the pandemic, the agency was single-minded in its determination to focus on delivering the best quality service possible and remaining as organizationally cohesive as was feasible: everything else was considered secondary, if important at all. This posture went hand in glove with patterns of workplace conflict and patterns of demand for the WRC's services marked more by continuity than discontinuity with the pre-pandemic world of work and employment. As Ireland emerged from the pandemic, a similarly hard-nosed approach was adopted to how the Commission should function in a post-COVID economy. The WRC emphasized the need for stocktaking from the pandemic experience so that any positive developments emerging from the forced adaptations it was obliged to make could be mainstreamed into its work. Thus, remote and hybrid hearings have become a significant feature of adjudication, without any radical change occurring in the work of the Commission.

Lessons on the nature of the public policy process

In the introductory chapter, it was suggested that analysing the creation of the WRC would provide interesting insights into the dynamics of public policy making, particularly in four areas: (1) how policy change comes about; (2) how public sector leadership should be understood; (3) how public policy is developed and implemented overtime, particularly when it is being delivered through a public agency, and (4) why organizational legitimacy is important to the functioning of public agencies, particularly those that have been newly created. On the first issue, the organizational shaping and reshaping of public workplace conflict resolution agencies provide illuminating insights into the dynamics of policy change. Two main views dominate discussions about how and why change occurs to public policy regimes. One view suggests that far-reaching or transformative public policy change – that involves a decisive move away from established methods of doing things or what political scientists call a punctuated equilibrium – is a rare event (Streeck and Thelen 2005). Institutional persistence and continuity are seen as working against any type of radical change. On this view, self-reinforcing mechanisms lead to patterns of activity and ways of doing things being internalized by people to such an extent that they cannot countenance any radical departure from established institutions or behaviour. Because public policy regimes are considered to be 'path dependent', it is assumed that any type of radical change will only occur due to some form of exogenous or external shock, with the severity of the shock determining the character and rate of policy change.

A contrasting view suggests that the embeddedness of public policy regimes should not be exaggerated, as people are not prisoners of inherited institutions and ways of doing things but have the capacity to take 'mindful' action. On this view, change can occur to public policy regimes in the absence of any external shock: policy change can be endogenous rather than exogenous. Endogenous change can take a variety of forms, but it is usually incremental and gradual in nature. One form of slow-burning change is what may be called 'hybridization': institutions are reformed to perform different tasks or to carry out particular activities in different ways, but the overall ethos and integrity of the institutional system remain more or less intact (Boyer et al. 1998). Another form is what can be called 'path creation'. On this view, a move away from an established path can amount to planting the seeds of an entirely new path, which ultimately involves a decisive departure from the old ways of doing things. Normally, this scenario emerges as a result of continuous gradual change radically changing established institutions by stealth. Another possibly – and we have seen how this happened to the public regime for workplace conflict resolution in Ireland during the 1990s – is that a process of policy change results in policy fragmentation: established policy regimes either lose functionality or become disorganized.

In the literature, the tendency is to juxtapose exogenous and endogenous change as binary alternative pathways that tend not to co-exist together: either change is radical or it is incremental. However, this study suggests that the relationship between radical and incremental change is less binary in reality. Over the years, the evolution of the public regime for workplace conflict resolution has involved both radical and incremental changes that are entangled with each other. Thus, for example, it can be reasonably argued that were it not for the incremental changes introduced in the 1990s causing increased fragmentation rather than improved efficiency of the conflict resolution system, the need, or at least the conditions for radical change that resulted in the creation of the WRC, would not have happened. Thus, in examining how public regime change occurs, it is important not to distinguish too sharply between exogenous and endogenous influences for change: these two dynamics are likely to co-exist in one way or another in public regimes, making it hard to predict in advance the nature and direction of change.

A prominent feature of this study is that radical changes were spurred when the conflict resolution system reached critical junctures, creating the conditions for decisive 'turning points' in the institutional architecture and functioning of the system. A series of 'turning points' are evident along the road to the WRC. As earlier chapters show, it took the global financial crisis and acute fiscal pressure on the State to turn long-smouldering frustrations surrounding the increasing fragmentation of conflict resolution into a radical blueprint for action and reform. Near consensus already existed that the prevailing conflict resolution system was dysfunctional, inefficient and costly. This was especially salient to the leaders of the LRC and NERA, Kieran Mulvey and Ger Deering. But, the political prioritization of public service reform during the crisis allowed these senior professionals to spur reform and prevented remaining sceptics and opponents from mounting significant resistance – particularly, when a new Minister, Richard Bruton, actively and forcefully supported reform.

Earlier, during the 1970s and 1980s, another turning point was reached when the effectiveness of the Labour Court was called into question by a mounting industrial relations crisis, triggered by escalating industrial conflict, price and wage inflation and a high level of unofficial industrial action. These developments led to contested reforms of labour law, and less controversial reforms of conflict resolution, in which conciliation was separated institutionally from adjudication through the creation of the LRC. Concerns about the operation and effectiveness of the Labour Court had been voiced for some time before the sharp escalation of strike activity and related trends triggered the turning point that precipitated the creation of the LRC in 1991.

Neither of the turning points leading to the LRC and WRC had provoked politically sponsored proposals for radical change in the core voluntarist tenets of collective bargaining and dispute resolution. The turning point that involved the creation of the Labour Court was in this respect different. Sean Lemass's original reform vision, inspired by the impending ending of the wartime Emergency, envisaged a radical change in the fundamentals of collective wage bargaining and conflict resolution stretching back to before the foundation of the State. Lemass sought to centralize wage determination within a neo-corporatist deliberative process, aligned with binding quasi-judicial dispute resolution. Strongly influenced by arrangements for wage regulation during the Emergency, Lemass sought to prevent a return to what he viewed as the disorderly methods of collective bargaining and limited dispute resolution arrangements that had prevailed before the War. Lemass's reform proposals, anticipating a wage scramble and soaring industrial conflict when wage controls were removed, were tempered if not derailed by strongly embedded support for voluntary wage bargaining, especially on the part of trade unions. The Labour Court created in 1946 retained the legacy of voluntarism. The Court was nevertheless highly significant in bringing into being the first integrated national conflict resolution system of wide prevalence.

The earliest turning point examined in this book involved changes in dispute resolution accompanying the rise in industrial conflict and social radicalism during the early decades of the twentieth century. The rudiments of voluntary industrial relations and dispute resolution had emerged during the closing decades of the nineteenth century, following a long historical accumulation of political, economic and legal changes in the United Kingdom. The conduct of industrial relations in Ireland was strongly influenced by developments in Britain – Ireland sharing laws, major unions and some large employers with the United Kingdom – and trade boards were established to regulate wages in several low-pay sectors. However, dispute resolution interventions by the UK Board of Trade seemed largely marginal to developments in Ireland and coexisted with more frequent ad hoc initiatives by the 'great and the good', both local and national.

Prevailing dispute resolution practices proved inadequate to the challenges posed by mass unionization, pressure for union recognition, demands for wage rises, resistance to wage cuts and social radicalism inspired by Syndicalism and the iconography and methods associated with the Russian Revolution. While state-sponsored repressive measures were evident during major industrial disputes during the early twentieth century – epitomized by police mobilization and violent clashes with strikers during lockouts in Wexford and Dublin – the apogee of state repression was reached during the War of Independence and Civil War. From 1918, The Dáil and Irish Governments adopted repressive measures, spearheaded by the IRA and army to suppress disputes, defend private property and quell social radicalism. The Dáil Department of Labour's attempts to institute a system of conciliation and arbitration were the key institutional development of the period. The Department's staff and agents around the country intervened in disputes on a considerably more widespread basis than the Board of Trade had done.

The Department's resources were strained by the spiking of conflict and social radicalism between 1918 and 1923 in the face of rapidly growing unionization, campaigns to increase and defend wages and challenges to private property and land ownership. The Department largely improvised dispute resolution arrangements on the British model and also harnessed the underground Dáil Courts. Thus, developments in the early twentieth century marked a turning point by institutionalizing a system of conflict resolution built on the British voluntarist model. This was reinforced by repression where disputes were seen as economically highly damaging or socially threatening. The Irish Free State carried over the dispute resolution activities of the Dáil Department of Labour through the work of conciliation staff in the Department of Industry and Commerce. Legislation predating the creation of the State was also used to establish a number of joint industrial councils and industrial courts, as well as to extend the system of trade boards.

The evolution of the conflict resolution regime in Ireland continued involving not only sustained periods of 'muddling through', when pragmatic adaptations were made to existing institutions, but also 'critical moments' when systematic policy making was required to introduce transformative changes to existing ways of doing things. Thus, just as is the case with radical and incremental change, this study suggests that 'muddling through' and systemic policy making should not be juxtaposed too much. The evidence suggests that not only do public policy regimes have the capacity to engage in both forms of policy making, but also that the boundaries between the two can be blurred. It was years of muddling-through policy making, creating fragmented public conflict resolution systems, that provoked more systemic policy making to map wholesale transformations. Thus, as the dysfunctionality of the system of conflict resolution was becoming increasingly evident from the early 2000s and also remained inert to policy proposals, leaders of the LRC and NERA were formulating radical blueprints for reform that would subsequently chart the way towards the complete reconfiguration of conflict resolution when the reform opportunity presented itself with the arrival of the global financial crisis.

For some time the case for reform of conflict resolution and specifically of the Labour Court had been canvassed before the industrial relations crisis of the 1970s and 1980s created the conditions for the establishment of the LRC. Earlier, Lemass's experience of the pre-war fragmented and limited system of collective bargaining and conflict resolution and wartime experience of wage coordination and control were instrumental in leading him to propose a new departure when the transition to peacetime industrial relations threatened industrial chaos and major economic dislocation.

The study also highlights the importance of leadership not only to policy change, but also to the wider public policy process. Turning points do not arise spontaneously when a policy regime arrives at a critical juncture. Rather, decisive action is required to ensure transformative change programmes are introduced in otherwise propitious circumstances. This study highlights the decisive contribution of Lemass to the creation of the Labour Court in circumstances where an industrial relations cataclysm was otherwise anticipated with the transition to free collective bargaining after the wartime Emergency. The study also shows that were it not for two leading conflict management professionals skilfully using the context of the financial crisis to push for wholesale reform of the public workplace conflict resolution regime, it is questionable whether the WRC would have been created. The actions of the two professionals also raise the matter of how leadership should be viewed in a public administration context. A huge publishing industry has emerged in the past two decades or more extolling the importance of leadership to organizations. Effective leaders are portrayed as all singing and dancing: they inspire and motivate their employees, they anticipate and respond to internal and external threats, they pursue opportunities while carefully managing risks and they handle crises and unanticipated events quickly and assuredly. Leaders are viewed as possessing a dazzling array of qualities; they are authentic, great motivators, problem-solvers, effective communicators, inventors of the future and so on (Pfeffer 2015). Private sector organizations are seen as the natural incubators for the nurturing of leadership, but a growing and influential literature argues that similar types of leadership styles and capabilities are required in public sector organizations if they are to flourish and be successful (Vandenabeele et al. 2014).

This study, however, speaks to a different type of public sector leadership, which is of older vintage and places the emphasis on different types of organizational activities. The classical work of Philip Selznick (1957) is widely considered to be influential in the construction of this alternative model of public sector leadership. According to Selznick, the role of public sector leaders is not to run a public sector organization as a 'rational instrument to do a job', which is the orientation of most private sector firms, but as 'a responsive, adaptive organism'. The role of the public sector leader is not only to infuse the public sector agency or department with a particular set of values, but also to be the guardian, champion and protector of these values thereafter. A key part of these roles is to ensure that the values of an agency or department do not lag behind changes in the internal or external environment. Thus, the public sector leader does not only have the responsibility to develop the distinctive character and mission of a public sector agency, but also to ensure that it adapts to changing operating conditions.

Essentially, Selznick was promulgating the idea that public sector leadership is not the mirror image of leadership commonly found in private sector organization but has features that require a distinctive set of skills and attributes. Over the years, the core thinking behind Selznick's writing has been reformulated and refashioned in numerous ways. Perhaps, the most influential articulation of his thinking today is 'public service motivation theory'. Perry and Wise (1990) define public service motivation as 'an individual's predisposition to respond to motives grounded primarily or uniquely in public institutions and organizations' (p. 368). The idea is that public agencies have an organizational purpose that in most cases seeks to deliver services that improve the well-being of people and a society. Public sector leaders – and employees – become imbued with this ethos and thus become committed to ensuring the agency performs its tasks as effectively as possible (Esteve et al. 2016). The actions of Mulvey and Deering to advance the reform of the public conflict resolution system approximate most closely to this model of public sector leadership rather than any alternative that emphasizes individual leadership traits or styles. While the LRC seemed destined to become the fulcrum of a reconfigured conflict management system, it nevertheless faced abolition as an independent agency. NERA's Director quickly developed the view that the institution's objectives were not well served by the prevailing configuration of conflict resolution agencies and that progress required the dissolution of the institution and the transposition of its functions within a new conflict resolution system

The study suggests that the relationship between a public agency such as the WRC and its parent government department and indeed the wider political process exerts a strong influence on not only how public policies are formed, but also how they are implemented. A feature of almost all advanced democracies over the past three decades has been the phenomenal growth in semi-independent public agencies, or 'quangos', charged with delivering a public service of one kind or another. These agencies usually only have an arms-length relationship with the direct institutions of government, civil service departments and the like (OECD 2021). A huge research agenda has emerged that seeks to understand how policy competence and authority are conferred on these public agencies and how matters of accountability and transparency are maintained in the context of policy delegation. Thus, for example, research has sought to show whether public agencies solely pursue the objectives set for them by government or if they use their relative autonomy to develop a policy agenda that goes beyond these objectives. Undoubtedly, agency theory has been the dominant theoretical framework used to investigate these fairly complex research questions.

When a government department decides to create a semi-autonomous public body, agency theory suggests that a principal-agent relationship has been created. The challenge that immediately arises is to design a relationship that ensures that the activities of the agent (the public body) are fully aligned with the objectives or interests of the principal (the government department). Because agency theory assumes that both the principal and agent pursue their own self-interests, have access to different (and inherently limited) forms of information and have contrasting risk-taking preferences, it is almost taken-for-granted that the principal-agent relationship will not be constructed in a fully optimal manner: the interests/objectives of the principal (government department) will not be fully aligned with those of the agent (public body). As a result, conflicts of interest emerge, as the agent (public body) starts to prioritize and pursue its own goals instead of the objectives of the principal (government department). The heavy use of agency theory to examine the arms-length relationship between government departments and semi-independent public bodies has resulted in two topics dominating the research literature on the matter. One branch of research seeks first to uncover the extent to which the interests of principals and agents diverge in particular circumstances and then assess the consequences of this sub-optimality for public service delivery. The other branch focuses on assessing the most effective monitoring mechanisms and incentive systems that can be put in place to make the actions of the agent as compatible as possible with the objectives of the principal.

Thus, the predilection of agency theory is to view the relationship between government departments and public agencies as riven with conflict, or at least as possessing only a minimal compatibility of interest. Although the theory is hugely influential, it is questionable whether it can be usefully employed to explain the cooperative arms-length relationship that this study has revealed between the WRC and the Irish Government, particularly the Department of Enterprise, Trade and Employment (DETE), which is directly responsible for the conflict resolution system. Little of interest or insight is likely to be revealed by using the principal-agent framework to examine the relationship between the WRC and its parent department DETE. An alternative although less influential theoretical framework that may more successfully account for the near absence of any competing interest or opportunistic behaviour from the relationship is 'stewardship theory' (Davis et al. 1997). In contrast to the principal-agent framework, stewardship theory suggests that the arms-length relationship between a government department and a public body is more often than not characterized by a high level of reciprocity and alignment of interests (Esteve et al 2016). The thrust of the theory suggests that the WRC, even though operating fairly autonomously, will act in a committed and responsible manner to implement the policy objectives of the department and government in relation to workplace conflict resolution. In practice, this indeed has been the case: the WRC and its leadership have consistently sought to operate within the organizational and policy parameters set for it by the Government.

Although stewardship theory more accurately captures how the relationship between the WRC and the government has unfolded since it was established in 2015, it probably doesn't tell the full story as to why both have stayed so consistently aligned with each other. Stewardship theory places a strong emphasis on intrinsic motivational factors such as trust, reputational enhancement, and discretion and autonomy of the people who work for both the principal and the agent. Having people who are collectively minded and committed to the mission of the organization is thus seen as the main reason why a stewardship dynamic and mentality emerge within a principal-agent relationship (Hayter et al 2018). While there may even be a surfeit of mutual trust between the WRC and the DETE, as well as the wider machinery of government, this is probably not the main factor that accounts for the persistence of congruent relations between the two. A more convincing explanation is that both realized that it was beneficial to each other to build and sustain cooperative relations. On the one hand, the DETE recognized that it was beyond the internal reach of the department directly to deliver effective workplace resolution services in a manner that would gain the full commitment of employers and employees. Such a task required a public agency that was relatively autonomous of government. On the other hand, the WRC has been acutely aware that it required the full imprimatur of government for it to gain organizational legitimacy amongst its multiple stakeholders and to have the capacity to deliver authoritative conflict resolution services. The stewardship dynamic that pervades the relationship between the WRC and Government was constructed by both on the hard anvil of institutional self-interest.

Finally, the study provides greater understanding of the importance of organizational legitimacy to the functioning of public agencies. Fitz Scharpf (1999) the celebrated German political scientist, suggests that legitimacy is two dimensional – one dimension relates to output legitimacy and the other to input legitimacy. Broadly, output legitimacy refers to the ability of an organization to accomplish effectively the tasks it was set up to do. The consensus is that the WRC enjoys a high level of output legitimacy – it consistently resolves thousands of adjudication cases each year and retains the panache to conciliate complex collective disputes. Input legitimacy relates to the acceptability an organization enjoys amongst stakeholders, clients and the wider public. The more acceptability enjoyed by an organization, the more its activities are considered to be desirable, proper and appropriate. In some countries such as New Zealand and Australia, the input legitimacy of the public dispute resolution bodies has at times been challenged. Employer organizations far from viewing the public dispute resolution bodies as acceptable have openly contested their purpose and have launched sustained campaigns to have their role and functions drastically curtailed, if not abolished altogether. In Ireland, individual employers may grumble about the WRC, particularly if they have to attend an adjudication hearing or dispute its outcome, but the role of resolution agencies has never been questioned: the WRC is widely recognized as performing an important role in the country. Having high levels of output and input legitimacy marks off the WRC from public dispute resolution agencies in other countries.

Current strategic challenges

Possessing legitimacy does not insulate the WRC from having to face numerous strategic challenges in developing and delivering its services. Of current strategic challenges three will be highlighted: the first arises from the ongoing juridification of grievance resolution, the second from the continuous growth of private conflict resolution and the third from a complex of changes to work and employment.

The juridification of adjudication

The juridification of adjudication, highlighted by the Zalewski challenge Supreme Court judgement, seems only likely to intensify, and will continue to throw up operating challenges for the Commission (Supreme

Court 2021). In 2020, the parties to adjudication availed of some form of third-party representation in 52 per cent of cases. Lawyers accounted for 50 per cent of third-party representatives – nearly double the combined level of representation by unions and IBEC officers (WRC 2021b). The legal division of the WRC has gained more staff and has received a new organizational focus and level of priority. Structures and procedures have been put in place to provide more comprehensive and systematic training for adjudicators – there is talk of obliging adjudicators to engage in accredited training programmes. New processes have been put in place to furnish adjudicators engaged in specific cases with speedier, better quality advice and guidance. Business analytic methods are being used to identify key patterns and outcomes in relation to adjudication cases so that established policies and procedures can be fine-tuned. Projects have been established between the adjudication team and social partners aimed at improving the manner in which hearings are conducted. All these activities amount to a significant ramping up and formalization of the legal support provided for adjudication and of the core process of conducting adjudication hearings. To a large extent, these changes were necessary to ensure that the adjudication service was delivered competently, professionally and in accordance with the law. The WRC is not alone in experiencing creeping juridification, the Labour Court has been affected by the same development, arising from the growing share of individual employment rights appeals in its caseload (Kerr 2014), and latterly from more frequent legal challenges to collective pay fixing institutions within its remit: joint labour committees/employment regulation orders and registered employment agreements/sectoral employment orders.

The danger of growing juridification for the WRC is that legal formalization will squeeze out the soft, problem-solving dimension of adjudication and allow the legalistic mentality of allowing people 'to have their day to court', associated in particular with the Employment Appeals Tribunal, to take hold inside the WRC. Adapting to the greater legal formalization of adjudication without inculcating the organization with excessive legalism is probably the most pressing strategic challenge facing the senior management team of the WRC and the day-to-day work of adjudicators. While the WRC takes the view that changes in adjudication procedures, hearings and ways of reporting decisions introduced in the wake of the Zalewski judgement have largely settled the matter, legal formalization seems set to continue and with it the possibility of longer and more complex hearings and increased pressure on parties to be legally represented in proceedings. The risk of judicial review has also risen as a consequence of these developments. Compounding these challenges is the significant incidence of remote and hybrid hearings following on from changes to service provision during the COVID pandemic, bringing new challenges in areas such as the presentation of evidence. One of the widely recognized features of the LRC had been the freedom of Rights Commissioners to combine mediation with adjudication and apply the knowledge gained from frontline experience to the specifics of individual cases. This has now been lost, not alone due to the decoupling of mediation from adjudication but also from the exigencies of being obliged above all to apply the law, increasingly in hearings where parties are legally represented and where lawyers are insistent that the legal rights of clients be respected and vindicated. The evidently greater success of complainants when represented by lawyers in such areas as employment equality seems set further to encourage legal representation and with it the further juridification of hearings (McGreal et al. 2021).

The continuing growth of private alternative dispute resolution

Beyond the borders of the WRC developments in ADR within firms and public sector organizations continue apace. Some of these, such as the creation of private dispute resolution arrangements for settling collective disputes, involve the defection of major clients from the WRC. From the early 2000s, private dispute resolution arrangements in which independently engaged panels of adjudicators provide conciliation and adjudication to resolve collective disputes (and sometimes individual grievances) have grown in incidence. Some 11 such arrangements have been documented in private sector and state-owned firms and in public agencies, ranging from Luas, Aer Lingus, DAA, the Irish Aviation Authority, Inland Fisheries Ireland, the Central Bank, Bord na Móna, Coillte and GE Healthcare (Roche 2021; 2022a; 2022b). More recently, other such arrangements have been established in the pharmaceutical firm, Hovione, the Irish Management Institute and in Iarnród Eireann. The majority of private dispute resolution arrangements seek to confine dispute resolution within the organizations involved by delivering binding recommendations and decisions; others provide a route to the WRC and Labour Court in what are intended to be exceptional circumstances. In some cases, such as Bord na Móna and Iarnród Eireann, the WRC was instrumental in supporting the establishment of new inhouse dispute resolution arrangements and provided the chair (Bord na Móna). While demonstrating multiple innovative features, private dispute resolution bodies have been found to be variably effective (Roche 2022a). Some have become dormant (the Central Bank) or collapsed as a result of changes in management (Aer Lingus). Yet, their emergence and growth point towards the determination of some traditional heavy users of the WRC to develop innovative in-house equivalents of both the Commission and the Labour Court. The WRC like the LRC before it appears ambivalent about private dispute resolution, supporting new arrangements as contributors to good employment relations but sceptical as to their likely longevity and effectiveness and concerned that malfunctions will increase the challenges it may face in resolving disputes.

The provision of other conflict resolution services of different kinds by private practitioners addressing individual grievances and collective issues also continues to grow (Kenny 2019) leading to what has been referred to as an evolving 'dual conflict resolution system', comprising state agencies and private providers (Roche 2018). With the rising incidence and range of such services, the WRC is losing the virtual monopoly of private dispute resolution enjoyed by public agencies since the foundation of the state. A range of private providers have entered the field – often involving highly trained, experienced and respected practitioners. The WRC has been challenged to consider how best to position itself around these external developments and how it might support new approaches to conflict resolution within organizations (Roche 2018; Stratis 2019). Some critics have pressed the case for formalizing the principle that internal workplace conflict resolution procedures should be exhausted before individual complaints are accepted by the WRC (Stratis 2019: 5). An experienced lawyer and mediator has also raised the issue of whether collective work stoppages should enjoy legal immunities only where conventional disputes procedures or ADR practices have been exhausted (Connaughton 2019 and see also Stratis 2019: 10).

The WRC, like the LRC before it, continues to adopt a largely passive approach to the development of different forms of ADR beyond its borders, sometimes by long-established service users. While the 'disguised antipathy' that may have been a feature of the LRC is not evident in the case of the WRC, neither has the growth of the private conflict resolution sector been viewed by the WRC as a challenge, concern or pathfinder, pointing towards wider positive reforms. Should the sector continue to grow, the WRC may be obliged to shift its stance towards proactively encouraging the development of private conflict resolution, consistent with its mission of fostering good employment relations. Such a shift might in turn involve the WRC in monitoring, benchmarking and promulgating good practice in private conflict resolution. This is the posture that has been adopted by sister bodies internationally such as the Advisory Conciliation and Arbitration Service in the United Kingdom, the Federal Mediation and Conciliation Service in the United States and the Fair Work Commission in Australia. All such agencies in different ways have actively promoted or sponsored ADR and related workplace innovations, sometimes through formal programmes and designated resources (ACAS 2014; Clews 2021; Robinson et al. 2005). Unlike some of these bodies, the WRC is prevented from charging for any services delivered, raising concerns about how expanded services could be resourced. The Commission may also be sensitive to possible challenges that new services would compete with private providers on unequal and unfair terms – a criticism that has been levelled against ACAS in the United Kingdom, which unlike the LRC is enabled to charge for some services. Yet, the WRC, like the LRC, has delivered training and diagnostic services within its statutory remit, is enabled to develop services to foster good workplace relations, can undertake research and develop codes of practice. As such, many of the tools for a more proactive role in fostering, monitoring and assessing ADR are currently available to the Commission.

Various forms of ADR are commonly encountered in large non-union and particularly multinational firms (Teague et al. 2015). While such firms generally seek to resolve conflict inhouse, some have availed of the conciliation and facilitation service of the WRC, working discretely to provide assistance to non-union parties seeking support. It remains the case, however, that non-union firms are heavily underrepresented among the users of the collective conflict resolution services of the WRC – and sometimes show an antipathy towards managing or resolving conflict in any formal manner (Doherty and Teague 2011). The criticism sometimes ranged against the LRC – and more generally extended to all actors in Irish employment relations – that it needed more effectively to accommodate models of employment relations based on direct engagement between employers and employees, unmediated by representative organizations, may still be levelled against the WRC. This is not because the WRC stands aloof from such firms but because relatively few of them see value in using the services available. As the incidence and workforce share of non-union firms grows, the WRC is faced with the strategic challenge of making its services more visible, attractive and widely available to this sector. The upshot is that the WRC faces growing competition from private providers within its traditional domain and creeping marginalization as the workforce grows in non-union firms often reluctant to engage with its services.

Changes in the economic and work environment

The establishment of the Labour Court and the creation of the LRC as a spinoff agency occurred in a world of work and employment marked by a relatively high level of continuity. Both agencies delivered services in periods of growth and recession, during cycles of high and low industrial conflict, in times when collective bargaining was centralized and decentralized and when pay movements were more or less affected by inflation. At the same time, widely prevalent working arrangements were based on attendance in factories, offices and other work locations where pay, working time and work organization were largely standardized, where there were clear and recognizable distinctions between employers and employees, where seemingly unlimited scope existed to expand production or service provision without concern as to the effects on the environment or climate and where changes in technologies favouring automation and latterly digitization where largely incremental.

All such established parameters of work and employment are under challenge. Labour market actors, whether employers, unions or public policy makers, have been forced to adjust to new challenges and priorities. The WRC can scarcely be insulated from the effects of the same challenges, or from the need to consider whether services forged in different economic and work conditions need to be adapted and reconfigured to respond to new external challenges and pressures (WRC 2022c).

Not surprisingly, the WRC anticipated that significant challenges would arise from ongoing multi-faceted changes in the labour market, work and economic environment. The expansion of remote and hybrid work, the sharp rise from 2021 in inflation and interest rates, the effects of climate change and the impact of artificial intelligence (AI) on jobs were among the developments seen as likely to impact on the Commission's future work. Quite to what extent and in what ways conflict resolution services and the enforcement of employment standards may be affected by these changes remained to be established by the WRC (WRC 2022a).

While the 'great return', involving many employees resuming attendance at worksites, often on the insistence of employers, has been evident in Ireland as in many countries, it is also clear that work patterns will not revert fully to their pre-pandemic forms. Preferences for hybrid and remote working, revealed in surveys during the pandemic, have largely continued and are shaping post-pandemic work patterns. Other innovations such as the trialling of four-day working weeks point towards possible further innovations in work patterns. The Irish Government sought to spur the growth of hybrid and remote work by supporting work hubs, where workers can share access to premises and technologies, and by committing to significant levels of remote and hybrid work across the public service. As discussed earlier in this book, the WRC was mandated under the Work Life Balance Act 2023 to prepare a code of practice on remote and flexible working requests by employees. Alleged breaches of the code may lead to complaints to the WRC that then become subject to mediation and/or adjudication.

The sharp increase in the rate of inflation following the ending of the COVID-19 pandemic and the war in Ukraine and the use of high interest rates as a counter-inflationary measure impacted significantly on pay bargaining, as unions sought pay rises that compensated at least in part for price rises. This expanded the repertoire of pay bargaining by including union demands and employers offer of lump-sum or once-off payments, non-taxable vouchers, improvements in fringe benefits. Higher pay offers were also conceded in response to union claims and sometimes union demands that existing pay agreements be reopened (*Industrial Relations News*, 12 January 2023). While the incidence of pay disputes referred to the WRC and Labour Court rose, the rise was no higher than several earlier peaks that occurred during less inflationary years since 2011. The WRC's conciliation service also remained highly effective in resolving pay disputes in the private sector during the period of highest inflation. The service also brokered public service-wide pay agreements in 2022 and 2023 against the background of high inflation and ballots for industrial action by public service unions. While the rate of inflation fell in 2023 and was projected to decline further, the WRC anticipated that inflation and high interest rates might for some time yet affect continue to affect the dynamics of pay bargaining and also the conduct of conciliation.

Measures to curb climate change through reductions in carbon emission have already impacted on industrial relations through job losses in high carbon emitting industries such as turf production and high-emission electricity generation. The running down of such industries has involved 'fair transition' programmes and related measures to support displaced workers and the communities in which they live. While current fair transition arrangements have been assigned to a parallel Fair Transition Team for the Midlands Region, headed by former LRC CEO and WRC Director General, Kieran Mulvey, the WRC has also been involved in dispute resolution around closures and job losses in Bord na Móna, primarily through its role in chairing the firm's private dispute resolution body, the Joint Industrial Relations Council. With the State's plans to become carbon neutral and to achieve emissions reductions and institute carbon budgets across industrial sectors, restructuring programmes and job losses seem likely to occur on a more widespread basis. Proposals for managing the transition to a low carbon economy and the just transition assign a major role to tripartite social dialogue (NESC 2020; ICTU 2022). Yet, significant implications also arise for the WRC, primarily in the areas of providing facilitation and conciliation, especially in sectors likely to be heavily affected: fossil fuels, electricity generation, parts of manufacturing and transport (NESC 2020: 9).

The recent acceleration of innovations involving digital technologies, particularly AI, has given rise to sometimes apocalyptic predictions of job losses and shifts in employment in a 'Fourth Industrial Revolution' (McKinsey Global Institute 2017). One high-profile forecast predicts that AI could displace some 300 million jobs in the United States and Europe (Goldman Sachs 2023). Highly skilled, professional and service jobs are commonly seen to be among those vulnerable to applications involving AI. Significant increases in employment also are seen likely in the development, application, marketing and sales of the new technologies. The effects of 'digital transformation' on work and employment are likely to be more wide-ranging both sectorally and occupationally than the low-carbon transition (NESC 2020: 9). Again, social dialogue is accorded considerable importance in managing digital transformation in Ireland (NESC 2020: ch. 3). Given the anticipated widespread work and employment effects of the accelerating development and application of digital technologies, the WRC is again likely to be involved in facilitating change and restructuring programmes. This work may involve providing conciliation in disputes concerning the employment effects of the new technologies and in adjudicating employment grievances and rights complaints arising from the application of AI technologies. Over and above the effects AI will have on employment, the content of jobs, the boundaries between jobs and the pace or intensity of work are also likely to be affected, not least in high union density service sectors like the public service, health and education. The OECD predicts that AI will entail a high degree of work reorganization, involving both the automation and creation of work tasks. It is also expected to increase work intensity and worker productivity and holds the potential to increase worker autonomy and control (OECD 2023: ch. 5). Many of these anticipated changes involve alternations to work processes and associated potential conflict flashpoints which fall within the services, skills and experiences of the WRC. What may now change are the sectors and occupations that will be affected, as well as the speed, extent and depth of the changes that may be wrought by the growing application of AI. The Commission may also be involved in promoting social dialogue as well as in providing facilitation and conciliation across these areas. Individual employment rights are also likely to be affected and even extended (e.g. the recent emergence of the 'right to disconnect' from digital devices during leisure periods), leading to a further growth in demand for adjudication and mediation.

Changes in the economic and work environment are beginning to focus the WRC's forward planning. They also highlight the extent to which the agency, notwithstanding its effectiveness and success, is deeply rooted in a work, employment and wider economic model that may be changing rapidly and radically. The anticipated scale and nature of some of the changes may clash with the culture of incrementalism and pragmatism that has characterized the functioning of Ireland's core conflict resolution agencies since the establishment of the Labour Court. The WRC is nevertheless aware that as the work and employment model on which conflict resolution has long been based comes under challenge it may need to adapt its services to the pressures and demands of a new model of work and employment.

The strategic lessons for other Anglo-American countries

In the first chapter, it was emphasized that domestic institutional structures and political priorities as well as the specific organizational character of prevailing public conflict resolution agencies would heavily influence how each Anglo-American country responded to the changes to work and employment that are posing major challenges to the established conflict resolution landscapes. These domestic conditions and circumstances determine whether attempts at renewing public workplace conflict management regimes are bold and transformative or small scale and incremental. However, this study of the creation of the WRC and its endeavours to establish organizational legitimacy suggests that irrespective of whether a reform programme may be radical or incremental, it must address three interrelated themes.

Probably, the first and most important theme that needs to be addressed is the strategic orientation of any modernized mission for a public dispute resolution agency. Any attempt at strategic renewal would not only need to set out the clear and specific purpose of a refreshed agency but also provide well-articulated reasons for the adoption of new goals and activities. It would also need to map out a plan to establish organizational legitimacy. If there is one lesson above any other from the Irish case, it is that the effectiveness of a public agency depends on credible commitments existing between it and the relevant parts of Government: each must trust the other and have confidence in the other's ability to carry out assigned tasks. Thus, a key part of organizational legitimacy in any national context involves the public agency and Government forging a common purpose on the nature and scope of public interventions to resolve workplace conflict. An important litmus test of the strength of such a common purpose is its ability to endure beyond electoral cycles. Another key dimension to organizational legitimacy is building up support and buy-in from stakeholders and clients. Through continuous stakeholder engagement, a public agency can deepen external understanding and alignment with its purpose and activities. Aligning stakeholder behaviour with organizational goals is indispensable to creating a cohesive and unified external environment for the resolution of workplace conflict.

The second theme is what can be called policy orchestration. This involves devising a set of complementary policies and services that enable the public agency to realize the goals that it has set for itself. Policy orchestration sounds much easier than it is to deliver. Agencies not only have to ensure that the design of policies is narrowly focused on the problems that they are seeking to address, but also that the internal capabilities exist to implement policies effectively. The Irish case highlights that establishing an effective adjudication service to address individual rights-based disputes is far from easy and cannot be completed in a short period of time. Implementing focused policy interventions is likely to be better realized in a public agency that has eliminated internal organizational silos that discourage cross-functional learning and cooperation. The Irish case emphasizes the multiple benefits that arise from fostering an overarching, inclusive internal organizational culture. Greater cooperation, flexibility and willingness to solve internal tensions and problems are amongst the main positive spin-offs that arise when a supportive, cohesive organizational culture is present.

A third theme is policy learning. Across countries, public conflict management agencies need to make strategic decisions about the resources they are going to devote to the promulgation of state-of-the-art conflict management policies for organizations and to evaluate the effectiveness of their own policies and programmes. Promoting state-of-the-art policies is designed to provide organizations with the know-how to upgrade their conflict management systems. Workshops can be organized to increase understanding of particular conflict management policies such as investigations or mediation. More ambitiously, pilot schemes could be set up involving groups of volunteer firms to encourage the diffusion of multiple ADR policies in a controlled and orderly manner. The benefit of such pilot schemes is that they give rise to significant demonstration effects, with organizations not participating in the pilot learning from those that have participated. A range of complementary policies could also be adopted should as writing practitioners guides on how to set up a conflict management system or introduce mediation at the workplace. Bubbling beneath the surface of these policy learning initiatives is the big strategic question of how dedicated should a public conflict management agency be to promoting economy-wide norms about what constitutes good conflict management practices at the workplace. So far many agencies have avoided answering this question systematically. However, sooner rather than later, a shrinking client base alongside the growth of private forms of conflict management are likely to require them to confront this complex question directly.

Policy learning is not only about the external promotion of knowledge and understanding of workplace conflict management. It is also about the internal capacity to evaluate and draw lessons from the various programmes and services that the agency delivers. Learning-by-monitoring processes come in various shapes and sizes, but they all seek to provide an accurate assessment of the degree to which and for what reasons a particular policy is succeeding or failing. Evidence is produced that allows an informed assessment to be made about the type of recalibration needed to correct any shortcomings, close any delivery gaps, or simply to strengthen an effective policy even further. Learning-by-monitoring and evaluation processes can be very resource intensive, which probably explains why so many public conflict management agencies do not conduct such exercises in an integrated, systematic manner. Nevertheless, the benefits of monitoring and evaluation in terms of improving decision-making and enhancing policy delivery are unquestionable. Thus, the big strategic task for public agencies in this area is to develop methods of evaluation that are not over-engineered or over-burdensome but that enable future improvements in organizational performance.

Conclusions

In Chapter 1, it was stated that a key purpose of this book was to throw light on the factors enabling alignment between public conflict resolution agencies and fast changing labour markets. This analysis of the Irish case, particularly the rise of the WRC, suggests that three factors are critical to maintaining alignment. One is the presence of political consensus. A number of huge benefits arise if the work of a public conflict resolution agency is not politically contested and instead enjoys cross-party political support. First of all, it ensures that the mandate or mission of the public agency endures beyond the lifetime of one government. Secondly, it leads to the activities of the public agency having the strong *imprimatur* of Government, with the effect of enhancing the status of the agency amongst firms, employees and citizens. Thirdly, it enables credible commitments to be fostered between the public agency and the relevant arms of government. Both must have an assurance about the behaviour of the other side, but at the same time must provide an assurance about its own behaviour and abilities. Credible commitments arise when these assurances are believed. With the presence of credible commitments, the public agency has sufficient leeway and autonomy to develop its work while the Government remains at an arms-length distance, trusting the agency to remain within the boundaries of its mandate.

The second critical factor making it more likely that a conflict resolution agency keeps pace with the changing nature of workplace conflict is legitimacy. A conflict resolution agency can be considered to have a high level of legitimacy when its mandate is not contested to any significant degree by external stakeholders and when there is a strong unity of purpose internally about the strategic pathway being travelled by the agency. If a public agency experiences a high level of contestability, its operational effectiveness is inevitably going to be impaired as it repeatedly has to try and persuade firms, trade unions and other users that its (shifting) work is valuable. Similarly, if there is no internal shared understanding and consensus about the strategies being pursued, then the agency is unlikely to have the focus and commitment to make work programmes fully successful. Low contestability and strong internal shared understandings are the ingredients for a conflict resolution agency acquiring high legitimation. Agencies that enjoy high legitimation can focus on remaining aligned with the dynamics of workplace conflict, new and old, in an unencumbered way. The third critical factor is pragmatic policy development and implementation within the conflict resolution agency. Pragmatic policy development rests on the assumption of the fallibility of conflict resolution programmes: there is recognition that the policies and services offered by the agency may not wholly effectively address the problems they were created to resolve. Thus, the internal organizational

DNA of the agency encourages not only the on-going review of existing programmes to assess their efficacy, but also the continuous investigation of the plausibility of different policy alternatives. Pragmatic policy making is about etching out continuous improvements. The story that unfolds about the WRC in this book suggests that the presence of these three factors makes it more likely that a public agency has sufficient internal capacity and flexibility to remain in tune with the changing nature of workplace conflict.

As to the evolution of Irish public agencies charged with addressing workplace conflict, this book suggests that their organizational character has progressed through both small- and large-scale changes. The two recent landmark episodes in this evolution were the creation of the LRC in 1990 and the setting up of the WRC in 2015. The motivation for the creation of LRC was first and foremost to bring greater order and stability to relations between trade unions and employers against a background of growing industrial conflict and the clogging up of the Labour Court. As a result, the LRC was an avowedly collective industrial relations institution. For nearly 25 years, the LRC was the dominant public agency for addressing workplace conflict in Ireland. It gained widespread public legitimacy for its repeated ability to settle successfully large-scale industrial relations disputes. A major restructuring of public dispute resolution agencies for workplace conflict in 2015 witnessed the demise of the LRC and the creation of the WRC. A significant event, the setting up of the WRC brought to a close the era when managing collective industrial relations was the main organizing principle for public action on workplace conflict. Although it continues effectively to address collective industrial relations disputes, this sphere of activity is no longer front and centre of the WRC's work or strategic vision. A conscious effort is being made to create a new type of public agency for addressing workplace conflict. The WRC is nestled firmly within the wider family of statutory agencies charged with delivering government programmes and services, governed by a board that reflects this new dispensation. The Commission is focused on how to operate an effective and efficient adjudication service for individual employment grievances – by far the largest area of WRC activity – against a background in which decisions of the higher courts threaten the growing juridification of its work. No longer is negotiating settlements to collective industrial disputes the fulcrum of the public regime governing workplace conflict, instead it is creating accessible adjudicatory processes for the vindication of employment rights.

Changes and adaptations to public agencies charged with addressing conflict at work have been motivated by a range of factors. Sometimes, changes of a radical nature have occurred – as was the case with the creation of the WRC – through serendipitous policy entrepreneurship, responding to a growing sense that existing agencies were collectively working ineffectively or suboptimally. More usually, change was introduced in an ad hoc and incremental manner to address a perceived gap in the public regime for dispute resolution or to accommodate a new emerging conflict method. The expansion of Rights Commissioners from a problem-solving service for small-scale industrial relations disputes to a quasi-judicial body for the vindication of individual employment rights, or the introduction of a mediation service for the resolution of equality cases, are examples of this type of change.

Perhaps, the most remarkable feature of change to Irish agencies for the resolution of workplace conflict is that it has never been driven by political ideology. In some Anglo-American countries, most notably Australia and New Zealand, the nature and purpose of public agencies have been buffeted to-and-fro by the flowing and ebbing tides of neoliberalism and counter ideologies. In Canada, where conflict resolution agencies are rooted in provinces, similar but more muted pressures have been evident, particularly in the most populous province of Ontario. In the United States and the United Kingdom, public agencies with similar remits to the WRC have experienced marginalization, often influenced by changes in the political appreciation and priority of the services they provided. The Irish agencies for resolving workplace conflict have never been caught on the high seas of contested political ideology. The work and activities of these agencies have consistently enjoyed cross-party support among the major political parties.

Functioning against the relatively tranquil backdrop of political consensus has unquestionably contributed to the pragmatic approach to decision-making and policy development that has been a strong characteristic of the main public dispute resolution agencies over the years. It is as if pragmatic problem-solving that has been an enduring feature of conflict resolution since the creation of the Labour Court in 1946 is baked into the organizational character of the WRC. While the Commission faces a series of challenges, in forthcoming years, the prevailing process of organizational adaptation and renewal is likely to continue inside the WRC. The precise nature or pace of the changes that will be introduced cannot be predicted in advance but is highly likely that they will be introduced in a largely politically uncontested manner and in a way that does not deviate too strongly from its pragmatic problem-solving traditions. And for a public agency charged with addressing workplace conflict that is as good an approach to the future as any.

Note

1 Information provided by the Workplace Relations Commission.

References

ACAS (Advisory Conciliation and Arbitration Service) (2014), 'Reframing Resolution: Managing Conflict and Resolving Individual Employment Disputes in the Contemporary Workplace', https://www.acas.org.uk/reframing-resolution-managing-conflict-and-resolving-individual-employment-disputes-html

Ahern, B. (2010), 'Address to the Conference on July 16, 2010', in Kerr, A. (ed.), *The Industrial Relations Act 1990 20 Years On*, Dublin: Round Hall Thompson Reuters, pp. 1–10.

Allen, K. (1991), *Fianna Fáil and Irish Labour 1926 to the Present*, London: Pluto Press.

Arrington, L. (2016), *Revolutionary Lives: Constance and Casimir Markievicz*, Oxford: Princeton University Press.

Autor, D. and Reynolds, E. (2020), 'The Nature of Work after the COVID Crisis: Too Few Low-Wage Jobs', Brookings Institution: The Hamilton Project.

Avgar, A., Colvin, A., Katz, H., Roche, W.K. and Teague, P. (2023), 'The Changing Role of Public Agencies in Workplace Conflict Resolution in Six English-speaking Countries', *Industrial Relations Journal*, 54(4), forthcoming.

Barrero, J. M., Bloom, N. and Davis, S. J. (2021), Why Working from Home Will Stick NBER Working Paper No. 28731, April.

Barry, B. (2016), 'Resolving Disputes under the Workplace Relations Act 2015: A Survey of Practitioners One Year On', address to Employment Law Conference, University College Dublin, 1st October (unpublished).

Batt, R., Nohara, H. and Kwo, H. (2010), 'Employer Strategies and Wages in New Service Activities: A Comparison of Coordinated and Liberal Market Economies', *British Journal of Industrial Relations*, 48(2): 400–435.

Bercholz, M. and FitzGerald, J. (2016), 'Recent Trends in Female Labour Force Participation in Ireland', *Quarterly Economic Commentary*, Dublin: Economic and Social Research Institute, September, pp. 1–34.

Berresford Ellis, P. (1985), *A History of the Irish Working Class*, London: Pluto Press.

Bew, P. and Patterson, H. (1982), *Sean Lemass and the Making of Modern Ireland 1945-66*, Dublin: Gill and Macmillan.

Blanchflower, D.G. (2019), *Not Working: Where Have All the Good Jobs Gone?* Princeton: Princeton University Press.

Boehme, S. (2015), 'Skeptics of the Screen: Irish Perspectives on Online Dispute Resolution', MA Dissertation, Maynooth University (unpublished).

Bonner, K. (1989), 'Industrial Relations Reform', in Kelly, A. and Murphy, T. (eds.), *Industrial Relations in Ireland: Contemporary Issues and Developments*, Dublin: University College Dublin, pp. 261–279.

Boyer, R., Charron, E., Jürgens, U. and Tolliday, S. (1998), *Between Imitation and Innovation: The Transfer and Hybridization of Productive Models in the International Automobile Industry*, Oxford: Oxford University Press.

Boyle, J.W. (1988), *The Irish Labour Movement in the Nineteenth Century*, Washington DC: The Catholic University of America.

Bragazzi, T. (2012), 'The Rights Commissioner Service – A Unique Response to a Pressing Need', in Sheehan, B. (ed.), *The Labour Relations Commission: Recalling 21 Years, 1991-2012*, Dublin: Labour Relations Commission, pp. 165–176.

Brouwer, S. and Huitema, D. (2018), 'Policy Entrepreneurs and Strategies for Change', *Regional Environmental Change*, 18(5): 1259–1272.

Bruton, R. (2011), 'Address by Richard Bruton, TD, Minister for Jobs, Enterprise and Innovation at the Opening of the High-Level Conference on the Resolution of Individual Employment Rights Disputes at the School of Law', University College Dublin, 1 July, Dublin: Department of Jobs, Enterprise and Innovation.

Buckley, O. (2016), 'Address to Employment to Employment Law Conference', University College Dublin, 1st October (unpublished).

Buckley, O. (2018), 'From "We" to "I": How Irish Workplaces are Handling the Move from Collective to Individual Disputes, address at Business School of University College Cork', May (unpublished).

Cairney, Paul. (2017), 'Three Habits of Successful Policy Entrepreneurs', *Policy & Politics* 462: 199–215.

Calleary, D. (2010), 'Address to Conference on July 17 2010', in Kerr, A. (ed.), *The Industrial Relations Act 1990 20 Years On*, Dublin: Round Hall Thompson Reuters, pp. 11–16.

Cashell, M. (2011), *A History of the Rights Commissioner Service 1970-2010*, Dublin: Labour Relations Commission.

Central Bank (2021), *Quarterly Economic Commentary* (Q1): Dublin: Central Bank.

Chubb, B. (1992), The Government and Politics of Ireland, London, Routledge

CIPD (Chartered Institute of Personnel and Development) (2020), 'The Impact of Covid-19 on Pay, Jobs and Employee Concerns', Dublin: CIPD, June.

Clews, S (2021), 'Resolving the Conflict Within: Becoming Your Own Mediator', https://www.acas.org.uk/resolving-the-conflict-within-becoming-your-own-mediator

Cohen, Nissim. (2016), 'Policy Entrepreneurs and Agenda Setting', in Zahariadis, N. (ed.), *Handbook of Public Policy Agenda Setting*, Northampton, MA: Edward Elgar.

Colvin, A.J.S. and Darbishire, O. (2013), 'Convergence in Industrial Relations Institutions: The Emerging Anglo-American Model?' *ILR Review*, 66(5): 1047–1077.

Commission of Inquiry on Industrial Relations (1981), *Report of the Commission of Inquiry on Industrial Relations*, Dublin: Government Publications.

Committee on Vocational Organization (1943), *Report of the Committee on Vocational Organization*, Dublin: Stationery Office.

Connaughton, M. (2019), 'Ireland's Voluntarist IR System: A Case of If It Isn't Broke Don't Fix it', address delivered at DBEI/ILO Conference to Celebrate the 100th Anniversary of the Philadelphia Declaration. Dublin, 17 September 2019 (unpublished).

Costello, F. (2003), *The Irish Revolution and its Aftermath, 1916-1923*, Dublin: Irish Academic Press.

Cronin, J.E. (1979), *Industrial Conflict in Modern Britain*, London: Croom Helm.

Central Statistics Office (CSO) (2018), *Labour Force Survey*, Quarter 4, Dublin: Central Statistics Office.

Central Statistics Office (CSO) (2019a), *Equality and Discrimination*, Dublin: Central Statistics Office.

CSO (2019b), *Labour Force Survey*, Quarter 4, Dublin: Central Statistics Office.

CSO (2020a), 'Business Impact of Covid-19 Survey', Dublin: Central Statistics Office, May.

CSO (2020b), 'Business Impact of Covid-19 Survey', Dublin: Central Statistics Office, September.

CSO (2021a), 'Pulse Survey: Our Lives Online', Dublin: Central Statistics Office.

CSO (2021b), 'Industrial Disputes, Quarter 3 2021', Dublin: Central Statistics Office.

DAA (Dublin Airport Authority) and Fórsa (2020), 'Pay Stabilisation and Road to Recovery Agrement between Daa and Fórsa Trade Union', Dublin: DAA and Fórsa Trade Union.

Dáil Eireann (1921), *Dáil Debates* 17th August, Dublin: Houses of the Oireachtas.

Dáil Eireann (2014), *Dáil Debates* 8th October and 12th November, Dublin: Houses of the Oireachtas.

Dáil Eireann (2015), *Dáil Debates* 12th January and 13th May, Dublin: Houses of the Oireachtas.

Dáil Eireann (2018), *Dáil Debates* 18th October, Dublin: Houses of the Oireachtas.

Dáil Eireann (2022), 'Joint Committee on Enterprise Trade and Employment Debate 2nd March', Dublin: Houses of the Oireachtas.

Dáil Eireann Secretariat Department of Labour (1920–1922a), 'DE2/5, National Archives of Ireland'.

Dáil Eireann Secretariat Department of Labour (1920–1922b), *Interim Report of the Proceedings of the Department of Labour, DE2/5, 19 August 1919 to 25 October 1919*, National Archives of Ireland.

Dáil Eireann Secretariat Department of Labour (1920–1922c), 'Ministry of Labour Trade Disputes', DE 2/5, June 1920, National Archives of Ireland.

Dáil Eireann Secretariat Department of Labour (1920–1922d), 'Department of Labour Conciliation Boards', DE 2/5, September 1920, National Archives of Ireland.

Dáil Eireann Secretariat Department of Labour (1920–1922e), *Report of the Working of the Labour Department*, DE 2/5, March 1921, National Archives of Ireland.

Dáil Eireann Secretariat Department of Labour (1920–1922f), *Report of the Working of the Department of Labour Under the Following Ministers, Madam Markievicz TD, Alderman T. Kelly TD and J. McGrath TD (Substitutes)*, DE 2/5, Period from 7 July 1920 to 26 September 9 1920, National Archives of Ireland.

Dáil Eireann Secretariat Department of Labour (1920–1922g), *Labour Department Report*, DE 2/5, August 1921, National Archives of Ireland.
Dáil Eireann Secretariat Department of Labour (1920–1922h), *Report of the Activities of the Labour Department*, DE 2/5, 11 January 1921–18 April 1922, National Archives of Ireland.
Dáil Eireann Secretariat Department of Labour (1920–1922i), 'List of Decisions at Ministry Meeting', DE 2/5, 6 April 1921, National Archives of Ireland.
Dáil Eireann (1946), *Dáil Debates* 25th June, Dublin: Houses of the Oireachtas.
Dáil Eireann (1947), *Dáil Debates* 15th and 22nd October, Dublin: Houses of the Oireachtas.
Daly, M. (1992), *Industrial Development and Irish National Identity 1922-1939*, Dublin: Gill and Macmillan.
Davidson, R. (1978), 'The Bord of Trade and Industrial Relations 1896-1914', *The Historical Journal*, 12(3): 571–591.
Davis, J.H., Schoorman, F.D. and Donaldson, L. (1997), 'Toward a Stewardship Theory of Management', *Academy of Management Review*, 22: 20–47.
Deering, G. (2011), 'Delivering the Programme for Government: Vision of a World-Class Equality, Employment Rights and Industrial Relations System – A Discussion Paper', March (unpublished).
Department of Finance (2009), *Report of the Special Group on Public Service Numbers and Expenditure Programmes*: Volume 2 Detailed Papers, Dublin: Department of Finance.
Department of Enterprise Trade and Employment (DETE) (2004), *Report of the Review Group on the Functions of the Employment Rights Bodies*, Dublin: Department of Enterprise Trade and Employment.
DETE (2005), *Outcome of Consultations Regarding the Employment Rights Bodies Group Report*, Dublin: Department of Enterprise Trade and Employment.
DETE (2008), *The Future of the Employment Rights Bodies*, Dublin: Department of Enterprise Trade and Employment.
DETE (2021), *Work Safely Protocol, Dublin: Department of Enterprise, Trade and Employment*, November.
Department of Jobs, Enterprise and Innovation (DJEI) (2011a), 'Consultation on the Reform of the State's Employment Rights and Industrial Relations Structures and Procedures', Dublin: Department of Jobs, Enterprise and Innovation, 15 August.
DJEI (2011b), 'Summary and Analysis of Responses to the Consultation on the Reform of the State's Employment Rights and Industrial Relations Structures and Procedures', Dublin: Department of Jobs, Enterprise and Innovation, October.
DJEI (2012a), 'Blueprint to Deliver a World-Class Workplace Relations Service', Dublin: Department of Jobs, Enterprise and Innovation, April.
DJEI (2012b), 'Legislating for a World Class Workplace Relations Service: Submission to the Oireachtas Committee on Jobs, Enterprise and Innovation', Dublin: Department of Jobs, Enterprise and Innovation, July.
DJEI (2012c), 'Blueprint Consultation Responses', Dublin: Department of Jobs, Enterprise and Innovation, June.
Department of Finance (1944a), 'Letter from the Secretary of the Department of Finance to the Secretary of the Department of Industry and Commerce',

Correspondence and Discussions Leading to the Introduction of the Industrial Relations Bill 1946, Emergency Wages Division' National Archives of Ireland, LC1, IR19, 5 October.

Department of Finance (1944b), 'Memorandum to the Government by the Minister of Finance on the Proposal of the Minister of Industry and Commerce to Appoint a Commission of Inquiry into Wage Policy and Allied Matters', Correspondence and Discussions Leading to the Introduction of the Industrial Relations Bill 1946, National Archives of Ireland, LC1, IR19, 26 October.

Department of Industry and Commerce (1944a), 'Memorandum for Government', Correspondence and Discussions Leading to the Introduction of the Industrial Relations Bill 1946, National Archives of Ireland, LC1, IR19, 23 October.

Department of Industry and Commerce (1944b), 'Observations on Post-war Wage Policy', Correspondence and Discussions Leading to the Introduction of the Industrial Relations Bill 1946', Emergency Wages Division 'Correspondence and Discussions Leading to the Introduction of the Industrial Relations Bill 1946, National Archives of Ireland, LC1, IR19, 25 July.

Department of Industry and Commerce (1945a), 'Rough Heads of an Agenda for Discussion Between the Federated Union of Employers and the Irish Trade Union Congress', Correspondence and Discussions Leading to the Introduction of the Industrial Relations Bill 1946, National Archives of Ireland, LC1, IR19, not dated.

Department of Industry and Commerce (1945b), 'Memoranda Between Officials', Correspondence and Discussions Leading to the Introduction of the Industrial Relations Bill 1946, National Archives of Ireland, LC1, IR19, May.

Department of Industry and Commerce (1946), 'Letters and Memos Pertaining Meetings with the ITUC and CIU', Correspondence and Discussions Leading to the Introduction of the Industrial Relations Bill 1946, National Archives of Ireland, LC1, IR19, 14 February to 1 March.

Department of Labour (1983), *Discussion Document on Industrial Relations Reform*, Dublin: Department of Labour.

Department of Public Expenditure and Reform 2020, Building Momentum – A New Public Service Agreement 2021-2022, Dublin: Department of Public Expenditure and Reform.

Doherty L. and Teague P. (2011), 'Conflict Management Systems in Non-Union Multinationals in the Republic of Ireland', *International Journal of Human Resource Management*, 21: 57–71.

Doherty, L. and Teague, P. (2012), 'Fit for Purpose? Reforming Our Industrial Relations and Employment-Standard Setting Agencies', in Sheehan, B. (ed.), *The Labour Relations Commission: Recalling 21 Years, 1991–2012*, Dublin: Labour Relations Commission, pp. 177–192.

Doherty, L. and Teague, P. (2013), *The Essential Guide to Alternative Dispute Resolution in Ireland*, Dublin: Irish Business and Employers' Confederation.

Dowling J. and Pfeffer, J., (1975), 'Organizational Legitimacy: Social Values and Organizational Behavior', *Pacific Sociological Review*, 18(1): 122–136.

Duffy, K. (2010), 'The View of the Labour Court', in Kerr, A. (ed.), *The Industrial Relations Act 1990 20 Years On*, Dublin: Round Hall Thompson Reuters, pp. 62–71.

Dunphy, (1995), *The Making of Fianna Fáil Power in Ireland 1923-1948*, Oxford: Clarendon Press.

Employment Appeals Tribunal (2011), 'Employment Appeals Tribunal's Response to the Consultation Document on the Reform of the State's Employment Rights and Industrial Relations Structures and Procedures', Dublin: Employment Appeals Tribunal.

Employment Bar Association (EBA) (2011), 'Submission of the Employment bar Association of Ireland to the Minister for Jobs, Enterprise and Innovation, Mr. Richard Bruton, TD, on Reform of the State's Employment Rights and Industrial Relations Structures and Procedures', Dublin: Employment Bar Association, 13 September.

Equality Tribunal (2005 to 2013), *Annual Reports*, Dublin: Equality Tribunal.

Esteve, M., Urbig, D., van Witteloostuijn, A. and Boyne, G. (2016), 'Prosocial Behavior and Public Service Motivation', *Public Administration Review*, 76: 177–187.

Fórsa (2020), 'Largest Ever Employee Survey Reveals Huge Appetite for Remote Working', https://www.forsa.ie/largest-ever-employee-survey-reveals-huge-appetite-for-remote-working/

Fórsa (2021), 'Fórsa Wants Immediate Dialogue on Public Service Remote Working', https://www.forsa.ie/forsa-wants-immediate-dialogue-on-public-service-remote-working/

Fox, A. (1985), *History and Heritage: The Social Origins of the British Industrial Relations System*, London: Allen & Unwin.

Girvin, B. (1989), *Between Two Worlds: Politics and Economy in Independent Ireland*, Dublin: Gill and Macmillan.

Glynn, I. and O'Connell, P. (2017), 'Migration', in Roche, W.K., O'Connell, P. and Prothero, A. (eds.), *Austerity and Recovery in Ireland: Europe's Poster Child and the Great Recession*, Oxford: Oxford University Press, pp. 311–326.

Goldman Sachs (2023), *The Potentially Large Effect of Artificial Intelligence on Economic Growth*, New York: Goldman Sachs.

Government of Ireland (2002), *Programme for Government*, Dublin: Government Publications.

Government of Ireland (2006), *Towards 2016: Ten-Year Framework Social Partnership Agreement 2006–2015*, Dublin: Government Publications.

Government of Ireland (2010), *National Recovery Plan 2011–2014*, Dublin: Government Publications.

Government of Ireland (2011), *Programme for Government*, Dublin: Government Publications.

Government of Ireland (2021), *National Remote Work Strategy*, Dublin: Government of Ireland.

Hann, D. and Teague, P. (2008a), *The Role of the Rights Commissioners in the Irish Employment System: Solving Problems and Vindicating Rights*, Dublin: Labour Relations Commission (unpublished).

Hann, D. and Teague, P. (2008b), *The Employment Appeals Tribunal*, Dublin: Labour Relations Commission (unpublished)

Hann, D. and Teague, P. (2012), 'Individual Employment Rights and the Renewal of Economic Citizenship: Lessons from the Rights Commissioners in Ireland' *Work, Employment and Society*, 26(4): 623–637.

Hayter, S., Link, A.N. and Scott, J.N. (2018), 'Public-Sector Entrepreneurship', *Oxford Review of Economic Policy*, 34(4): 676–694.

Health and Safety Authority (2005), *Code of Practice for Employers and Employees on the Prevention and resolution of Bullying at Work*, Dublin: Health and Safety Authority.

Hodgins, M., Pursell, L., Hogan, V., MacCurtain, S., Mannix-McNamara, P. and Lewis, D. (2018), *Irish Workplace Behaviour Study*, Dublin: Institute of Occupational Safety and Health.

Horgan, J. (1987), 'The Future of Collective Bargaining', in Kelly, A. and Murphy, T. (eds.), *Industrial Relations in Ireland*, Dublin: University College Dublin, pp. 168–174.

IMF (International Monetary Fund) (2010), *Memorandum of Economic and Financial Policies and Technical Memorandum of Understanding*, Washington, DC: International Monetary Fund.

Industrial Relations News. Issues Cited in Text and Published in Dublin.

Irish Business and Employer's Confederation (IBEC) (2011), 'Submission to the Minister for Jobs, Enterprise and Innovation: Consultation on the Reform of the State's Employment Rights and Industrial Relations Structures and Procedures', Dublin: Irish Business and Employer's Confederation, 16 September.

IBEC (2020), *HR Update Survey*, Dublin: IBEC, October.

IBEC (2021a), *Returning to Work Survey*, Dublin: IBEC, May.

IBEC (2021b), *HR Update Survey*, Dublin: IBEC, October.

Irish Congress of Trade Unions (ICTU) (2022), *Just Transition Alliance Joint Declaration, by founding members: Congress, Siptu, Forsa, Friends of the Earth, Stop Climate Chaos, TASC*, Dublin: Irish Congress of Trade unions.

ICTU (2011), 'Congress Response to Consultation Document for Reform of the State's Rights and Industrial Relations Structures and Procedures', Dublin: Irish Congress of Trade Unions, September.

'Industrial Efficiency and Prices Bill 1947', Dublin: Houses of the Oireachtas, https://www.oireachtas.ie/en/bills/bill/1947/29/

'Industrial Relations Act 1946', Dublin: Irish Statute Book, https://www.irishstatutebook.ie/eli/1946/act/26/enacted/en/html

Insititue of Directors (IOD) (2022), 'The Latest Quarterly IOD Director Sentiment Monitor Survey for Q1 2022 Finds That Business Leaders are Split on Right to Request Remote Working Bill 2022', Dublin: IOD.

Kenny, T. (2019), 'Workplace Mediators in Ireland: A Qualitative and Quantitative Study, Thesis Presented for the Degree of PhD', Dublin: University College Dublin (unpublished).

Kenny, T. (2021), 'Adapting to Mediation Online: The Irish Experience', *Journal of Mediation and Applied Conflict Analysis*, 7(1): 1–19.

Kerr, A. (2014), 'Changing Landscapes: The Juridification of the Labour Court', 38th Countess Markievicz Memorial Lecture of the Irish Association of Industrial Relations, https://www.ul.ie/iair/sites/default/files/2014%20Lecture%20by%20Anthony%20Kerr.pdf

Kostick, c. (1996), *Revolution in Ireland: Popular Militancy, 1917 to 1923*, London: Pluto Press.

Kotsonouris, M. (1994), *Retreat from Revolution: The Dáil Courts, 1920-24*, Irish Academic Press.

Lee, J. (2012), *Ireland 1912-1985: Politics and Society*, Cambridge: Cambridge University Press.
Labour Court (1989), *Annual Report 1989*, Dublin: The Labour Court.
Labour Relations Commission (1991), *Annual Report 1991*, Dublin: Labour Relations Commission.
Labour Relations Commission (1996), *Annual Report 1996*, Dublin: Labour Relations Commission.
Labour Relations Commission (2008), *Annual Report 2008*, Dublin: Labour Relations Commission.
Labour Relations Commission (2009), *Annual Report 2009*, Dublin: Labour Relations Commission.
Labour Relations Commission (2010), *Annual Report 2010*, Dublin: Labour Relations Commission.
Labour Relations Commission (2011), *Annual Report 2011*, Dublin: Labour Relations Commission.
Labour Relations Commission (2013), *Annual Report 2013*, Dublin: Labour Relations Commission.
Labour Relations Commission (2015), *Annual Report 2015*, Dublin: Labour Relations Commission.
Lemass, S. (1942), 'Labour Policy', Planning for Post-war Situation: Industry and Commerce, Department of an Taoiseach, National Archives of Ireland, S12886.
Lemass, S. (1944a), 'Memorandum to Secretary', Correspondence and Discussions Leading to the Introduction of the Industrial Relations Bill 1946, National Archives of Ireland, LC1, IR19, 13 July.
Lemass, S. (1944b), 'Letter to Cathal O'Shannon, General Secretary of the Irish Trade Union Congress' Correspondence and Discussions Leading to the Introduction of the Industrial Relations Bill 1946', National Archives of Ireland, LC1, IR19, 7 December.
Lemass, S. (1945a), 'Memorandum of Meeting with the Irish Trade Union Congress' Correspondence and Discussions Leading to the Introduction of the Industrial Relations Bill 1946', National Archives of Ireland, LC1, IR19, 14 February.
Lemass, S. (1945b), 'Memorandum on Full Employment', UCD Archives, 16 January.
Lindblom, C. (1959), 'The Science of Muddling Through', *Public Administration Review* 19(2): 79–88.
Locke, R., Kochan, T. and Piore M. (1995), 'Reconceptualizing Comparative Industrial Relations: Lessons from International Research,' *International Labour Review*, 134(2): 139–161.
MacCarthaigh, M. (2017), *Public Sector Reform in Ireland: Countering Crisis*, London: Palgrave Macmillan.
Maguire, M. (2005), *The Civil Service and the Revolution in Ireland, 1912-38*, Manchester: Manchester University Press.
Mandate, (2020), *The Shopfloor*, August, Dublin: Mandate.
McCarthy, C. (1977), *Trade Unions in Ireland, 19894-1960*, Dublin: Institute of Public Administration.
McCarthy, C. (1978), 'Problems in the Field of Dispute Resolution', 3rd Countess Markievicz Memorial Lecture of the Irish Association of Industrial Relations. https://www.ul.ie/iair/sites/default/files/1978%20Lecture%20by%20Charles%20McCarthy.pdf

McDermott, D. (2019), 'Radical EU Change to Irish Legal Framework for Resolution of Employment Disputes', *Industrial Relations News*, 28th February.

McGee, R. (2012), 'Conciliation: Art? Mystery? Magic? Just Get Then Fixed and Out', in Sheehan, B. (ed.), *The Labour Relations Commission: Recalling 21 Years, 1991-2012*, Dublin: Labour Relations Commission, pp. 55–66.

McGinley, M. (1997), 'Industrial Relations in the Public Sector', in Murphy, T. and Roche, W.K. (eds.), *Irish Industrial Relations in Practice*, Dublin: Oaktree Press, pp. 227–276.

McGinnity, F., Grotti, R., Kenny, O. and Russell, H. (2018), *Who Experiences Discrimination in Ireland?* Dublin: Economic and Social Research Institute.

McGinty, B. (2010), 'The Employer's Perspective', in Kerr, A. (ed.), *The Industrial Relations Act 1990 20 Years On*, Dublin: Round Hall Thompson Reuters, pp. 72–88.

McGreal, Roche, K. and Markey, R. (2021), *Assessing Award Quantum in Published Employment Equality Decisions*, October 2015 to July 2022, Dublin: Legal Island.

McKinsey Global Institute (2017), *Jobs Lost, Jobs Gained: Workforce Transition at a Time of Automation*, McKinsey Global Institute.

Middlemas, K (1979), *Politics in Industrial Society: The Experience of the British System Since 1911*, London: André Deutsch.

Mintrom, M., (2019), *Policy Entrepreneurs and Dynamic Change*, Cambridge: Cambridge University Press.

Mintrom, M. and Norman P. (2009), 'Policy Entrepreneurship and Policy Change', *Policy Studies Journal*, 37(4): 649–667.

Mitchell, A. (1974), *Labour in Irish Politics*, Dublin: Irish University Press.

Morrin, D. (2012), 'The Labour Relations Commission Advisory Service', in Sheehan, B. (ed.), *The Labour Relations Commission: Recalling 21 Years, 1991-2012*, Dublin: Labour Relations Commission, pp. 151–164.

Morrissey, T. (2007), *William O'Brien 1881-1968*, Dublin: Four Courts Press.

Mortished, R.J.P. (1947/1948), 'The Industrial Relations Act 1946', *Journal of the Statistical and Social Inquiry Society of Ireland*, 18: 471–690.

Mulvey, K. (2010), 'The View of the Labour Relations Commission', in Kerr, A. (ed.), *The Industrial Relations Act 1990 20 Years On*, Dublin: Round Hall Thompson Reuters, pp. 45–61.

Mulvey, K. (2011), 'All Changes, Changed Utterly – New Times, New Engagements and New Solutions: How the Employment Relationship is Changing', 19th John Lovett Memorial Lecture, University of Limerick, 10 March.

Murphy, T. (1997), 'The Resolution of Industrial Disputes', in Murphy T. and Roche, W.K. (eds.), *Irish Industrial Relations in Practice*, Dublin: Oak Tree Press, pp. 276–310.

NESC (National Economic and Social Council) (2020), *Addressing Employment Vulnerability as Part of a Just Transition in Ireland*, Dublin: National Economic and Social Council.

National University Galway and Western Development Commission (2020), *National Remote Working Survey*, Galway: National University Galway and Western Development Commission, October.

O'Brien, J. (1980), *A Study of National Wage Agreements in Ireland*, Dublin: Economic and Social Research Institute.

O'Connor, E. (1980), 'Agrarian Unrest and the Labour Movement in County Waterford, 1917-1923', *Saothar*, 6: 40–58.
O'Connor, E. (1988), *Syndicalism in Ireland, 1917-1923*, Cork: Cork University Press.
O'Connor, J. (2010), 'The Industrial Relations Act 1990: A Missed Opportunity', in Kerr, A. (ed.), *The Industrial Relations Act 1990 20 Years On*, Dublin: Round Hall Thompson Reuters, pp. 89–95.
O'Mahony, D. (1965), *Economic Aspects of Industrial Relations*, Dublin: Economic and Social Research Institute.
Organization for Economic Cooperation and Development (OECD) (2001), *Public Sector Leadership for the 21st Century*, OECD Publishing, Paris,
OECD (2023), *The Impact of AI on the Workplace: The Main Findings from the OECD AI Surveys of Employers and Workers*, Paris: OECD.
Owens, E. (1996), 'The Labour Court: Past, Present and Future', 21st Countess Markievicz Memorial Lecture of the Irish Association of Industrial Relations, https://www.ul.ie/iair/sites/default/files/1996%20Lecture%20by%20Evelyn%20Owens.pdf
Perry, A. (2018), 'Contribution to Panel Discussing Internal Dispute Resolution Bodies', Annual Conference of *Industrial Relations News*, University College Dublin, March (unpublished).
Perry, J.L. and Wise, L.R. (1990), 'The Motivational Bases of Public Service', *Public Administration Review*, 50: 367–373.
Pfeffer, J. (2015), *Leadership BS: Fixing Workplaces and Careers One Truth at a Time*. New York: Harper Business.
Privalko, I., Russell, H. and Maitre, B. (2018), *The Ageing Workforce in Ireland: Working Conditions, Health and Extending Working Lives*, Dublin: Economic and Social Research Institute.
Pulignano, V. (2023), 'The Transformation of Work: Changing Employment Governance Regimes', in Bianchi, P., Labory, S. and Tomlinson, P.R. (eds.), *UK Handbook of Industrial Development*, Cheltenham: Edward Elgar, 90–105.
Quinn, K.P. (1952), 'The Industrial Relations Act, 1946', MA thesis presented to the National University of Ireland, Library, University College Dublin.
Radio Telefis Éireann (RTE) (2016), 'Head of WRC Admits that Service in Not yet World Class', and 'Employment Law Body Criticizes WRC', 1 October and 30 September, RTE.ie website.
RTE (2017), 'Woman Awarded €7.5K Compensation Over Halligan Interview', 8 November, RTE.ie website.
Regan, J. (1999), *The Irish Counter-Revolution 1921-1936*, Dublin: Gill and Macmillan.
Robinson, G., Pearlstein, A. and Mayer, B. (2005), 'Dyads: Encouraging Dynamic Adaptive Dispute Systems in the Irganized Workplace', *Harvard Negotiation Law Review*, 10: 339–382.
Roche, K.S. (2012), *Richard Corish: A Biography*, Dublin: Original Writing Ltd.
Roche, W.K. (1987), 'The Formation of the Irish Trade Union Movement and Aggregate Organizational Developments Since 1945', Paper prepared for the Dues Project, university College Dublin (unpublished).

Roche, W.K. (1997), 'Pay Determination, the State and the Politics of Industrial Relations', in Murphy, T. and Roche, W.K. (eds.), *Irish Industrial Relations in Practice*, Dublin: Oaktree Press, pp. 145–226.

Roche, W.K. (2007), 'Social Partnership in Ireland and New Social Pacts', *Industrial Relations: A Journal of Economy and Society*, 46(3): 395–425.

Roche, W.K. (2009), 'Social Partnership in Ireland: From Lemass to Cowen', *Economic and Social Review*, 40(2): 183–205.

Roche, W.K. (2015), 'The Emergence of a Dual Dispute Resolution System: Private Facilitators in Irish Industrial Relations', *Industrial Relations Journal*, 46(4): 293–311.

Roche, W.K. (2016a) 'Turning Third Party Intervention on its Head: Assisted Bargaining and the Prevention of Workplace Conflict in Ireland', in Saundry, R., Latreille P. and Ashman I. (eds.), *Reframing Resolution: Innovation and Change in the Management of Workplace Conflict*, London: Palgrave Macmillan, pp. 216–236.

Roche, W.K. (2016b), 'The Development of Conflict Resolution Practices in Irish Workplaces', *Administration*, 64(3/4): 61–92.

Roche, W.K. (2018), 'Towards a New Architecture for Resolving Workplace Conflict', Address Delivered at the Launch of the HR Research Centre, Cork University Business School, 16 May.

Roche, W.K. (2021), 'The Genesis of Private Dispute Resolution in Irish Industrial Relations', *Industrial Relations Journal*, 52(1): 82–106.

Roche, W.K. (2022a), 'How Effective is Private Dispute Resolution? Evidence from Ireland', *Industrial Law Journal*, Oxford University Press, Advanced Access Publication.

Roche, W.K. (2022b), 'Extending the Boundaries of ADR: Private Dispute Resolution in in Economic and Industrial Democracy, early view https://doi.org/10.1177/0143831X221086016

Roche, W.K. and Higgins, C. (2016), 'Networked Dispute Resolution: The National Implementation Body in Irish Industrial Relations', *Advances in Industrial and Labor Relations*, 22: 161–188.

Roche, W.K., O'Connell, P. and Prothero, A. (2017), *Austerity and Recovery in Ireland: Europe's Poster Child and the Great Recession*, Oxford: Oxford University Press.

Roche, W.K. and Teague, P. (2015), 'Modes of Concession Bargaining and their Antecedents in the Great Recession: Evidence from Ireland', *Industrial Relations Journal*, 46(5–6): 434–445.

Saint-Martin, D. and Rothmayr Allison, C. (2011), Rationalism and Public Policy: Mode of Analysis or Symbolic Politics?' *Policy and Society*, 30(1): 19–27.

Scharpf, F. (1999), *Governing in Europe: Effective and Democratic?* Oxford: Oxford University Press.

Scott, R. (2001), *Institutions and Organizations*. Thousand Oaks, CA: Sage.

Selznick, P. (1957), *Leadership in Administration: A Sociological Interpretation*. New York: Harper & Row.

Sheehan, B. (2009), 'McCarthy's Body Not Enamoured of IR Bodies, Social Partnership', *Industrial Relations News*, 22nd July.

Stratis (2019), 'The Journey Towards a 'World Class' Workplace Relations System – Where Are We? Stratis Consulting 'White Paper – 2020 Vision' Assessment', Dublin: Stratis.

Streeck, W. and Thelen, K. (2005). Introduction: institutional change in advanced political economies. In W. Streeck, & K. Thelen (eds.), *Beyond Continuity: Institutional Change in Advanced Political Economies.* Oxford: Oxford University Press.

Supreme Court (2021), 'Zalewski v Adjudication Officer and WRC, Ireland and the Attorney General' [2021] IESC 24, Dublin: The Supreme Court.

Teague, P. (2009), 'Path dependency and Comparative Industrial Relations: Conflict Management Systems in Sweden and the Republic of Ireland', *British Journal of Industrial Relations*, 47(3): 299–520.

Teague, P. (2013), *Resolving Workplace Disputes in Ireland: The Role of the Labour Relations Commission*, ILO, Geneva, Working Paper No 48.

Teague, P. and Currie, D. (2016), 'Economic Citizenship and Workplace Conflict in Anglo-American Industrial Relations Systems', *British Journal of Industrial Relations*, 54(2): 358–384.

Teague, P. and Doherty, L. (2009a), 'Professor Paul Teague and Liam Doherty PhD Consultation Response', in Department of Jobs, Enterprise and Innovation, 'Blueprint Consultation Responses', Dublin: Department of Jobs, Enterprise and Innovation, pp. 183–191.

Teague, P. and Doherty, L. (2009b), 'Reforming Our IR Institutions: A Snip in the Wrong Direction', *Industrial Relations News*, 22nd July.

Teague, P., Roche, W.K., Gormley, T. and Currie, D. (2015), *The Management of Workplace Conflict: ADR in Ireland*, Dublin: Institute of Public Administration.

Thelen, K. (2004), *How Institutions Evolve: The Political Economy of Skills in Germany, Britain, the United States and Japan*, New York: Cambridge University Press.

Thelen, K. (2009), 'Institutional Change in Advanced Political Economies', *British Journal of Industrial Relations*, 47(3): 471–498.

Vandenabeele, W., Andersen, L.B. and Leisink, P. (2014), 'Leadership in the Public Sector: A Tale of General Principles and Particular Features', *Review of Public Personnel Administration*, 34(2): 79–83.

Wallace, J. (2010), 'The Industrial Relations Act 1990: An Industrial Relations Perspective', in Kerr, A. (ed.), *The Industrial Relations Act 1990 20 Years On*, Dublin: Round Hall Thompson Reuters, pp. 17–44.

Wallace, J., Gunnigle, P. and McMahon, G. (2004), *Irish Industrial Relations*, Dublin: Gill and Macmillan, 3rd Edition.

Wallace, J., Gunnigle, P. and McMahon, G. (2013), *Irish Industrial Relations*, Dublin: Gill and Macmillan, 4th. Edition.

Walsh, A.M. (2017), 'The Monday Interview: For the Sake of our Country We Had to Cut Public Pay', Irish Independent, 13 March.

Weil, D. (2008), 'A Strategic Approach to Labour Inspection', *International Labour Review*, 147(4): 349–375, http://www.oit.org/public/english/revue/download/pdf/s3_weil.pdf

Workplace Relations Commission (WRC) (2015), *Annual Report 2015*, Dublin: Workplace Relations Commission.

WRC (2016a), *Annual Report 2016*, Dublin: Workplace Relations Commission.
WRC (2016b), *Statement of Strategy 2016–2018: Assisting the Recovery in a Changing and Challenging Environment*, Dublin: Workplace Relations Commission.
WRC (2017), *Annual Report 2017*, Dublin: Workplace Relations Commission.
WRC (2018a), *Annual Report 2018*, Dublin: Workplace Relations Commission.
WRC (2018b), *Workplace Relations Commission: Stakeholder and Service User Research*, Dublin: Workplace Relations Commission.
WRC (2018c), *Statement of Strategy 2019-2022: Fair and Compliant Workplaces and Equal Treatment in Services*, Dublin: Workplace Relations Commission.
WRC (2019a), *Employment Equality Complaints January to June 2019*, Dublin: Workplace Relations Commission.
WRC (2019b), *Annual Report for 2019*, Dublin: Workplace Relations Commission.
WRC (2021a), *Code of Practice for Employers and Employees on the Right to Disconnect*, Dublin: Workplace Relations Commission.
WRC (2021b), *Review of WRC Adjudication Decisions and Recommendations – January to December 2020*, Dublin: Workplace Relations Commission, Dublin: Workplace Relations Commission.
WRC (2022a), *Strategy Statement 2022–2024*, Dublin: Workplace Relations Commission.
WRC (2022b), *Review of Adjudication Decisions and Recommendations, January-December 2020*, Dublin: Workplace Relations Commission.
WRC (2022c), 'Research Recent Labour Market Developments', Dublin: Department of Enterprise Trade and Employment Tender Document, 20 December.

Index

Note: *Italic* page numbers refer to figures and page numbers followed by "n" denote endnotes.